Michael McGirr is the author of *Things You Get For Free* and fiction editor of the journal *Meanjin*. He was raised in Sydney but grew up in Melbourne. He now lives in a small town somewhere between the two where he is enjoying his middle age with his wife and their three children.

Also by Michael McGirr

Things You Get For Free

BYPASS

THE STORY OF A ROAD

MICHAEL McGIRR

PICADOR
Pan Macmillan Australia

This project has been assisted by the Federal Government through the
Australia Council, its arts funding and advisory body.

First published 2004 in Picador by Pan Macmillan Australia Pty Limited
This Picador edition published 2005 by Pan Macmillan Australia Pty Limited
St Martins Tower, 31 Market Street, Sydney

National Library of Australia Cataloguing in Publication Data:

McGirr, Michael, 1961– .
Bypass : the story of a road.

ISBN 0 330 42190 5.

1. McGirr, Michael, 1961 – – Journeys. 2. Bicycle touring –
Anecdotes. 3. Hume Highway (N.S.W. and Vic.) – History. 4.
New South Wales – Description and travel. 5. Victoria –
Description and travel. I. Title

796.640994

Typeset by Midland Typesetters, Maryborough, Victoria
Printed by McPherson's Printing Group

Papers used by Pan Macmillan Australia Pty Ltd are natural, recyclable products made from
wood grown in sustainable forests. The manufacturing processes conform to the environmental
regulations of the country of origin.

FOR JENNY

The Hume Highway has been known as both the Great South Road and the North-Eastern Highway. It is has been both Sydney Road and Melbourne Road. In various times and places it has been George Street, Broadway, Liverpool Road, Camden Valley Way, Remembrance Drive, Argyle Street, Auburn Street, Hume Street, Cullerin Road, Yass Street, Yass Valley Way, Comur Street, Sheridan Street, Dean Street, Young Street, Wagga Road, Wodonga Place, Conness Street, Tone Road, Murphy Street, Parfet Road, Ryley Street, Bridge Street and Royal Parade. Parts of it are the Old Hume Highway and parts of it are the Hume Freeway. All of these names are used in this book and others as well. Often it is just called 'the road'.

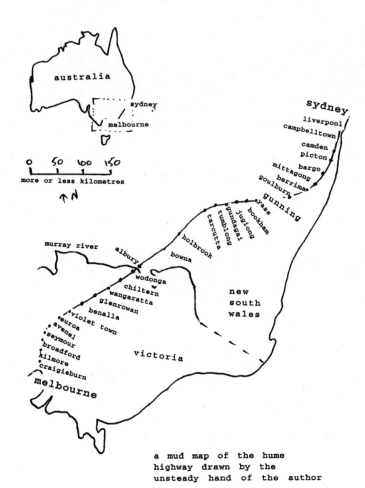

australia

sydney

melbourne

0   50   100   150

more or less kilometres

↑ N

sydney

liverpool
campbelltown
camden
picton
bargo
mittagong
berrima
goulburn

gunning

yass
bookham
jugiong
gundagai
tumblong
tarcutta

holbrook

murray river   albury   bowna

new
south
wales

wodonga
chiltern
wangaratta
glenrowan
benalla
violet town
euroa
avenel
seymour
broadford
kilmore
craigieburn

victoria

melbourne

a mud map of the hume
highway drawn by the
unsteady hand of the author

Give a man a road and he has a library
MARY GILMORE, *Hound of the Road*

Sancho answered, 'There's no road so
smooth that it ain't got a few potholes.'
CERVANTES, *Don Quixote*

One

Nobody had heard of Cliff Young. In late 1982, his application to run in a foot race from Sydney to Melbourne turned up on Martin Noonan's desk. Noonan thought it was some kind of joke. Young was sixty-one years of age. He came from the western districts of Victoria. He was a potato farmer and still lived at home with his mother, Mary. She was eighty-nine and kept fit by cutting wood.

Noonan was helping to organise an event for elite athletes. He was the state marketing manager for Westfield, an empire of shopping centres which made a fortune by providing places where people could be bored in comfort. Westfield was already contributing to the fitness of the nation by getting its citizens to push trolley loads of consumer goods from the checkout to the carpark. They got an extra workout when the wheels of the trolley went in four different directions at the same time.

Noonan, a dedicated runner himself, wondered if Westfield could sponsor something in Melbourne a bit like Sydney's City to Surf, an annual race which attracts over 50,000 entrants.

Melbourne used to call it the City to Sewer because the finishing point, Bondi Beach, had trouble in those days with effluent outflow. For various reasons, the City to Surf idea was not going to work in Melbourne. Melbourne had a city but no surf. A similar distance to the Sydney event would have taken runners from the city to the northern suburb of Fawkner, best known for its memorial park, but the City to Cemetery concept was hard to sell. This was despite the fact the City to Surf often kills at least one of its entrants, usually somebody well on in years who has decided that by keeping fit they will live forever. The plan went on the shelf.

A year later, Noonan heard that fellow runner John Toleman wanted to stage an event to showcase the abilities of two athletes he admired, George Perdon and Tony Rafferty. Perdon was fifty-eight and Rafferty was forty-four. They had both run from Perth to Sydney, a distance of over 4,000 kilometres. They were rivals. Noonan got in touch and said that Westfield was interested in employing Toleman to direct an event which would be open to as wide a field as possible. Westfield would put up a prize of $10,000 and meet the running costs for a race between Australia's two largest cities. It became a race between Australia's two largest shopping centres, Westfield Parramatta, in Sydney's western suburbs, and Westfield Doncaster, in Melbourne's east. Before long, twelve competitors had come forward. Cliff Young was among them.

Young was part of a movement. In the early eighties, the whole world was running long distances. The craze was accompanied by fad diets, an obsession with shoes and a library of literature which explored the dark territory between psychology and sweat. There was a bestseller called *The Loneliness of the Long Distance Runner*. The attraction of running, many said, was the isolation. So they joined 'fun runs' in which tens of thousands jostled each other in the quest for solitude. Eventually the fad died when runners discovered that their knees were unable to read all those books.

Noonan, a serious runner, was on the Pritikin diet. Cliff Young wasn't. He told Noonan that he needed oil in his diet to keep his bones lubricated. He also said that he did most of his training running round the paddocks in gumboots.

Young had been running seriously for only three years. Before that, he'd tried hang-gliding but found it was too dangerous. He had played football for his local team, Colac, until he was forty and was disappointed to have been retired on account of his age. When his application arrived, Noonan thought he better take Cliff out for a bit of a run to make sure he was up to the task.

Not only was Cliff in remarkable physical condition but he was a natural wit. He had an answer to everything. He said that where he came from it rained for nine months of the year. Then the winter set in.

A press release went out saying that one of the competitors trained in gumboots. From that moment, Young had a toehold in the public imagination. He was running against technology. At the media launch of the event, a journalist asked Cliff why he wasn't wearing gumboots today. Cliff said that he'd been given a pair of new-fangled fancy runners. They were so good, he said, that it took him 200 metres to slow down and stop.

On 27 April 1983, the field set off at a cracking pace along the road from Sydney to Melbourne. They did the first 42 kilometres, the length of a marathon, in less than three hours. Cliff took a wrong turn. He said later that he was lucky he didn't run to Darwin by mistake. Another competitor pointed him in the right direction.

DON'T JUST DO SOMETHING.
SIT THERE.
— Bumper sticker, Hume Highway

You don't come to a small town to hide. There are cities for that. If you want to move to a town like Gunning the best place to start is where most people come to rest: the local cemetery. The sign out on the freeway says the population of Gunning is 1,000 but that's an exaggeration. Until 1993, when the town was bypassed, its main street was part of the road between Australia's two largest cities, Sydney and Melbourne. Suddenly it became the main road between the post office and the pub. Towns such as Gunning, where I live, were offered signage on the new freeway to let travellers know they still existed. The bigger the town, the bigger the sign, so rather than quietly disappear, Gunning fibbed. The sign on the way into town, which says that the population is 530, is more honest. Once upon a time, somebody announced a new arrival by changing 530 to 531, an item of graffiti which has never been removed. People like it. It suggests that the place is growing.

There are more people buried in Gunning than living here. Some of the graves, especially those belonging to children, are eloquent because they say so little. Two separate plots are marked simply, 'Baby Lees.' Another is occupied, if that's the right expression, by both Selina Waters who died in 1921 at the age of ninety-three and Miriam Hillier who died in 1927 having lived for just three weeks. Henry Lanham, who lived ninety-two years, is buried next to Maurice Lanham, who lived eight years. There are many instances of this. They make you think. Even a long life is short.

There are names in the cemetery of families who have been in the district for generations. The best advice to any newcomer wanting to fit into a small town is to go to the cemetery, find a common name, and nail it with a hyphen onto their own. Around Gunning, the name of Hume would do as well as many and better than most.

One of the most imposing tombs is sacred to the memory of Elizabeth Hume, died 1847, mother of Hamilton Hume, the man after whom the road between Sydney and Melbourne is named. In the same resting place is John Kennedy Hume, Hamilton's brother. It says that he was murdered at Gunning in January 1840, aged thirty-nine, 'whilst rendering assistance to his neighbours to capture a party of bush rangers headed by the notorious Whitten'. Whitten had come to town looking for a police informer. Gunshots were fired at the Grosvenor Inn and John, not far from town on the property 'Collingwood', heard them, rode in to see what was up and got caught in the fray. His epitaph concludes: 'he left a widow and nine young children to bewail his loss.' One of the children was born after his death.

I didn't realise I was considering moving to Gunning until I found myself saying as much to one of the locals. He looked a little surprised. There wasn't much hype in the property market at the time.

'You want to live in Gunning?' the man asked.

'Well, maybe.'

'Gunning?' he arched an eyebrow. If it was such a strange idea, I wondered why he was living here himself.

He sent me down to the pub. Gunning used to have five hotels but the Telegraph is the only one still in business, its name a reminder of the days when communication between here and the outside world was wonder enough to call for a drink. He told me to look at a small framed photo inside the door. The photo, dated a couple of years earlier, showed the main street covered in ice and snow.

'Did you see it?' he asked later.

'Yes.'

He was pleased.

'There's one thing you can't see in that photo.'

'What's that?'

'You can't see the fucking wind.'

The prevailing wind in Gunning comes from the west and, on its day, it's a force to be reckoned with. But it can be as much friend as foe. It fights back the sound of the trucks which, around the clock, grunt along the Hume Freeway a kilometre or more on the eastern side of the town. On a still night, they rumble and snort on the edge of consciousness.

Gunning is defined as much by something which is not here as by anything that is. The road has gone away. Until the bypass was built, the road brought over 3,000 trucks a day through the main street. People talk about it like a difficult child who has moved out of home, leaving fond memories of chaos. One of the local identities, for example, was a refugee from the kitchen of a celebrated French restaurant in the city, who opened a cafe on the main street and found that the hungry followed him. People enjoy the memory of elegant diners at one table and truckies at the next, and boast that this was the town which bridged the gap between filet mignon and a steak sandwich. The food was great but you couldn't hear a champagne cork pop. Conversations paused while trucks changed gears.

Traffic moved slowly in the main street.

'At least you got to read the bumper stickers,' one resident told me. 'Because it was impossible to talk.'

A farmer with a property on the road a few miles out says that they never went to church on Good Friday. It wasn't that they didn't want to. They went to church most Sundays. But on Good Friday, with holiday traffic on the move, it was impossible to get out the gate.

Some of the stories have grown. You believe what you can, like the one about the local hairdresser who would never cut styles she judged to be unroadworthy. Her salon was opposite the French restaurant and she lived in fear that her customers, relaxed by her attentions, would pull out into the path of a truck. She refused to do work which required hair to balloon over the ears of her patrons, particularly their left ears, because this would block their line of sight when they were reversing. None of her perms was ever involved in an accident.

Every story in Gunning seems to touch the road. Major public celebrations and major public tragedies, such as a fatal car accident, are measured by the same yardstick. If the road gets closed, it is serious. Like Pall Mall, the road was closed on the day Elizabeth II was crowned. It was closed again in 1988 for a street party for the bicentenary of European settlement in Australia. People wore period costume, although there was some confusion about the period. Farmers who dug out the suits they had worn to their weddings or to long-forgotten events in the 1950s were applauded for their efforts. Besides, every party, if it goes long enough, will eventually flush out Elvis impersonators.

Other stories shed light on the way fortune rises and falls in everyday life. Like the story of the local grazier who wanted to quarry rock from his land to sell for the foundations of the freeway, and became the centre of a furore on which the dust is yet to settle. Or the story of a new bridge that was built not far away on the old highway. When it was opened, a generation or more ago, a truck was involved in an accident on the approach and its load of biscuits was scattered far and wide. The sheep in nearby paddocks might have contracted diabetes except for the school kids who sacrificed an afternoon's learning in order to help themselves to the biscuits. The Department of Roads wanted to call the bridge after some worthy gentleman or other, but from that day it has always been known as the Biscuit Bridge. There is no sign on it because it doesn't need one. Everyone knows.

A senior resident, Edna, speaks about the day the bypass was opened. In the morning, the trucks hooted as they edged through town for the last time. This was the day of liberation and people waved. Everyone went out to the opening ceremony and waved again as the trucks went through the new route for the first time. A marquee had been set up nearby to serve refreshments to dignitaries and school children were seated in neat rows on the shoulder of the freeway to listen to speeches. It was only when they got home that their parents realised how close the road contractors had run their deadline. The kids all had wet bitumen stuck to their pants. For days, mothers were on the phone to each other working out the best way to get the road off their children's bums. The shoulders of the old road had been loose. They threw gravel at strangers and kicked up dust. The new road was made of sterner stuff.

'When we came back that day,' says Edna, 'the town had gone quiet.'

Now, as you come off the freeway and approach the town from the south, the first thing you find is an abandoned petrol station, the doors of its former rest rooms flapping in the wind. Often you see sheep and cattle chewing on the grass that has grown through the cracks in the concrete where vehicles used to stop to fill up. Further down, another service station has given up selling petrol and has turned its attention to domestic needs, making its living fixing lawn mowers and supplying bottled gas for cooking and heating. It's not uncommon for one of the two surviving fuel outlets to open at 7 a.m. and find a car sitting in the driveway without enough petrol to get to the next pump, fifty kilometres away. The driver will be annoyed that the road still tolerates businesses which do not open every hour of the day, every day of the year.

The freeway has no sense of day and night, winter or summer. In the roadhouses, it is always the same temperature and breakfast is always available. Gunning, on the other hand, has moods and seasons. In my first year here, the freeway was closed at different times by both fire and snow.

The road brings the whole world to town. In the days after 11 September 2001, a Moslem family went through their prayers in the shade of the trees around the service station. They were from another world, yet the rundown Ford Falcon into which they neatly folded themselves after they had prayed was a phrase from the local dialect.

Another time, I was sitting in the Chinese restaurant which adjoins the hotel when a motorbike gang arrived wanting to be fed, every member kitted in club colours, mostly black, mostly leather. Before long, a mobile phone rang. It was answered by a junior member who consulted a more senior member before finally the bikie boss agreed to take the call. He moved his beard to one side before he could speak. There were no pleasantries.

'Fuck.'

He wasn't happy. The table fell silent.

'Fuck.'

The whole restaurant fell silent.

'Jesus Fucking Christ.'

The news was obviously bad. I imagined that he was learning of the infidelity of his woman or, worse, that some part he needed for his Harley was unavailable until next week. The only other prospect was that a gang battle had erupted and wasn't going well. That didn't bear thinking about.

The call ended.

'Fuck me dead,' he said as he tossed the phone back to an underling.

There was a respectful silence.

'What's the problem?' one of the others finally ventured.

'The dollar just fell below fifty cents.'

Towards the end of 2000, for reasons which I still can't properly articulate, I bought a three-bedroom fibro chateau in Gunning. I had never lived on my own before. Back then, the house cost about the same as a second-hand Falcon although the car would have come with air-conditioning which the house certainly didn't. But I needed a roof over my head and I liked the idea of a place from which nobody could throw me out. The way I was feeling, it could have been anywhere. Maybe I saw an affinity between myself and a town which looked like it was struggling. The agent told me, with refreshing candour, that I might never get my money back. It's the way things had been going, he said.

I wasn't fussed. I was putting aside my work as a Catholic priest and leaving the Jesuit order after twenty-one years as a member of that community. When you leave a religious order such as the Jesuits, it's a bit like getting divorced, sacked and evicted all on the same day, except that it is a decision you make for yourself, though that doesn't make the experience any more simple. It's not as easy as it sounds and it doesn't even sound easy. In need of security in every way, I decided to scratch together as much money as I could lay my hands on and buy as much property as it would buy. My friends Jonathon and Richard found themselves helping to load my belongings into a small truck and taking me by the hand to this small town they had passed through but never noticed. I wanted a place to hide, somewhere to rest an exhausted spirit. It didn't matter what the place looked like, nor even where it was. There was an irony in thinking I'd rest for a while beside the Hume Highway. The road is a monument to restlessness.

Unlike a river, a road does not begin at a place but at a time.

Work commenced on the Great Wall of China, which is actually a road – the only one visible from the moon – when a group of people felt threatened by outsiders.

The poet Horace called the Appian Way 'the queen of long distance roads'. By 244 BC it stretched 600 kilometres south of Rome. It was a wonder in its time but a mere run to the shops by the standards of the Pan American Highway which stretches 24,000 kilometres from Alaska to Patagonia.

The Appian Way did not begin in Rome, a place, but at the moment somebody decided to leave Rome, at the psychological moment at which a city decided to exert control over places. Pine and cypress trees were grown alongside it to shade both the troops and the trade for whom it was built as the road's traffic followed the expansion and contraction of an empire. Roads are political. Building them is a sign that somebody is the boss. Hitler built the autobahn to impress underlings. Osama Bin Laden built roads in Sudan in the early nineties after he had been exiled there, to let people know that he was a force to be reckoned with. There are men who concrete the driveway every time the daughter brings home a new boyfriend.

The Appian Way stretched further in time than it did on the ground. It survived its builders and most of its users: one of its jobs was to provide an avenue along which the dead could be safely buried beyond the walls of the city. Romans used the metaphor of a river, the Styx, to talk about the meaning of death but they used a road to talk about the dead. Many of the tombs along the Appian Way carried warnings to the living about the certainty of death and the uncertainty of doctors. There were thousands of them.

The Hume Highway has come, in its own way, to share this purpose. It carries numerous memorials, mostly to the young, some of whom died in accidents on the road itself, some in battle-fields on the other side of the world. Like a cemetery, the Hume is sacred space. Unlike a cemetery, it is noisy and respects no peace. For the most part, the freeway does nothing for the imagination. But the Hume is sacred space in the way a shopping mall or a courtroom or an operating theatre is sacred space. If people ever find stillness there, it is the kind of deep stillness in which they are changed. If they pray there, the words find them.

The Hume Highway begins at the moment in 1824 when two travellers, Hamilton Hume and William Hilton Hovell, left Gunning to head south to Port Phillip, now the site of Melbourne. An obelisk on the side of the old Hume Highway, a mile or two from our town, marks the occasion. It turned out to be a difficult journey which took the two men and their six companions, all with a convict record, to the brink. It was not made any easier by the fact that Hume and Hovell did not hit it off.

Hume, born in 1797, was nine years younger than Hovell. He was one of the first generation of Europeans born on Australian soil and is arguably the first 'native', as opposed, in the usage of the day, to 'black native', to have shown much interest in finding out what lay inside the country where he was born. He was a natural bushman with an instinct for survival in hostile environments, a fact which was significant in getting the party home without loss of life – a rare achievement in the history of Australian frontiersmanship. But Hume had a chip on his shoulder about where he had come from. In 1826, when he returned from his celebrated journey, he wrote to Governor Brisbane and said that he had had no problem 'presuming myself (altho' an Australian) capable from experience of undertaking such an expedition'. The word *altho'* has his fingerprints all over it.

Hume had started exploring country unfamiliar to Europeans when he was seventeen. In 1813, he and his brother, John Kennedy Hume, then aged fourteen (the man who was to be shot by bushrangers in Gunning), got as far south-west from Sydney as Berrima. They reported that decent grazing land was on offer down that way, welcome news to the people who mattered. The boys' mother was not so easily impressed. She forbade John from leaving home again.

Perhaps Elizabeth had already given up hope of restraining her eldest, Hamilton. Over the next ten years, he was part of a number of expeditions and his name became known among that group of entrepreneurs and speculators, dreamers and escape artists, still introduced to primary school age children as 'explorers'. His travels began rolling out the course of what was to become the Hume Highway, a road which began life as a track linking properties increasingly distant from Sydney. In 1818, in company with Charles Throsby and James Meehan, Hume negotiated streams, gorges, rocky terrain and forests to get as far as Marulan. It took three arduous weeks to get there from Liverpool, currently a south-western suburb of Sydney. Marulan is now best known as a truck weighing station on the Hume Freeway. You can drive back to Liverpool in ninety minutes.

In 1821, Hume was part of a group of four which pushed on beyond the Goulburn Plains onto the Yass Plains. John Kennedy Hume, who had evidently outgrown his mother's advice, was with them. They established a station called 'Woolloobidallah', which later changed its name to 'Collingwood', where John was still living when he was shot by the bushranger in 1840 on a night he should have listened to his mother and stayed home.

But back in 1824, Hamilton Hume, William Hovell and crew left 'Collingwood' for Western Port. They got to Corio Bay and, in so doing, became the first Europeans to travel overland between Sydney and Melbourne. They were not the last. In 1824, 'Collingwood' marked the frontier of European enterprise. Now it's on the outskirts of Gunning. That's assuming the town is big enough for skirts.

The property is still in the Hume family although the sign on the gate is minuscule for a place which is so venerable, at least in Australian terms.

'Collingwood' shares its name with an inner suburb of Melbourne and that suburb of Melbourne has given its name to one of the country's best known Australian Rules football teams. The eponymous Collingwood was one of Nelson's admirals. In the early eighties, the South Melbourne football club relocated to Sydney, heralding the start of a national football league, a phenomenon which has been difficult for smaller suburban teams but which has brought benefits to the communities which line the highways linking interstate football grounds. When the teams travel, so do the supporters. This is great for burger outlets but difficult if your property is called 'Collingwood'. John Emery, the current owner, got sick of enthusiastic supporters souveniring his sign on the way to Sydney, so he got one about the size of an envelope which they were less likely to notice. Eventually, the highway did the decent thing and went somewhere else.

You also have to look for the homestead, a building which dates from the 1830s and which is camouflaged by a stand of elms. Elms have a high opinion of themselves. They will impose their children on you without warning or apology, breeding in all directions at once as their roots send suckers into the world. They are subject to strange perversions and will surface through the floorboards of bedrooms and bathrooms to catch the occupants unawares. They will also show a willingness to repent, coming up through the floors of old churches and standing in silence among the groaning woodwork.

John Emery says that the elms were already getting in the way in the 1890s and he has records of his grandmother needing to have them lopped in 1900, by which time they were already old. John can remember a period in which he and his father worked long hours into the night, having already spent the day with their sheep, to build a trench to a depth of four feet around the perimeter of the house's courtyard. They filled it with concrete, the only stuff likely to keep the suckers at bay.

Melbourne is proud of the elms which line the avenue which leads into the city from the north. Gunning is older than Melbourne although Melbourne has, admittedly, grown faster. There are people around Gunning who will tell you in a stage whisper that Melbourne's famous elms are just suckers on the roots of ours. The roots tunnelled their way south faster than the road.

It's conceivable that the elms on 'Collingwood' go back to the first days of what is always called European settlement but should be called European restlessness. If the trees were introduced by either of the explorers, the most likely culprit was Hovell.

Hovell may have to share the honour of being the first to travel overland to Port Phillip, but he stands alone as the first to cover his tracks with litter. Hovell sowed clover everywhere they went and was especially fond of peach trees, writing in his journal that 'in every place we have stopped all night, and the Soil good, I have planted Peach Stones'.

Hovell dropped exotic seeds with one hand and hacked into existing trees with the other. The first line of the journal he kept after leaving Gunning notes that he 'commenced marking the trees as we passed along'. It was day one and Hovell was already nervous: the markings were meant to help them find their way back. Hume, who had better instincts for country, thought this was ridiculous and, once Hovell's arm got tired from all the chopping, refused to help. So did the lesser beings travelling with them.

Hovell had been a naval captain. On land, however, he was all at sea. He was born in Yarmouth, one of those places best known for the people who left it rather than those who stayed, and was twenty-seven when he arrived in the colony from England in 1813 with his first wife and two young children. The governing metaphor of the new colony was monetary. Free settlers who had the dignity of being born on English soil were known as 'sterling'. Hume was a 'currency lad'. Both men had short fuses.

One familiar lesson to draw from the Hume and Hovell expedition is the power of the person who gets to tell the story, the one whose words are left standing. Hovell had been introduced to Hume and given joint responsibility for the expedition partly because he was willing to contribute towards its cost. Both men took a big risk at this level and neither ever thought that the government had rewarded them adequately. But Hovell was also recommended as a 'man who is capable of taking observations', meaning both that he was an experienced navigator, albeit on water, and that he could keep a journal. Hume was a man of few words who kept his record of the journey in the form of a skeleton map.

Hovell wrote reams along the way in a leather-covered notebook about fifteen centimetres by eight centimetres. The diary begins innocuously with the words 'remarks on a journey' but is bound with a brass clasp, an indication that it was conceived from the outset as an item of value. Hovell dragged himself through each day's march but, every night, found sufficient energy to put pen to paper. He always refers to 'myself and Mr Hume'. The order of their names was important to him: no matter what was actually happening on the ground, in writing, his name came first.

Sometimes the journal reveals a sense of humour which was strangely out of sympathy with both the dire circumstances he was describing and the pathetic figure Hovell became in folklore. The vegetation they found south of the Murray was so dense that at times the team had to move on their hands and knees, visibility reduced to a few metres:

> *Mr Hume had his face so nearly covered with brambles and boyers that it appeared as if it had been done by the fair hand of some Amazonian damsel.*

One man had his trousers torn to pieces in the scrub:

> *leaving him in that state that had there been any doubt of his manhood before, these doubts were now removed.*

Hume and Hovell are the patron saints of all who fight on a journey, of everybody who just wants to get there and get home.

In the late spring and summer of 1824, the pair moved southwest looking like a pair of angry beacons: Hume with a shock of red hair, Hovell burying himself in his journal. The party left Gunning on 17 October and within a week had managed to cross the Murrumbidgee. On 8 November, they became the first Europeans to sight the Australian Alps from the inland side, but they didn't waste much time enjoying the view. Hume and Hovell were already at each other's throats.

They decided to go their separate ways, despite the greater

danger this would involve, and then proceeded to argue over every piece of equipment. Hume spent years embroidering the incident. Late in life, he was saying that they would have cut their only tent in two, except Hume eventually let Hovell have it rather than render it useless. He claimed that they fought physically over the possession of a frying pan until it broke. This has become the image of the pair that has stuck in the popular imagination: two blokes having a domestic miles from home.

In rest stops all along the Hume Highway, you still see pilgrims following their example, arguing over maps, food, body odour or what somebody said to the in-laws they have just fled. At any time, there are fifty thousand people doing a lap of Australia in some kind of mobile accommodation. Known as 'grey nomads', they are mostly newly retired and the mobile home has taken a significant bite out of their superannuation. It may be the long-awaited adventure of a lifetime, but to somebody who encounters them on the road, these travellers often look like the restless damned which Dante knew, tracing a circle in an outer darkness in which they are never able to escape themselves. Hume and Hovell are their patrons. It's a pity the pair didn't think to exploit the money to be made from travel psychology.

Hovell could only see the new country with old eyes. As he went, he filled it with mental furniture he had lumbered from the other side of the world. Grasslands 'look like Meddow land in England', Port Phillip reminds him of the County of Norfolk, and when the party caught a lobster, Hovell wrote, 'I cannot perceive any difference between it and the Lobsters in England.'

The diarist coped with stress by absenting himself emotionally. He was not really there, fantasising instead about the bliss of the natives who have 'neither House rent nor taxes to provide' and are 'happy within themselves'. On one occasion, the man driving Hume's bullock cart was nearly killed when the ground gave way on the side of a range they were negotiating. Hovell responds as if he'd read about this incident in *The Times*: 'it will be here proper to mention the superiority of Bullocks to Horses in Mountain travelling.' Only once does Hovell mention anyone other than Hume by name. The lucky chap was James Fitzpatrick. But he does name his dog, Rolla, and is quite emotional when it goes missing. He mourns the loss of another dog, 'a very industrious little fellow', and is almost inconsolable when a favourite bullock, 'poor old Captain', has to be killed to feed the 'men', who appear as a lesser species scarcely worth such a sacrifice. He praised the creature which up to then, as leader, had to 'make a road for the others' – the first recorded roadwork on what was to become the Hume Highway.

There are countless references in the journal to the manner in which Hovell was tormented by mosquitoes (whose name he never seems to spell the same way twice) and other insects. He envies the natives who 'go naked and lay in the dirt and smoak'. Even here, however, Hovell's sense of humour is still in evidence. He calls his nemesis the Devil Fly 'becaus they have the power to tormant us and they at the same time are almost invisible'. He refers to them as 'old friends'. Hovell's sense of humour, although tinged by a feeling of superiority, is his redeeming feature:

> for the last few days we have been much troubled by the
> Misketo and the Devil fly, I am now covered with them,
> which, I suppose is the reason of my thinking to Mention it.

To the extent that either Hume or Hovell are noticed at all, Hovell gets a shocking press. Australians have tended to side with the local-born Hume whose name is all over the map of south-eastern Australia, an inevitability once that name got attached to the country's main street. A quick look through the phone book will turn up literally hundreds of businesses which are his by association, even if they got their name in the first instance because of the road. Some of them are expected: Hume Motors, Hume Driving School, Hume Mufflers, Hume Service Station, Hume Smash Repairs, Hume Truck Wreckers, Hume Tyre Dealers, Hume Caravan Accessories and so on. Then there are Hume Building Society, Business Solutions and Bottle Shop. Doors, Dry Cleaning and Demolitions. Fences, Furniture and Funerals. Everything from Hume Locksmiths to Hume Insurance Brokers, from Hume Primary School to Hume Palliative Care. Hovell, on the other hand, has very little.

THIS IS NO TIME FOR THE PRESENT
— Bumper sticker, Hume Highway

Gunning has public secrets. A couple of years after I moved here, I was talking with a group of older women, graziers mostly, the kind of people I would hardly have met in the city, but was thankful that I had. They had weathered long summers and dry winters but, for all that, I thought, would never tolerate a cup without a saucer or a bed without a bedspread. I warmed to them at once and mentioned I was interested in the road.

'Do you know about Hot Dog?' one asked.

I didn't.

'Oh, you must know about Hot Dog.'

She found someone else to tell me the details.

'Hot Dog was a comfort stop for the truck drivers,' said the second woman. 'It was on the Highway just out of town on Pinch Hill.'

Pinch Hill is no longer signposted but its name goes back to Hume and Hovell.

'Oh,' I said. 'A comfort stop. You mean there were toilets there.'

'No. No.' The second woman went to find a third who could tell me more.

'Not toilets,' the third said. 'It was a brothel.'

The brothel ran under the guise of a hot-dog stand, behind which there were a number of caravans where drivers could find comfort of sorts. The women who told me this did so without condemnation. There was even a touch of wry amusement as well as compassion; they said that the women who worked there didn't have much of a life. Another told me that, when you thought about it, Hot Dog wasn't a bad name for a brothel. I was already thinking about it.

Later that day, I called into the general store to buy a paper.

'I believe you've been hearing all about Hot Dog,' said Marilyn, across the counter.

Hume was not a romantic but he liked roads and trusted their makers. The three convicts he had assigned to him for the 1824 expedition, Harry Angel, James Fitzpatrick and Claude Bossawa, all had experience as road builders. No sooner had Hume returned than he was writing, in 1825, to the *Australian*, saying he was willing to bet £500 that he could take a horse and cart along the full length of the journey he had just struggled to complete on foot.

Roads are a significant part of bringing a strange land to book, the act of domestication that needs to follow conquest. Both Hume and Hovell lived for years on the side of the road that became their monument, almost as if they wanted to keep an eye on their legacy. Hovell retired to Goulburn where he became a magistrate, one of the first local councillors, a member of the board of the hospital and commissioner for crown lands. He complained about people asking him for help at odd hours, but he did make his paddock available to local cricketers.

His house was on Auburn Street, part of the road which in 1928 was named the Hume Highway. By that stage Hovell was dead enough not to care. He was buried in 1875, having made it to ninety years of age, and shares a grave with his second wife, Sophie. Until the bypass was built around Goulburn, their resting place lay within view of the Sydney Road. Every afternoon, the bluestone walls of the Goulburn jail throw a blanket of shadow across them.

Hume bought a property near Yass at precisely the point at which the expedition had camped on its first night out of Gunning. This was where he chose to live out his days with his wife, Elizabeth, watching the flow of traffic along the road steadily increase as land was taken up and people prospered. Like Hovell, he became an *éminence grise* in the area and his house, Cooma Cottage, is now owned by the National Trust. It, too, has been bypassed.

Every day, travellers pull off the new Hume Freeway and stop in Gunning. They don't stay long. The minute the car door opens, a portable world is suddenly decompressed. Pillows fall out. Drink bottles and chip wrappers escape. The tail end of an argument jumps into the street. A nappy bag is released from the boot. People hold mobile phones to their cheeks like face sponges. The engine dies and the whole street can hear the car stereo, announcing what planet these people come from: classical, heavy metal or country. The ones who've spent miles listening to nursery rhymes get looks of pity. Travellers refuel, find a toilet, get something to drink then suck everything back inside the body of the car. A car on a long trip is like a bag with too much stuff in it.

People stop for directions. In the height of summer, I saw a mini-bus with half a dozen Asian tourists stop outside the post office. The signs back to the freeway give the names of the next towns: Goulburn in one direction and Yass in the other. But they don't say anything about Sydney or Melbourne. The tourists looked confused. The driver waited for a customer to emerge from the post office. It was one of the locals, a man who never leaves a shop without an elaborate ritual of hitching his pants up as he goes. He always looks like he's still getting dressed.

'Sydney,' the driver asked him. 'Please. Sydney.'

'Sydney,' the man repeated with excessive care.

'Yes. Sydney.'

The rest of his passengers were fanning themselves in the shade of the war memorial.

The local made a show of thinking. He was already rehearsing the story for the pub.

'Sydney. No. Sorry. This ain't Sydney.'

It's hard to know if the response is proud or cruel.

The mini-bus zipped up and pressed on.

A road is the antithesis of a river. A river rises in one place and finds its way eventually into a body of water: a sea, a lake or another river. The current indicates its direction. It may do unruly things. It can burst its banks and, over time, change its course. But a river rests in a place, on its bed. Humans tend to describe the world in their own image and likeness: the furthest point of a river from its head is its mouth.

It's not so easy to see a road as made up of human parts, although, ironically, the first bypass was performed on the Hume in 1967, the year the world's first successful coronary bypass was performed in Cleveland. Both procedures had the same root cause: congested arteries. Only one part of the human body is regularly used to describe the shape of a road. A road has shoulders. It is there to do a job, to bend its back, to carry loads. A river has a mind of its own. A road is a beast of restless burden.

The Greek philosopher, Heraclitus, used the image of a river to explain that all things are in a constant state of change. One of his fragments says 'upon those who step into the same river, flow other and yet other waters.' Plato, in a dialogue called *Cratylus*, later gave those words the meaning that is commonly attributed to them:

> *Heraclitus is supposed to say that all things are in motion and nothing at rest; he compares them to the stream of a river, and says that you cannot go into the same water twice.*

This often gets abbreviated to 'you cannot step into the same river twice'. In other words, by the time you put your second foot in a river, the water which welcomed your first foot has already moved on.

Bitumen, in contrast, may melt in the heat but it doesn't really go anywhere. You can set foot on the same road twice. But you won't be the same person when you do. You'll have aged, even if just a few minutes. People often use roads to measure the change that has taken place in their own lives. They will think back on previous trips along a road and remind themselves of the time they passed that way when they were children, or before they had children of their own or before their children had children.

The Hume is an exception to the rule. It is a bit like a river. It has changed course so many times that you do wonder if you can set foot on the same road twice. You can go looking for forgotten pieces of the old road, which are still there, from every period of its existence, often in surprising places, and wonder if you are looking for something like a memory. Or you can just sit still on its banks and eventually the whole world will pass by. You can find anything on the Hume, almost every part of Australian history has been over it at some point. You have to ignore the signs which keep you going at 110 kilometres an hour and resist the urgency of the road to move you from one end to the other as quickly and painlessly as possible. You have to go slowly.

A bicycle is the perfect vehicle for exploration.

A bicycle with an unfit rider is even better.

A bicycle with an unfit rider who thinks he has seen this road a thousand times is best of all. One who wouldn't have lasted a day with either Hume or Hovell.

There was one living in Gunning. He couldn't sit still on his own.

THE OLDER I GET, THE BETTER I WAS
— Rear window sticker, Hume Highway

I had lived in Melbourne for seventeen years as a member of various Jesuit communities. In that time, I had jobs which took me to every part of a large city and I was occasionally asked to speak on issues, normally ones about which I knew much less than I thought I did, on the radio and in the papers. One day I might be giving a talk on one side of town and the next day I might be saying a wedding or a Mass on the other side. I could count on running into people I knew anywhere in the metropolis and there was always somebody else I could drop off and see before I finally went home. I belonged nowhere because I belonged everywhere. I lived on the road.

I am sure that the work I was doing mattered to people but there's a difference between thinking your work is important and thinking you are important because you do the work. I am afraid I was beginning to think that I was important because of what I did. The city felt small to me. When I got to Gunning, population 500, it was overwhelming by comparison.

Melbourne had become a different place for me in the time since I had left. The whole city had become focused in my mind on one small flat in Ripponlea which was where my friend Jenny lived. As I grew close to her, I felt less anxiety to know everybody else. A truck driver is tiny in relation to his or her rig; but without the driver, the truck is just an empty husk. A city is like that. The person you share it with is one individual among so many. But, for me, the city had become a husk without her.

They call them push-bikes for a reason. The bloke who sold me mine ran bicycle tours and took an interest in the trip I was planning for the end of 2001, advising me, first and foremost, to invest in a decent saddle. The Chinese frame that fell within my budget would be fine, he said. Not brilliant, but it should do the job. On the other hand – he hoped I didn't mind if he was frank. Not too many Chinese, he said, had a bum like mine. It would require support.

He spoke as softly as a counsellor, insinuating an entire underworld into one word. I nodded. But I still thought the saddle supplied by the manufacturer looked supportive enough. My childhood bike, after all, only had one diaphanous piece of plastic between my end and that of the bike and I had cycled to university every day for five years on a saddle that looked so severe that I seldom bothered to chain up the bike. I just found a place in the rack next to one that looked more accommodating.

'You will be travelling alone?'

'Yes. I think so.'

'You will need something behind you, if you don't mind the expression.'

I wasn't being co-operative. I was wary of a shop full of what looked to me like unnecessary gadgets and accessories with which I thought Paul was trying to load me up for a future garage sale.

Another customer arrived and showed his grandson a secondhand bike that he wanted put aside for the boy's birthday. We got chatting.

'It's my birthday the day after tomorrow,' I volunteered.

'How old will you be?'

'Forty.'

Both Paul and the grandfather looked at me like I was too old to be buying cheap Chinese bikes. Anybody still riding at my age ought to have learnt a few lessons by now and be investing in an alloy frame, preferably one made in Europe. There's a point at which you either get serious about something or give it away. Forty-year-old stamp collectors don't rip the corners off envelopes. They carry small lists of elusive items in secret parts of their wallets. Paul and his other customer eyed the bike I had chosen like they knew a mid-life fling when they saw it.

'Don't worry,' said Paul, 'I look after everybody. I even look after the old folks in the retirement centre up the road.'

'That's good of you,' I said.

'Yes. I fix the spokes on their wheelchairs.'

The grandfather left with the boy who was looking disdainful at the prospect of a second-hand bike.

'But the grips on your handlebars are good,' Paul went on.

'Is that important?'

He was smiling now.

'It will be more comfortable when you have to get off and push.'

Mum watched me pack on the verandah of her home in North Sydney. She asked me why I needed so much stuff.

'Running repairs.'

'What about this?'

She held up an incriminating copy of *Anna Karenina*.

'Something to read?'

'Won't that be dangerous?'

'I mean when I stop.'

She waved me goodbye. A few minutes later, she passed me in

the car as she was going up to the shops to buy the Sunday papers, and then passed me again on her way home, by which stage I had already dismounted and was pushing my way up the first hill. I waved back cheerfully but Mum was keeping her eyes steadfastly on the road. I wanted to get to the top before she remembered she had forgotten to get milk and came back for it.

At the top of the hill, I cruised past our family church where an old friend was standing outside, dressed up and ready to start saying Mass. I recognised some of the parishioners as they filed in and felt a pang. Not so long ago I'd have been saying Sunday Mass myself. I hadn't seen my friend for ages, but I didn't stop. He looked like he had things to do.

So did I. I trained my eye on a blue line which had been painted on the road outside the church to mark the course the marathon had followed in the Sydney Olympics the year before. The minute I got onto that, I felt more athletic; it helped that the road started to ease itself downhill. I was moving now. There ought to have been crowds cheering me, not just a few Sunday morning stragglers minding their own business, some still on their way home from parties, others out for a leisurely jog. I stopped on the cycle way of the Sydney Harbour Bridge and rang Jenny in Melbourne, where she was still in bed.

'Five kay down and nine hundred to go,' she said, her voice wiping sleep from its eyes.

I felt like I was cycling towards her. But it was too early to tell her that.

The good thing about riding in slow-moving traffic is that you feel like you are making progress. Within an hour, I had left the place where Governor Macquarie, who was good at tidying things up, had an obelisk built in 1817 to define the starting point of all roads in the colony, and had reached Ashfield where I turned onto the Hume Highway itself. There is a point in every city where the number of coffee shops and cafes is suddenly exceeded by the number of automotive businesses, a point where latte land gives way to a fantasy on wheels. This is what delineates the inner city from the suburbs and every year in Sydney the place moves a little further west. At the time I was riding, it was easy to locate. It was marked by a hybrid business in Enfield where you could get your vehicle washed while you had a cappuccino. I asked if they did bikes which they didn't – not even, they said, if I supplied my own coffee.

The road I was on passed through Bankstown, named after Sir Joseph Banks, the botanist on the First Fleet, and through Bass Hill, named after George Bass. In 1795, George Bass and Matthew Flinders came up the George's River and 'discovered' the Bankstown area in a dinghy called the *Tom Thumb* which was about the size of a family sedan. They were both in their early twenties and in rude good health but that did not inhibit them from finding a young man called Martin to do the rowing. That may have been his first name or last name. He doesn't figure much.

Later, in a more commodious vessel, Bass and Flinders would circumnavigate Tasmania, and Bass had the moody strait of water between Tasmania and the mainland named in his honour. Flinders was good at getting around things. He went on to be the first to circumnavigate Australia. By the time Flinders got back to England in 1810, his wife had been waiting for his return for thirteen years, the last six of which he had spent as a prisoner of the French on Mauritius, where he had dropped in for repairs on his ship and found the service poor. By the time he got home, his dinner was well and truly cold. He sat down to write his memoirs and no sooner had they been completed than he died. The first copies were rushed to his bedside. His wife's reaction is not recorded. She had to read the book to find out how he'd spent their marriage.

There is a plaque at the side of the road here at Bass Hill to mark the achievements of Banks, Bass and Flinders, reminding readers that Banks 'continually advocated and was principally responsible for the settlement of Australia'. You have to be looking to find the plaque. Roadside businesses change hands all the time and the first thing a new tenant does is expunge all evidence of the previous one. An area like this doesn't give much away about its past.

On the corner of Henry Lawson Drive, though, I found the badge of a BMW which must have been in an accident there a long time before because the logo had faded. It could have been there for years, maybe even long enough for the people involved in the accident to have got through the phone queue at their insurance companies and to have reached a human operator. I picked up the BMW badge and strapped it to the frame of my bike, knowing it would earn me more respect on the roads of Sydney. It covered the warning labels which looked a bit like they held the bike together and which I was already tired of reading. The one warning against using the bike for either serious sports or for stunts was grating on me.

This part of the Hume Highway is not used much now by traffic heading from Sydney to Melbourne. The following Sunday would see the opening of the final freeway extension which meant that you could now drive out of the city without seeing any of it.

Australia has a curious ritual for welcoming major new roads. For the day or two after they are completed, the appropriate authority invites people to come and walk all over them. People walked across the Sydney Harbour Bridge when it was opened in 1932 and some of them, including my mother, were still fit enough to join the crowd which walked through the Harbour Tunnel when that was completed sixty years or so later. The custom is hard to explain. It's a bit like celebrating the delivery of a new car by pushing it home from the dealer.

Anybody who is now heading towards Canberra or Melbourne will notice that the Hume Highway, as many knew it, has itself vanished. There is no longer a single set of traffic lights between Sydney and Canberra and, with that, one of the great tests of family and friendship has been taken away. Kids these days don't know what they are missing out on. There needs to be an interactive museum which provides the young with an experience of what the road to Melbourne used to be like before cars were air-conditioned, before kids had inboard DVDs to protect them from adult conversation and before parents had mobile phones to protect them from kids. The young need to know what the combination of hot vinyl upholstery and a hundred sets of traffic lights can do to the human spirit.

I passed over Prospect Creek before I realised it and had to double back, looking for Lansdowne Bridge, opened in 1836, the oldest part of the Hume Highway still in use. The road has been duplicated to provide four lanes and the original bridge now comprises the east-bound ones, the ones I hadn't come across. Lansdowne Bridge is a study in functional elegance. Its opening was a study in colonial kitsch. When the great day came round, the then Governor Bourke decided that he wanted to see a procession over the bridge which represented everything the settlers could be proud of. It was Australia's first *mardi gras*, a demonstration of colonial pride. Native-born boys were chosen to bring bullock drays across, followed by sheep, oxen, horses and goats, followed by floats displaying ox hides, wine, various preserved meats, oil, fruit and so on. After the procession, the public were encouraged to walk all over the new road. Governor Bourke was delighted and told the crowd that the bridge would last for centuries.

Some individual with a can of spray paint has left his or her mark next to the original inscription honouring David Lennox, the man who designed and built the bridge. The graffitti meant nothing to me. Lennox, on the other hand, is worth getting to know.

Following the death of his wife in 1832, Lennox, a stonemason from Scotland, decided to make a fresh start as far away as possible. At the age of forty-four, having left two young daughters in the hands of his sister, he arrived in Australia. There was plenty of work going and before long the irritable surveyor-general, Major Thomas Mitchell, discovered Lennox working on the masonry that was to front Sydney Hospital and the new Legislative Council. The pair got talking. Lennox already had considerable experience building bridges, having worked for a fellow Scot, the engineer Thomas Telford, one of Britain's most established road and bridge builders. Telford was among the first to realise that the secret of a good road was not so much how it coped with traffic as how it coped with water. Even a brush with that kind of expertise meant a lot in the colony.

Lennox suddenly found himself lifted a few rungs on the social ladder. Mitchell made him first Sub-Inspector of Roads and then Superintendent of Bridges. His first stone bridge was the Lennox Bridge west of Sydney in the approaches to the Blue Mountains. The one I was now looking at, Lansdowne, with an arch of 110 feet, came a little later. For this bridge Lennox got a bonus of £200 and his salary was doubled; the convicts who'd done all the work got extra rations on opening day.

Over time, Lennox built bridges in a number of places along what was to become the Hume Highway: at Berrima, Black Bob's Creek and Yass. Sadly, the others are no longer standing. Lennox died in 1873 and, like Jesus and Mozart and most of the convict bridge builders, ended up in an unmarked grave.

Nine months after the bridge was completed, it was still not open for traffic because the tollhouse hadn't been completed and, as everyone knows, a bridge without a toll has no real purpose. These days, all that remains of that building are three large boulders which sit beneath the windows of a cavernous family restaurant which now occupies the tollhouse site, one of those establishments where you pay one toll for all you can eat. Signs urged patrons to book early for Christmas.

It was time for lunch so I settled down inside.

There was a large family function in full swing alongside me. I think it must have been an engagement party as two young people were fascinated with each other and the rest were squabbling ferociously, apart from an older man who was lecturing the couple on politics. The nation had just been through a federal election so he was like a bloke who wants to talk football in the off season. The happy pair were not paying him much attention. They were on my side of the table, displaying their mutual admiration by secretly slipping corn crackers into each other's bum cracks. I guess it didn't matter when the food was so cheap. I finished my lunch and got out before they started on the jelly and ice-cream.

Warwick Farm Racecourse is one of Australia's *dercas* places. It's *sacred*, backwards. This was where my father used to come for the races and from which, as kids, tired and restless, we used to start counting the number of sets of traffic lights until we got home. A small sign near the gate which simply says 'Polo' gives a clue as to different reasons the venue has left its small scratch on history. This is the place where, during a polo match in 1990, the Australian media magnate, Kerry Packer, died. And then came back to life.

It's common that places such as Lourdes and Fatima, where people have claimed visions of a religious nature, become the destination for millions of pilgrims. It's funny that the same thing doesn't happen to places where people have the opposite kind of vision.

Packer, a renowned gambler, is always billed as 'Australia's richest man'. On the day of his heart attack, he hit the jackpot. Only five per cent of the ambulances in Sydney at the time were equipped with heart starters, also known as defibrillators, the machines which thud the heart back into action. You always see them on TV medical shows because they look so dramatic. A friend of mine had suggested I carry one on my bike just in case. But I had been to the doctor before setting out to check that I didn't need a bypass myself and besides, I needed room in my panniers for my current companion *Anna Karenina*.

On 7 October 1990, one of the small number of ambulances then equipped with a heart starter happened to be cruising along the Hume Highway at the gates of Warwick Farm when the call for help went out. By the time the paramedics reached Packer, his heart had not been beating for seven or eight minutes. He just made it. Yet within a week, he was back at work, making life unpleasant for journalists who tried to get shots of the man who had come back from the grave. He donated $3 million to the government to have defibrillators, which are now known as 'packer whackers', installed in every ambulance in the state.

Kerry Packer returned from the beyond with the ultimate investment advice.

'I've been to the other side,' he was reported as saying. 'And let me tell you, son, there's fucking nothing there.'

Mr Packer was fifty-three at the time of the incident. He was a young man to have achieved such enlightenment, an old man to be so poor.

People's passions are seldom boring but often hard to comprehend. In Liverpool, a vintage speedster club was having their Christmas swap-meet. People who'd spent their weekends restoring old speedsters, most no bigger than a go-car, some fifty or sixty years old, had brought them here on trailers to show off to someone who might understand their enthusiasm.

One of the participants told me that when she had travelled around Australia with her husband she started collecting teaspoons but found they made too much noise rattling around in the drawer of their mobile home. So she decided to collect labels from two-litre cartons of milk. Every part of Australia has a different dairy and every dairy has its own labels, so it was ideal. Her favourite was the one she got from Albury, on the Murray River, which featured a paddle steamer. She and her husband had married young and promised themselves they would retire at fifty. They worked for their dream and had managed to clock off and take to the road in a mobile home by the time her husband was fifty-one. They did all sorts of trips, the longest being eight months and the shortest eight weeks. It was just as well they did, she said. Her husband died of liver cancer at the age of fifty-six, the result, she believed, of something an unscrupulous builder had made him use on a job when he was in his twenties.

He had collected Austin A40s, and done them up, which made more sense than collecting snail shells, she said. She knew people at the speedway swap-meet. That was why she was here. Most of them, she said, had garages bigger than their houses.

'I tell people he's gone to the great swap-meet in the sky. It took a long time for me to be able to joke about it like that. But I do know he's up there somewhere.'

The development of the motor car created the motel, a term coined in California in 1925, when Arthur Hieneman opened the Milestone Motel, the first facility of its kind where, for $1.25 a night, travellers got their own kitchen and their own garage. Soon the self-contained unit was everywhere. TV replaced the conversation of the front bar as the main form of recreation for travellers and with that, it became more and more possible for people to pass through a place without actually being there. But they were also more likely to be safely on their way the next morning. Hieneman knew the importance of location. The Milestone was ideally situated at San Luis Obispo, on Route 101, halfway between San Francisco and Los Angeles. Since then, we have discovered that everywhere is halfway between two some-wheres, so everywhere there is a motel.

I trundled on and joined the freeway for the first time. It took me to Campbelltown where, lo and behold, I found a motel and asked for a room with a bath. The owner told me I was in luck. She had one. She didn't tell me the bath had been designed for amputees.

I extricated *Anna Karenina* from the spare tubes and T-shirts with which she had become intimate in the outer suburbs of Sydney. She held me for half a page before she got bored with me, turned over on her spine and fell asleep under her cover.

The next morning, I was moving slowly. It didn't seem fair. I have watched the Tour de France on TV and know that those cyclists regard a day's work as somewhere between 200 and 250 kilome-tres, often in mountainous terrain. I'd done about a quarter of that on a flat road but my legs didn't seem to understand reason and there was a pesky bone in my rear end which was making its presence felt. It had spent forty years tucked away inside my body without so much as a murmur. I didn't know it existed. Today, it was like a quiet child which had suddenly reached adolescence and was calling all the shots. Every other part of me was thinking of ways to tip-toe quietly around its tantrums. The bicycle man had been right. I needed more support.

I pushed the bike down the street and found a place for break-fast where it didn't take long to convince myself that the ordeal which lay ahead entitled me to bacon and eggs. Sitting at a table on the footpath, I watched Campbelltown stir into life on a Monday morning. Early visitors regarded Campbelltown, named in honour of Macquarie's wife, as a social backwater, and even when it celebrated its centenary in 1920, it was still a sleepy hollow. One writer said then that the place was a hundred years old and looked it, a township which had been forgotten because it was off the original south road. Things have changed. The area is now part of Sydney's growth corridor, a quarry for stories of both urban chaos and urban magic, a mine of both horror stories and fairy tales. The place is now 180 years old and looks about 18.

There were so many people about that I wheeled my bike around to the back of the Monte Carlo cafe and found a kerb which was about the right height to enable me to remount in relative dignity. I didn't want to perform for a street full of people dragging themselves to work.

Once I got going, I didn't feel too bad. I thought my bum would keep quiet if I ignored it for long enough, and eventually it fell into a kind of sullen numbness. I decided to get as far as possible before it started to complain again.

On the way out, I passed over the freeway, the traffic gliding under me at 110 kilometres an hour. Santa had recently been that way. He, or someone else, had added a touch of Christmas cheer to the speed limit signs. With a stroke of a paintbrush, '110' had become ' HO.' As you joined the freeway, they read ' HO HO HO'.

There was no break in the suburbs until I reached Narellan, where William Hovell, recently retired from the sea, received a land grant on arrival in the colony. The houses rolled on to Camden, which announced itself brazenly as the 'birthplace of the nation's wealth', a claim based on the empire founded here by John and Elizabeth Macarthur and their obliging flock of merino sheep, an enterprise which dramatically upsized the colonial economy. By 1820, the Macarthurs' wool was already fetching something like £1 a pound. Unimaginable sums of money were involved.

The wool, of course, had needed a road to get to port. Two early surveyors-general, the grim John Oxley and his successor, the even more grim Thomas Mitchell, both had property in the vicinity and both wanted to have the route of the road altered to run close to their front gates. Only a cad would suggest that self-interest was ever involved.

The bloke who helped the controversial Macarthur secure his grant of 5,000 acres in 1805 was Lord Camden, the Secretary of State for War and the Colonies, a curious combination of responsibilities. Perhaps Camden had a crystal ball and foresaw a time when his name would be immortalised in the windows of video shops and pizza parlours, despite the fact that John Macarthur was not in favour of a town being built where Camden now stands. He thought it would bring riff-raff to the area and pose a threat to his holdings. Macarthur, the Kerry Packer of his day, was used to getting his own way. His career marks the beginning of a major strain in Australian history: the tension between those in office and those in power. But this was one time when Macarthur did not prevail. Camden has got the parking meters to prove it.

There was a bike rack outside the post office and a seat where Santa came to rest his weary bones beside me. He had been trying to add a little merriment to the morning's business in the town but was finding the going tough. His beard was crawling with perspiration. An assistant arrived, who looked suspiciously like his wife, and helped him exchange his boots for thongs.

'That's a bit bloody better,' he said.

He noticed a child was listening and resumed his part.

'Ho. Ho. Ho.'

'Have you got any give-aways?' the child asked.

'Ho. Let's see. What about a lolly?'

The child was not impressed. It didn't help that Santa's satchel was a Coke cooler bag. The colours matched his outfit.

'Got any Coke?'

'If I did, I wouldn't be giving it to you. Ho. Ho.'

Santa started to ring his bell. He rang it like he was calling the next round of a title fight. Two babies started to scream.

'Merry Christmas,' said Santa humourlessly.

Santa pulled his cigarettes out of the side pocket of his cooler bag. The packet was red and white, so his entire ensemble was colour co-ordinated. He lit up and before long I noticed a strange smell. He had singed his synthetic beard with the lighter. It didn't seem to trouble him, he just brushed the stiffened fibres away with the back of his hand. There wasn't much left of the part of the beard below his mouth. That's what you get when you buy imported Santa suits. He needed a beard made from wool.

TRUCKS CARRY THIS COUNTRY
— Car sticker, Hume Highway

IF YOU CAN'T SEE MY MIRRORS, I CAN'T SEE YOU
— Truck sticker, Hume Highway

I was following the old Hume Highway. Between Camden and Picton, it negotiates a nasty bit of road over a sharp rise called Razorback – both a natural and psychological barrier until 1814 when Hamilton Hume managed to slip across. Like the Blue Mountains further north, the feature defined the early settlement. Before the freeway, it was regarded as the steepest section between Sydney and Melbourne.

Early travellers had a lot to say about the road in this part of the world. It was still bad in the 1840s when the traffic largely comprised vehicles laden with wool: the holes in the road were so deep that the drays regularly sank to their axles. Somebody once counted thirty drays passing by in a single day; they averaged six kilometres an hour. By 1846, there were two regular coach services south to Goulburn. On stretches like Razorback, the men got out and walked.

Before long, the road had forced me out of the saddle for the first time and I was walking myself. My pride was wounded but my bum was happy.

Suddenly, in a period of fifteen minutes, the weather turned around. The change began with a profound stillness which coincided with a long break in the traffic as if every living creature had decided at that moment to tip-toe off the stage, leaving me with the world to myself. Clouds rolled over and the light faded. It was cold and dark. Then thunder. The skies opened.

For the next half hour, I pushed into gale force winds as rain fell like glass. I was glad for my helmet, even more so when the hail started. The wind blew my glasses off my face. They landed in the gravel ten feet behind me and started edging towards the road. I turned around and, in that moment, realised what it would be like to be heading in the other direction, with that wind pushing the bike down that hill. Even on foot, I had trouble balancing and keeping myself upright. My shoes filled with water, my feet were freezing, my hands were numb, my pulse started racing and I was panting for breath. It might be okay to die of hypothermia on Mount Everest, I thought. But not on bloody Razorback.

I inched my way to the top and found what I was looking for. But I didn't stop long: there wasn't much to see, even in good weather. A simple blue sign on the side of the road declared that this was a memorial to the truck blockade of 1979. It didn't look like much of a memorial, to be honest. There was nothing except the sign, a place to pull a car over and an impressive accumulation of litter, most of it now dancing in the wind. Only the cigarette butts looked sullen and there were plenty of those. Cigarette butts don't budge for anything, even a cyclone.

You had to be in the know to realise that buried on this site is a 1967 W model Kenworth truck, a vehicle that was widely admired by the drivers of 1979. Digging a hole large enough for a truck of this size was easier said than done but, more than twenty years after the blockade, the ritual was important enough to be worth the effort.

The truck blockade of 1979, one of the more notable chapters in the history of the Hume Highway, deserves its curious memorial. For ten days before Easter that year, the road was blocked by the very people whose livelihood depended on it. They were like fishermen who were prepared to dam their own river rather than let it starve them.

In the end, the scale of the protest came as a surprise despite the fact that it had been brewing for a long time. For at least eighteen months there had been tension in the trucking industry, especially among owner-drivers, men who usually carried at least two hefty mortages and seldom had a house worth more than their truck.

In 1979, the truckies felt particularly hard done by. Their long list of grievances included load limits, cartage rates and the behaviour of the banks to which they were mortgaged. In the previous year, twenty per cent of the trucks on the road in New South Wales had been booked for overloading and drivers saw this as a cynical form of revenue raising. But the real bugbear was the road tax imposed by the New South Wales government. Many of the drivers were facing bankruptcy.

The seventies had marked an increasing awareness of truckie culture. There were songs about trucking, such as Slim Dusty's 'Lights on the Hill', which won the award for the song of the year at the first Australasian Country Music Awards in Tamworth in 1973 and soon became an anthem. It is about a driver who longs to get home to his own bed. Being a country song, the driver has to die at the wheel, a bit like a faithful soldier at his post. C.W. McCall's 'Convoy', a more upbeat, defiant number about truckies riding in triumph across the United States, reached number one on the American top forty in early 1976. There were Clint

Eastwood movies about gutsy drivers with nerves of steel. Truckies began to recognise themselves as part of a sub-culture. That sub-culture registered on the radar of the rest of Australia in April 1979.

On Monday afternoon, 2 April, a 35-year-old owner-driver from the outer Sydney suburb of Lethbridge Park, Ted Stevens, pulled into the parking bay on the top of Razorback. Two days before he'd told his wife that he was either going to get rid of the truck 'or I'll park it in the middle of the highway'. Stevens radioed other drivers to join him. He had worded up four friends, who were soon on the scene, but hadn't expected that he would catch a wave of angst. Within thirty-six hours, three hundred trucks were blocking the road. Another blockade was established further south on the Hume Highway, at Yass. Before long, there were blockades on every major road leading into Sydney. The city was under siege.

The state government didn't respond sympathetically. Four drivers were arrested. In the early hours of Wednesday morning, emergency legislation was rushed through parliament. A new Road Obstructions (Special Provisions) Bill which allowed authorities to forcibly remove the trucks and charge the drivers for the honour. The trucks stayed where they were.

John Laws, then as now a ubiquitous presence on talk-back radio, decided to help and paid a visit to Razorback in a helicopter. The drivers trusted Laws, whom many of them had as company on the road, although the newspaper reports of the day could not resist noting the discrepancy between Laws's appearance and that of the truckies. Laws wore 'trendy tobacco-coloured strides, open-necked shirt showing fine gold chains around the neck, gold watch and gold bracelet'. The drivers hadn't showered for days.

Laws also had the ear of the Labor premier, Mr Wran. Few politicians get anywhere in this country without heeding the potentates of talk-back radio. It beats me why prime ministers

don't take talk back on the floor of parliament and cut out the
need for focus groups, opinion polling and all that stuff. Wran
said he would hold off using his emergency legislation until he'd
heard from Laws. The following day, six drivers were taken by
helicopter to see the relevant minister for the first attempt at
talks. Later, Mr Wran got a helicopter down to see the drivers. The
TV stations had helicopters constantly in the air .

Meanwhile, Sydney was starting to feel vulnerable. Supplies of
fresh fruit and vegetables were in jeopardy. The papers reassured
readers that there would be plenty of milk, because that came to
the city by train, and plenty of eggs, because most of Sydney's hens
were batteried within the circle of the blockades. The dieting classes
were appalled that the city was now facing a cholesterol overload. It
was a curious siege when people were worried it would make them
fat. Cabbages were soon fetching a dollar each in Sydney.

By Saturday, there were 3,000 trucks blocking the road at forty
places around Australia. They dominated the news; only a few
paragraphs were spared for the election that would bring Mrs
Thatcher to power for the first time on the other side of the
world. Mr Wran said he doubted if there were enough police in
the whole of New South Wales to shift all those trucks. Ted
Stevens, who was bald apart from a dramatic moustache, had
become a national identity, known everywhere by his nickname,
Greendog. The public-relations battle was going his way. He knew
the impact of lifting the blockade, for example, to allow through
cargo that was to benefit charity.

For a while, there was a picnic atmosphere among the drivers.
No alcohol was allowed on the mountain. One journalist reported
that it seemed incongruous to see these men drinking soft drinks
and eating ice-creams in the heat as well as being careful not to
leave litter lying around. They were organising a roster to look
after rubbish.

Some women had travelled to join their men on Razorback. One, Barbara Frew, said that life on the road was tough on families. It had been a bit better until the baby came along because she used to be able to travel with her husband. 'The life is very hard on marriages. This is the second marriage for both of us.' A number of locals, from Camden and Picton, were bringing out food and inviting men back to their homes for a shower. Greendog Stevens said he'd been speaking on the phone to his wife and she was crying a lot but he was going to stay where he was until his truck rotted. Mr Wran told parliament that Stevens was 'no folk hero' but an anarchist who wanted to 'starve Australia into submission'.

The drivers also played tough. One man who tried to break the blockade was followed up the Hume to Liverpool where he was pulled from his truck by other drivers and bashed. Drivers employed by the major transport companies formed convoys and were escorted by police. The Prime Minister, Mr Fraser, said he was thinking of calling in the army because Wran wasn't getting it sorted.

Finally, however, the government conceded most of the drivers' demands. After ten days, the trucks started moving again and Sydney was saved from scurvy. One reporter observed that, before long, there was no evidence of the blockade left on Razorback other than hundreds of cigarette butts in the gravel on the side of the Hume.

Ken Coggan was the driver of the fifth truck from the top of the mountain during the blockade. He happened to be in the vicinity, carrying a load of fresh orange juice which the striking drivers started drinking until the owner of the load came along and locked the trailer. Eventually the juice had to be dumped. Twenty-something years after the event, Ken is one of the few owner–drivers in the blockade who is still in the business.

'I was younger then,' he says.

Ken has seen what the industry can do to people. The health of one of his best friends was shot to pieces by pills and the man now wears a colostomy bag and works in a motel on the coast; sometimes he rings Ken on his mobile to hear the latest from the road. The friend keeps saying he wants to get back behind the wheel, but Ken tells him he'd be mad. Drivers pop all kinds of stuff, he says, just to make the hours the industry demands. 'Sometimes they do it because they think it makes them heroes.'

Ken says he has never been into any of that. That's why he has survived and and so has his marriage. He counts his blessings. There are not too many drivers who can say the same. Ken left school at fifteen and was married at nineteen to a girl he met at the movies in Cootamundra.

'What's the secret of keeping a marriage together?'

'Honesty.'

I once travelled with Ken to Melbourne with twenty-five tonnes of raw chemicals in the trailer behind us. The chemicals were going to be turned into shampoo at the other end of the journey, part of Australia's effort in the war against dandruff. The front of Ken's truck was hardly the ideal environment in which to talk. It was noisy and there was an entire aisle between the passenger seat and the driver's seat. It was a place for one-word answers.

'Honesty,' he repeated.

Ken has had his moments. In thirty-six years on the road, he had been involved in two bad accidents.

One was on the Hume Highway, heading into Melbourne where a woman absent-mindedly did a U-turn in front of the truck. She was okay but the car was destroyed.

The other accident was worse. A woman whose marriage was breaking up decided to commit suicide by running her car under a truck. Ken was in the wrong place at the wrong time. He told me he can remember every detail of her car: make, model and colour. His truck went over on its side and he got wedged under the dashboard, from which position he had to be cut out. His back still gives him trouble. Some time later, he was in a shopping centre and he saw a woman who reminded him of the one who'd died. It freaked him out and he fled from the centre.

Ken drives the length of the Hume between Sydney and Melbourne six times a week, a total of 250,000 kilometres a year. Late on Friday night, he pulls into his yard which overlooks the freeway on the way into Gunning and goes down to the pub to unwind. On Sunday afternoon, he starts heading back towards Sydney to pick up another load. For the rest of the week, the Hume is home.

Ken grew up on a farm within a stone's throw of the Hume. Near Jugiong, not far north of Gundagai, there's a sign for Coggans Road which comes off the Hume and used to lead to the family property. As a boy, Ken lay awake at night listening to the highway. He can remember a time during heavy rain when his father went out to help trucks which had got bogged on the road and, with no means to shift themselves, just had to stay there until things dried out. Ken's father killed a couple of sheep for food because the drivers were so hungry, a memory which came back to Ken years later during the blockade on Razorback when local women arrived with home-made cakes and men turned up with meat for a barbecue.

Ken also remembers his father telling him about an old stone building on the side of the road at Coolac, less than 20 kilometres north of Gundagai, which was where Cobb and Co had changed horses in the old days. Ken's father knew old people who could remember those days. There is a living line of story on this road from stage coaches to prime movers.

In the cab that night we travelled together, I asked Ken why so many trucks have mermaids and girlie pictures on their mudflaps, visors, toolboxes or petrol tanks. Ken didn't know. He said there is a lot of pornography associated with the trucking industry. When we stopped for a meal break in Albury, he pointed out the range of magazines available, at least half of which came in wrappers.

There was an article in Ken's *Owner Driver*, a free industry magazine, about a priest who was raffling a truck to help pay for the new church his parish was building near the Hume, just north of Albury. The raffle was called 'Highway to Heaven II' and the Western Star Prime Mover, first prize, was worth almost $350,000 with tickets priced at $50. So the winner was going to do nicely. The article said this priest had once hitched a ride in a truck a couple of thousand kilometres to Perth across the Nullarbor Plain, which truckies call 'the big paddock'. The driver had told the priest that he only believed in three women: Mother Nature, Lady Luck and the Ladies of the Highway. But, said the priest to the interviewer, $50 spent in his raffle was 'a much better invest-ment than those ladies of the highway'. The priest's name was Father Casanova.

Ken Coggan told me that it's not uncommon for a driver to be approached by a prostitute. But there are also small signs of motherliness on the road. A hand-written sign in the truckies' section of the roadhouse in Albury asked drivers to let them know if they are having a shower so their meals could be kept hot. And I remember that the woman on duty was solicitous about gravy: she took time to put the right amount on the right part of the plate.

'There were plenty of prostitutes around during the blockade,' said Ken. 'That's one thing I remember. They did a good trade, too.'

Ken once transported a dinosaur skeleton for a museum. That was something a bit different. Another time he was offered $5,000 cash to deliver a load of pills but he walked away and hasn't even been back to the truckstop where the offer was made.

Ken didn't know what had become of Greendog Stevens. After the blockade, Stevens stopped driving. Ken said that Greendog was run off the road a couple of times and kept getting bricks through his windscreen from drivers who weren't happy with his stand. He disappeared and took up a singing career.

'Did the blockade change much?'

'It got rid of the road tax. So they just created a petrol tax. And the petrol tax is harder to beat. Blokes could lie about their mileage. But you pay the petrol tax at the bowser.'

As we'd neared Melbourne that night, Ken said that he wished he'd had the chance for more education and to travel more.

'You travel more than anyone I know.'

'This is not travel. This is driving.'

Then Ken shook my hand as I clambered down into the darkness, and said he was off to deliver his load to the shampoo industry after which he'd ring his son, who was also on the road, and finally his wife.

'I'll just pull over somewhere around midnight then head back the other way in the morning.'

The Hume Highway supports two cultures. Cars and trucks. Big wheels and little wheels. The two seldom come into contact, except tragically. Even if they find themselves at the same service station, cars and trucks have separate places to refuel. The trucks need more space and grumble to a stop under cavernous shelters of their own. The service stations of the Hume are like airports where light aircraft flit around in the shadow of 747s. Car drivers get intimidated by trucks. Bicycle riders get intimidated by cars. The small number who take to the road on foot, like Cliff Young, can be intimidated by bikes.

The funny thing is that the driver is also dwarfed by his or her truck. It's easy to look at the machine and forget about the person inside. If you pull in to a truck stop, the rigs lined up in the parking bays look pretty serious. Then you go inside and notice half a dozen quiet men sitting around plastic tables drinking flavoured milk and Coke. They don't take up much space.

I once watched a driver climb down from a machine to put an apple core in the bin. In the context, it seemed a small thing for him to fuss over. He lined the core up like a basketballer lines up a shot on goal. He missed the basket, so he danced across to the bin and, making a wide arc through the air with his arm, balanced it on top of the other rubbish. The performance was delicate, a small ballet. Then he hauled himself back into his truck which cleared its throat and got down to work.

SEX IS NOT THE ANSWER. SEX IS THE QUESTION. YES IS THE ANSWER.
— Bumper sticker, Hume Highway

ADVERTISE HERE
— Bumper sticker, same car

For a long time, one of the features of Razorback was the so-called Horderns Tree, an elegant Moreton Bay Fig, which, along with the slogan 'as I live I grow', was invariably pictured in the advertising of the Anthony Horderns Department Store. Horderns conducted business in an impressive building not far from Sydney's Central Railway, where it had a strong following among rural families. One of its busiest periods of the year there was always the week around Easter when farmers and graziers and their families came to town for the Royal Easter Show. The men and women of the soil had to cram an entire year's retail therapy into ten days.

The Horderns building is no longer part of the landscape and the tree which, in its day, was a tourist attraction in its own right, has died. It had once commanded an otherwise bald hilltop. Battling through the storm on my bike, though, I noticed that a young Moreton Bay Fig had been planted right on the side of the road. There were signs around it with the old motto: 'While I live I grow.' The new tree was a bonsai version of the original.

By the time I reached the top of Razorback, the rain had eased but the wind had freshened and was blowing into my face, pushing the storm rapidly towards Sydney. The only part of me that was dry was my bum and it was still having problems of its own. The hill down the other side of Razorback was steep, but, such was the wind, it felt like I was pushing uphill and Picton, at the foot of the hill, seemed like a distant prospect, let alone Melbourne which didn't even feel like it existed.

I finally did get to Picton and found a room in a hotel built in 1839 – one of a list of licensed premises in Australia which claim to be the oldest in some way, shape or form: the oldest licence, the oldest premises, the oldest purpose-built licensed premises, the oldest continually licensed premises, the oldest licensed premises continually in the same family and so on. The place I landed might have laid claim to the oldest carpet, the oldest bedspreads and the oldest unopened bottle of ouzo on the oldest top shelf. Instead, it boasted of being the oldest pub in New South Wales to be licensed as a brewery.

I was happy to drink to that before retiring to a room which had been originally occupied by soldiers in charge of convicts being escorted along the South Road to Berrima jail. If the room was one of the perks of authority, I thought, I was glad I wasn't a convict.

Maybe I was just cranky. I needed to get out of my wet clothes and lie down. I had a shower and listened on the radio to news of the storm which was sweeping across Sydney. There had been some injuries and the traffic was in chaos. The experts said that the storm had blown up south-west of Camden sometime around midday. I could have told them that. Nobody was asking me, though: my mobile phone hadn't rung for two days.

In the pub, I found a brochure advertising ghost tours. I thought that you'd hardly need to leave the premises where I was staying, but I rang the number anyway and spoke to Liz Vincent who happened to be a former resident of Gunning, a place, she assured me, with ghosts of its own. Picton, I learned, is particularly well supplied with supernatural residents and for the past six years Liz has taken visitors to their haunts. Ghosts have been part of her life for a long time. Liz believes in neither God nor heaven but rather that the people we love can scarcely bear to leave us and sometimes hang around as ghosts.

When Liz's mother died, she was able to smell the dead woman's perfume both at home and at work when nobody else could. Her father promised to send messages from the other side when he passed on and, according to Liz, has been in regular communication. This has helped her cope with her loss.

'I know he's there.'

A number of Picton's ghosts travel the Hume. There is a place on the old road over Razorback called Peach Tree Bend which, Liz says, many find disturbing. It is often deathly quiet; you don't hear any birds. I wondered if this was the place where I experienced the calm before the storm yesterday. Peach Tree Bend used to be the location of an inn. Apparently, in 1832, a convict by the name of Smithwick, already serving a life sentence, killed a bullocky on the site. Liz's next story was that, years after this, a team of bullocks went over the precipice at Peach Tree Bend and the driver was killed. Other victims of road accidents have been known to haunt the road. Liz Vincent believes that ghosts are restless beings who have not been able to find peace.

The old road has a ghostly presence of its own. Liz Vincent tells stories of cars which have driven off the highway on Razor-back and ended up in the bush, sometimes killing the occupants, because the car has tried to drive over an old route of the road. A phantom of the former road has appeared and deceived the driver, who has followed it as though it is real.

After a fitful night's sleep on one of the world's oldest licensed mattresses, I decided to discover more about the new Anthony Horderns tree. Snooping around Picton's nurseries, I found a man with a lot to say on the subject. He told me that the old tree had mysteriously died around the time that Anthony Horderns itself went out of business. He thought this was fitting. Sadly, he believed the original tree had been poisoned, and the rumour was that the people who owned the property had poisoned it themselves because they were sick of the trespassers who assumed it was a piece of public property. He didn't know whether or not to believe such stories. But he'd been part of a group which had hassled the local council to replant this piece of the area's history and had arranged for a suitable tree to be moved from Queensland at a cost of about $5,000. It was worth it, he said. A place needs its history, even if it has to be replanted.

MY WILD OATS HAVE TURNED INTO PRUNES AND ALL BRAN
— Bumper sticker, Hume Highway

Still pointed towards Melbourne, I pedalled slowly through Bargo which, in the early days, was known as Bargo Brush, a notorious hang-out for bushrangers. The 1850s saw the discovery of gold further south, around Goulburn, Braidwood and Araluen. In the history of Australia, gold has got people moving faster than anything. The volume of traffic increased enormously and locals were able to supplement their incomes by doing the repairs that were always needed on the South Road. Razorback became known as the gateway to a darker, less secure part of the world. There was a feeling of lawlessness beyond it, a tradition which has not died completely. I passed an anguished sign on a building site which said that the place had been vandalised and burgled the night before and that any help would be much appreciated.

Issues of road safety have limited the advertising signage on the new Hume, as on most major highways around the world. The high-water mark for billboards in the United States was during the mid-sixties when there were over a million of them all over the country. Then, at the time billboards began to be thought of as a safety hazard, TV came to the fore to pinch the advertising dollar. The number of billboards halved, although they had a brief reprieve during the seventies when they were one of the few places left for tobacco companies to promote their products. The Australian story is similar. There was a period in which cigarette advertisements were banned on TV and radio but still permitted in outdoor venues. There was even a strange period during which shop posters and outdoor hoardings were allowed, as long as they did not feature human beings.

In 1929, the Victorian government passed a law 'dealing with the erection of advertising hoardings and the exhibition of advertisements on or in the vicinity of any State Highway'. Even then, big money was involved. An advertising company challenged the validity of the law and the matter ended up in the High Court. Even as the case was being contested, fresh billboards were going up on the sides of highways. The High Court upheld the law and the billboards came down.

Victoria's Country Roads Board pointed out that similar laws restricting roadside advertising had been in force in England since 1907 and that forty-two states of the United States also had restrictions to some degree. The Board's annual report of 1930 made its case with naive indignation, bemused that the information on billboards had not been asked for by the public and was available elsewhere anyway:

> *Hoardings and advertisements are designedly erected where they will attract most attention. They therefore tend to distract the attention of the motor driver when he should concentrate on the road and the careful driving of his vehicle. In addition, they frequently obscure the landscape or mar the beauty of the surroundings.*

You no longer see many billboards on the Hume Freeway except in a few places where the road still comes within reading distance of private property, and advertising companies have leased land from the farmers and put up hoardings. Many of these have been leased in turn to fast food outlets and advise the weary driver how many minutes to the next shake, fry or tortured chook.

I counted the kilometres until I reached Mittagong, where a friend, John, had hidden the key to his house in a place I have sworn not to disclose. I was grateful for the opportunity to wash my clothes. John, a teacher, had taken an excursion of school children to Japan, an act of heroism worthy of praise – all the more so because it gave me the house and, with that, the entire run of John's bedside table to myself.

A proper bedside table is spacious, a window on the obsessions and neuroses of the occupant of the bed. It is generally covered by pills and potions, tonics and tablets, all of which suggest that the occupant hardly expects to wake. Either that, or it is buried under half-read books and magazines which suggest that the occupant hardly expects to sleep. John must have taken the contents of his table with him to Japan. I approved. Anybody travelling with a herd of teenagers needs all the comfort they can get. I could now put *Anna Karenina* to bed with due reverence, to sleep it off beside the lamp. She was starting to look a bit neglected after a few days in the pannier and I wondered if she'd have been happier sleeping with somebody else. She looked faithful but I was finding her hard to read.

I woke up the next morning with an odd sensation. I felt terrific.

This doesn't happen often and I was suspicious. But the feeling only grew as I rode out of Mittagong and rejoined the old road. A light misty rain was falling, not enough to fog my glasses but enough to provide a steady trickle of water over my lip and into my mouth. The air was sweet. The fog hung low. The miles clipped by.

Perhaps I had benefited from a good night's sleep. Perhaps, perish the thought, I was getting fit. I wasn't sure. I couldn't recall the last time I'd been in that condition.

I could have ridden forever.

I could not, however, ride past the Book Barn on the outskirts of Berrima, a place which offers an eclectic stock as well as a warm fug in which a damp cyclist can dry out in peace. Mikhail Gorbachev had visited some time before me and had signed a biography of Lenin which was now lying in state in a glass display cabinet. Seeing that the barn was so interested in Russian litera-ture, I dug my copy of *Anna Karenina* out of the bottom of the pannier where she was now sulking. This meant unpacking some of life's less literary necessities onto the floor. I thought I might be able to offload her for the price of a cup of coffee, but the barn was not interested in acquiring a rare paperback edition of which they already had two or three identical copies on the shelves. I tried to remonstrate that they were not, in fact, identical. The cover was falling off mine. But I was stuck with her.

I limited my own acquisitions to a copy of *Tao Te Ching* by Lao Tzu, an ancient distillation of Taoist wisdom whose origins lie, like the southern tablelands of New South Wales, shrouded in mist. The book satisfied two important criteria. It was small and it was cheap. I admired the Taoists for getting all their good oil into a work which makes both the Bible and the Koran look like they need a haircut. God, however, is a notoriously difficult author. He/she does not stick to deadlines, organises his/her own publicity and has scant regard for the laws of defamation. Above all, God is above all. God does not work with editors.

The Taoists pack a lot into a few words. Much of the *Tao Te Ching* relates to travel. Perhaps this is because one of the many interpretations of Tao, a word which, like God, defies interpretation, is 'the way'.

> *One who excels in travelling leaves no wheel tracks*

and

> *Let your wheels move only along old ruts*

and

> *The way that leads forwards seems to lead backwards*

Lao Tzu, whoever he, she or they may have been, lived too early to write bumper stickers, which is a pity because Lao Tzu had a natural talent for the genre. You can think about these one-liners all day. They deal with ambition, materialism, egotism and restlessness, all the stuff which has sadly been relegated to the fine print in the contracts which govern most lives. Lao Tzu has a delightful sense of humour and irony, preferring riddles to roadmaps.

The south road through Berrima owes a lot to Major Thomas Mitchell, a gentleman who followed the path of oat, which is tao spelt backwards. He ended life as Sir Thomas Mitchell and was keen on the title, having come to Australia because his military career in England was not progressing at the speed he believed was his due. Mitchell was a man of extraordinary energy. A lot of it went into building his own place in the world, but there was enough left over to build a few roads as well. Their names reflect his image of himself: the Great North Road, the Great Western Road and the Great South Road.

Among the old buildings of Berrima is the Surveyor General Inn, the oldest continually licensed hotel in the same building in Australia, just another one of the many pubs which claims to be the first under some rubric or other. It is named after Thomas

Mitchell – he'd become surveyor-general in 1828. Being on the Wingecarribee River, the site of Berrima was chosen for a settlement because it was one point on Mitchell's road where water was in good supply.

You catch glimpses of Mitchell's character in his relationship with his wife. He married Mary in 1818 when he was twenty-six and she was not yet eighteen. He seems to have squeezed courtship into the gaps left by his more pressing interests and, once married, it became clear that he had really wanted a staff member more than a wife. Soon after the wedding, he wrote to his mother that 'my wife is totally unfit for any domestic charge and her negligence in dress, house, etc. is incredible.' He believed his career had been 'defeated by my marriage'. Like Hume, however, Mitchell now has his name all over Australia, so in the end he did all right for himself.

Berrima is, like the Queen Mother, known for different things, but being old is the main one. Age and beauty are its major sources of income. Since the highway became the freeway and took another path, Berrima has prospered as an attraction for people who like looking at colonial architecture, browsing in gift shops and buying aromatherapy products. Never able to look a gift shop in the mouth, and despite the lessons of Lao Tzu, I had soon acquired a pair of glass earrings for Jenny towards whom I was cycling slowly.

Leaving Berrima then, the old road linked up to the freeway again and I passed a small sign to the Belanglo State Forest. The Hume was then joined by the Illawarra Highway, the main road from Wollongong and the south coast – just in time for the traffic of two highways, and me, to be lured into a major roadhouse complex. A roadhouse is a place where everything that can't be eaten has been laminated, and not all the food can be eaten.

The Sutton Forest roadhouse does well out of the snow season.

And, calling in here during the school term, I've often encountered busloads of children on their way to Canberra to inspect the national capital and to see parliament either in action or not as the case may be, mostly not. Apparently, most primary school age children at some time in their career make this pilgrimage in honour of civic education. This means a lot of buses and a lot of thickshakes.

Now, at the table beside me, two imposing buisnessmen were slurping thickshakes of their own.

I rang ahead and tried to book a bed at the only place in Marulan, the next town south, that had accommodation. Unfortunately, it was fully booked. I cursed myself for not arranging something earlier and turned to *Tao Te Ching* for comfort, where I found fresh aphorisms about the shortness of life and the transience of all discomforts.

Obviously it required more than these few hours, most of them spent in Berrima, to enter into the depths of this great contemplative tradition. It's all well and good to approach life with perfect composure and resignation, but not if you have to sleep in a ditch beside the Hume Freeway. The book said it didn't matter. It did matter.

'A sudden downpour cannot last all day,' says Lao Tzu. Yes, but it could last all night.

Lucky for me, a roadhouse staff member told me about a cheap-and-cheerful place to stay in Bundanoon so I set off on a detour of about 30 kilometres. A few days earlier, I would have done anything to avoid the extra mileage. Today, it seemed like a breeze. I enjoyed being on a quiet road for a change and felt buoyant in the saddle. The rain had stopped and the wind was favourable. I rapped out Christmas carols on my bicycle bell.

Mitchell's Great South Road, opened in stages between 1830 and 1843, followed precisely the route of the current Hume Freeway. It replaced a road called the Argyle Road, built between 1818 and 1833. The Argyle Road went through Penrose, Wingello and Tallong, the small communities I rode through the following day until I met up again with my old friend, the Hume Freeway, just shy of Marulan, home of Truckstop 31, a roadhouse which looks after truckies by providing bottles of twenty-six different sauces for them to choose from. The servery was lathered in placards which gave a sense of camaraderie between the staff and customers, the boys on one side and the girls on the other:

> *Of course I don't look as busy as the men. I did it right the first time.*

If Lao Tzu had been a truck driver, he might well have raised the standard of roadhouse repartee.

Be nice to your waitress. She's the last person to touch your food.

The road between Sydney and Canberra is subtitled 'Remembrance Way' and all the rest stops along it are dedicated to men who have won the Victoria Cross 'for valour'. The war heroes are honoured with a display explaining their achievement, which generally makes for disturbing reading. The one at Towrang, not far past Marulan, celebrates Sergeant Thomas Derrick, who won his award at the age of thirty for his 'refusal to admit defeat in the face of a seemingly overwhelming situation' in New Guinea in November 1944. Sadly, his star did not shine for long. He was killed within six months and is buried in Tarakan War Cemetery.

The toilet at the rest stop boasted about its reliance on natural processes. Unfortunately, nature was having a rostered day off and the toilet was out of order. So I set off to find a part of nature that was open for business. I ripped a couple of pages out of my diary, inadvertently taking those which described the wonders of Mittagong, and set off into the bush. Having put Mittagong behind me, I noticed that I had landed near an old bridge. This, it seemed, was the original Towrang bridge, proclaiming itself built in 1839 – possibly the work of David Lennox. It was the convicts who always did the building, which is, I suppose, how road lengths came to be measured in chains.

The only other people sharing the area were two backpackers from Europe. For $1,500 they had acquired a station wagon of doubtful reliability in Sydney and had crammed the luggage area with their belongings. This seemed to me to be cheating on the first premise of backpacking, that you take only what you can carry.

'Our packs were too small for all our stuff,' one explained.

'So were our backs,' added the other.

They told me they'd just finished studying a semester of social science at an Australian university located handy to beaches, a fact that is stressed in the marketing of its academic excellence to overseas students, and were now keen to have a look at 'your country'. There were surfboards on the roof so I asked why they were heading south when they seemed more interested in following the sun. They said that the steering on the car was 'not so good' so they had to follow a straight road, which, they had been assured, meant the rebuilt Hume. Later, they wanted to head into the west where, on their maps, they had seen roads that went for a lifetime without a bend. It would save them money not having to get the steering fixed. If worse came to worst, they knew a lot about wind-surfing and could rig up a sail on top of the car and use the wind to steer. It wouldn't be so hard. They were backpackers. Anything was possible.

One of them discovered that the toilet was locked, returned to the car, found the business pages of the day's paper, and headed off into the same wilderness which I had recently vacated, intending to clean up on the stockmarket.

'How far will you get tonight?' the other one asked me.

'I'll get as far as Goulburn. It's a big town.'

'Goulburn', he said, more quietly. 'That's where the jail is. We heard about it. It's where they put the backpacker killer.'

The Hume has a dark side. On 25 January 1990, Paul Onions set off to hitchhike from Sydney to Melbourne. Onions was twenty-three years old. He'd been discharged from the navy and had come to Australia from England on a working holiday, a member of the great tribe of backpackers who pace the earth in search of enlightenment on a shoestring budget. Onions thought that he might find work picking fruit; every February and March, the fruit growers on the Murray River employ an army, many of them backpackers from overseas, the rest itinerants of one kind or another.

At Casula, just past Liverpool, Paul went into a shop for a

drink and a bloke called Bill offered him a lift. Paul was delighted. I know the feeling. Hitchhiking makes you appreciate your luck. Mine has all been good. I should say it was all good because I haven't stuck my thumb out on a road in Australia since we were all forced to make the acquaintance of the same man whom Onions thought was friendly and helpful. Bill would do more to change the culture of the Hume than most. He made sure that travellers stayed safe within their own cars, listened to their own CDs and avoided strangers.

By the time they got to Mittagong, Paul noticed that Bill's manner had changed. He was no longer relaxed and easygoing but was sounding off about the extreme right-wing political causes he supported. Not much further down the road, Bill pulled a gun.

Paul jumped from the vehicle and ran for his life into the face of the oncoming traffic. He managed to get a car to stop.

Paul was both courageous and lucky. He was haunted by that incident for a long time; eventually, back home, he was to make a connection with a news story which was filtering from the Hume to England.

Backpackers are a significant part of the Australian economy. According to the surveys, they spend less per day in this country than those who stay in the best hotels, but they are here much longer and so end up spending more in total. There are almost half a million of them every year, worth $2.5 billion to the economy. They are also more likely to stay in places owned locally and they do all sorts of jobs which locals avoid, such as fruit picking, and then have the decency to spend the money before they leave these shores, making sure they are broke when they get home.

On one occasion long ago, I found myself in a backpackers' hostel in Cairns in North Queensland. Somebody had offered me a plane ticket they couldn't use and since I had no particular reason to be anywhere at the time, I accepted. The hostel was a rundown motel. There were four bunks in every room, the remains of a small bathroom and one or two signs of former elegance still visible beneath the rising damp. My only room mate was a young German. I had my copy of *Anna Karenina* with me, intending to read it, but I was restless. I put her aside with a sigh.

My room mate looked across the narrow divide between our bunks and grinned. He then imitated my sigh. I suspected the early signs of some form of mating behaviour so I set out to demonstrate the intellectual nature of my sigh by telling him about the book. Indeed, I decided to give it to him. The young man was touched. He rose in his boxer shorts, stood between our two bunks and delivered a speech of formal acceptance. He said that he would take the book back to his country as a memento of ours. His father knew Russian and he would appreciate it as well. It would be an heirloom.

Two days later, I was browsing in a book exchange in Townsville, further south. There I laid my hand on the very copy of *Anna Karenina* I had entrusted to the German traveller. I saluted his memory. He was a true backpacker. Undying friendship and assurances of gratitude counted for little beside the need to fund his next cup of coffee. I bought the copy back. It was now travelling second class at the bottom of my pannier.

Backpackers are explorers; they are ourselves when young and beautiful. In inner-city churches and cathedrals you will often see them sitting quietly, their backpacks in the aisles beside them. They could be there to admire the architecture or to escape the weather free of charge, but young people far from home also touch another nerve in us. Watching these two young travellers by the side of Remembrance Way, I thought of how many of them are searchers, and of how even some of their reckless behaviour reveals a vulnerability. They follow predictable caravan routes around the continent, somehow assuring the rest of us that this place offers a fairy-tale combination of safety and adventure, that the pilgrim's staff is still respected. But this image is fragile. Stories of young travellers in danger cut deep.

There is a long list of tragic incidents involving both backpackers touring Australia and Australian backpackers overseas. None of them has bruised the imagination as deeply as Ivan Robert Milat, the name of the man whom Paul Onions later identified as the one who'd aimed a gun at him on the Hume Highway in 1990. Although Onions managed to get away, the bodies of two back-packers were already lying in bushland nearby. Eventually, seven bodies would be found in the Belanglo State Forest, down a road which joins the Hume Highway close to Berrima, at a rest stop which honours a young war hero, Private James Gordon. The sign indicating the way to the forest is small, but it had aroused in me a kind of shudder. It is like a sign pointing the way to the under-world, more powerful than much bigger signs pointing to much bigger places.

Those seven people whose remains were found there had all been in their early twenties, all backpackers, all snatched from the side of the Hume.

In 1996, Ivan Milat, then aged fifty-two, was convicted of the murders. He has always maintained his innocence, but the case against him was formidable.

Milat was one of numerous siblings. His father was an alcoholic and capable of both violence and menacing silence. His mother struggled to keep things together. He grew up along the banks of the Hume in the outer suburbs of Sydney, a desolate world in which the strongest relationships many boys formed were with their cars.

As a teenager, Milat spent time in Mount Penang Juvenile Detention Centre. As an adult, he was brutalised in Grafton jail, an institution whose history is written in blood. He needed security. He became a control freak. He was a caffeine addict, a gun fetishist and intoxicated by extremist political rhetoric. He was also a road worker with a capacity for sheer hard labour. If the jackhammers were not available, he was one of the few who would grab a pick and just start swinging. Ivan Milat helped to build the new Hume Freeway. The road was his place of work but also his playground. It was not in his nature to go out and explore the world with a small bag of belongings. His only interest in the world was to dominate it. For that, he needed an arsenal.

Milat is now serving seven life sentences in the maximum security section of Goulburn jail, one of four major prisons along the route of the Hume Highway: Berrima, Kilmore and Pentridge are the others.

SO MANY ARSEHOLES. SO FEW BULLETS.
— Bumper sticker, Hume Highway

The Goulburn jail, complete with barbed wire and watch towers, is still very much in operation. Built in 1883, it dominates the view from the old Hume Highway as you wind into town.

It's difficult to romanticise the home of Ivan Milat. But it does get dramatised. The place is seldom out of the news for long: any horror story from the jail is good for ratings. When its new High Risk Management Unit (HRMU), a jail within a jail, was opened in the middle of 2001, the public was provided with details which included what the state's worst prisoners would be able to eat and when they would be allowed to eat it. There was information about how the unit was designed to foil any attempt at suicide: the mattresses would be fire-resistant and the shower curtains would be integrated into the ceiling. The appetite for such material is, it seems, insatiable. Journalists, sounding a bit like fazed travel writers, reported that showers would be restricted to two minutes and controlled from outside the cell.

The opposition spokesman said, predictably, that the place was a five-star resort. The premier, just as predictably, invited him to spend a night in it and see if that changed his mind. When the place was commissioned, the premier, Mr Carr said that it would accommodate 'the psychopaths, the career criminals, the violent standover men, the paranoid inmates and gang leaders'. Eighteen months later, the same premier said that if terrorists were ever found at work in Australia, this was where they'd be put. In those eighteen months, the rhetoric of world politics had changed. But fear is always in fashion.

Soon after the HRMU was opened, I spent a day in Goulburn jail with two of the chaplains, Kevin Flynn and Eileen Reardon. Kevin, a seasoned character, was the parish priest of Gunning.

When I first arrived in town, Kevin had dropped around within a matter of days. I told him I had left the priesthood the previous week. I think I was apologising. He interrupted.

'You must be hurting,' he said.

I was caught short.

'You must really be hurting.'

Until Kevin laid his finger on this tender spot, I hadn't realised how lost I was feeling. You don't need to say a lot to be truthful. My bottom lip started to wobble.

'That won't stop you getting me a cup of coffee,' he added.

I apologised that my place was small and that with all the packing boxes around the place, we had to sit outside. He told me not to worry and then went off on a tangent, saying that Ivan Milat lived his whole life in an area the size of two caravans. I was surprised that the name of Milat could come up so casually. I was expecting Kevin to start the normal denigration of the convicted killer. But he didn't.

'You know Ivan Milat?'

'I've spoken to him a few times.'

'What is he like?'

'His eyes. He has the softest eyes. The kindest eyes of any man I have ever met.'

When Kevin had gone and I got back to unpacking my life into a small fibro house in an unfamiliar town, I thought with relief that my mind must be an easy place to live compared to Milat's.

There must be at least seven people who'd think differently about Milat's eyes. Eight if you count Paul Onions, the one that got away. I decided then that if I was ever going to see Goulburn jail, I wanted to see it through the eyes of Kevin Flynn.

Kevin warned me that it would be boring. It was.

The prisoner in the reception building showed us the store of clothing which was issued to new arrivals. Everything was precisely the same shade of green. Green shirts, green socks, green underpants, green trousers, green jumpers, green jackets. As we move through the building, Kevin explained that people here, both prisoners and guards, spend the whole day waiting for something to happen. They were all bored, he said, and boredom eventually becomes poison. It gets on your nerves like sand in your shoe; you hardly notice it at first. So does frustration. A lot of the men had problems expressing themselves constructively. The first time Kevin said Mass in the jail, he'd been embarrassed because, when he asked somebody to read from the Bible, he found that none of the small number of men who'd turned up was literate.

Bushrangers have tended to be seen as either animals disguised as humans or gentlemen disguised as thugs: either above or below the normal pattern of human behaviour. It is hard to see them for who they were. One reason for this is that, unlike the explorers, bushrangers seldom left written records. A sustained journal by a bushranger would provide a way into minds which are generally inaccessible. On the other hand, the very capacity to write a journal might have changed the nature of the outlaw. The inability to express oneself is the cornerstone of social alienation.

Of recent times, there has been a stirring of interest in the journals and letters of Australian explorers, in their arcane, mannered, bombastic, vulnerable, confused, cute, despairing, callous and compassionate turn of phrase. The words they attached to their experiences tell a great deal about early encounters between the Australian landscape and the European mind and about how they altered each other. These days, we are as likely to be interested in the language explorers used as the maps they drew, in their words as much as their measurements. We are intrigued by the ones who actually didn't find very much but had a lot to say about not finding it.

Many of the early bushrangers were also explorers but they moved outside the frontier to stay out there. They were seldom willing or able to bring their experience to the written page. The vast majority were illiterate.

In Goulburn jail I watched as Kevin spent a typical day talking to the prisoners allowed into exercise yards. A lot of them ask for things; most of the time he replies affably that there isn't much he can do.

Many of the cells you'd see in Goulburn are a hundred years old and look like Hollywood's idea of crime and punishment. The yards are concrete enclosures, fenced by metal bars and barbed wire. When Eileen first came here, she said, the thing that got on her nerves was the complete absence of any trees or plants.

Both Kevin and Eileen told me that their job is to try and find some beauty in an ugly situation.

'Sometimes people say that criminals should be shot to save all the money it costs to run maximum security,' said Kevin. 'But if I stop believing that people can come good, I've got to deny my belief in redemption. It's not my job to decide if people are innocent or guilty. That's the court's job. I only try to help a prisoner accept himself and know he has dignity, no matter what. If I didn't believe that, I'd have to give my whole faith away.'

Kevin has trouble hearing, is a recovering alcoholic and has weathered deep hurt in his seventy or more years. Yet there is no sign of hardness around the edges of his soul. He has far more reason to be cynical than I have but he isn't. He has been less protected from the dark side of human nature, yet he isn't afraid of it. Perhaps that is one reason why he is still a priest and I am not. I am afraid of the dark. I'd rather not face it alone.

One last thing stays with me from that day:

Kevin indicates the unit where Ivan Milat is kept but he isn't going there today. I get the feeling that he doesn't want to run a freak show for my entertainment. As we pass, we notice a food tray leaving the unit. Nothing has been touched. Kevin says that the food is coming from Milat's cell where Milat is on a hunger strike. Kevin says that the officers would be happy to let him die and so, for that matter, would most of Australia. My own feelings are mixed at best. But Kevin lives in hope. Over the shoulder of the woman carrying the tray, I notice that the name of the building housing Milat is the Hamilton Hume Unit. The place where Milat is kept is literally fifty yards from William Hovell's grave, the longest fifty yards in the country.

The four prisons along the Hume Highway were all built in the nineteenth century and all have the kind of imposing stone facade which communicates as much to those on the outside as to those inside. Two of them, at Kilmore and Pentridge in Victoria, are no longer functioning as prisons. The old Kilmore jail is now in private hands and part of a tour known as 'the pure indulgence trail' which invites the astute traveller to enjoy all the fine things the region has to offer.

One of the lazy habits of popular history is a tendency to romanticise the criminals of the past and demonise the criminals of the present. This brings with it a tendency to tame or domesticate the jails of the past. At the time when Ned Kelly's father was held there in Kilmore jail, inmates always left with a legacy of bitterness. Now the manager apologises if she hasn't been able to get the heating quite right. A visitor has written in the guest book: 'If the coffee is this good in jail, then lock me up and throw away the key.'

The same sort of thing is true of Pentridge, the bluestone facade of which hovers over the Hume just north of Melbourne. Ned Kelly's headless body was buried here; the last man executed in Australia was hanged here. Pentridge has only been out of operation for a few years; the original walls will remain, but much of the land behind them is being turned into a new housing estate. For some time after Pentridge shut down, the doors which used to close on the cells in Jika Jika, the infamous maximum-security wing, were doing the rounds of charity auctions and sports fund-raisers. I was once at a function where one was sold for $300, the man who bought it announcing that he was going to put it on the door of his teenage son's bedroom. It had taken just weeks for this item to change from being an object of fear to an object of fun. When Pentridge was shut down, a group organised tours of the premises in order to raise money for worthwhile causes. The demand was so great that they had to keep extending the season. The line queued around the block. Melbourne had spent generations trying to keep out of the place; now they couldn't wait to get in. Some former prisoners agreed to conduct tours, some brought their wives and children to show them the place, and some stayed away.

These stories and the tale of Ivan Milat are only part of the elaborate relationship between crime and the Hume Highway.

Ben Hall was involved in sixty-four highway robberies, many of them along the road that was to become the Hume. He shared with Dick Turpin, the highwayman who tickled the romantic imagination, an ability to move so quickly across unmarked terrain that people thought he was able to make himself present in two places at once. In some ways he could. Hall mastered the art of guerrilla warfare, an art which depends on making your presence felt even when you are absent. Guerrilla warfare is the opposite of God who, for some unknown reason, makes his or her absence felt even when present.

Hall's busiest year was 1864. Hall was then twenty-seven, an old man in his line of work, and had been paranoid about the administration of law ever since his wife ran off with a policeman and he had been accused of a crime he did not commit. In November that year, as principal of the gang of Hall, Gilbert and Dunn, he was responsible for the death of Sergeant Parry when the gang held up the Gundagai Mail on the road between Jugiong and Gundagai. Gilbert pulled the trigger. You can see a cairn in Parry's honour at that place on the Hume.

A month later, the gang interrupted a wedding which was being held at Plumb's Inn on Narumbulla Creek, a stone's throw from Towrang. A member of parliament, William Macleay, was riding through and stopped to fight them off before the speeches and toasts could resume. The following year, 1865, Macleay was among those in the House voting on the Felons Apprehension Act, a grim expression of the apprehension felt by the colonists. It allowed the likes of Hall and Gilbert to be killed in cold blood and, before the year was out, they were.

Some of the bushrangers were as disturbed as Ivan Milat. In April 1865, the body of one 'Mad Dan' Morgan was dragged along the Hume into the police station in Wangaratta. It was not treated with much respect. Morgan had been illiterate, paranoid, trigger-happy and given to sudden bursts either of anger or compassion, both of which tended to find frenzied, uncontrolled expression.

He lived off the bush and spent most of his life in solitude, but could appear from nowhere. He loved setting things on fire, especially tents, especially with people in them. He was not a good man to find next to you in a camping ground.

Morgan was hunted and shot like an animal. In Wangaratta police station, a press photographer, knowing that crime may not pay but it sure sells, propped Morgan's eyes open with match sticks to get a sensational image. A gun was positioned in his hand and the image which resulted is suitably macabre. The police superintendent, wanting a souvenir, skinned Morgan's trademark beard and took it down the road to Benalla to show it off. Morgan's head was carried in a box along the highway, escorted by police, to Melbourne, a spectacle which residents of Seymour remembered for years.

The highway provides the essential ingredient for random acts of violence: randomness. It brings strangers together far from home. In the early days, wooded parts of the road were approached in fear, and the dark passage through Bargo Brush was notorious. In April 1842, John Lynch, aged twenty-nine, was hanged at Berrima jail. As in the case of Milat, there are circumstances which shed light on a profound darkness of spirit.

In 1832 John Lynch, aged nineteen, had been transported for seven years for the crime of 'false pretences', but, on arrival, a clerical error had him listed as a 'lifer'. He was put to work building roads while his own claim to inherit property in Ireland was forfeited because of his life sentence. He had reason for the chip on his shoulder.

But his behaviour towards his victims indicated a much deeper personality disorder. One day he was camping with a group of about half a dozen people by the side of the road at Bargo Brush. It was common for travellers in this neck of the woods to team up for their mutual protection. Lynch was driving a stolen dray.

Before long, a trooper arrived looking for the dray, but failed to recognise either it or Lynch, who was hiding beneath it. When the constable left, Lynch decided he was in danger.

As was his custom, Lynch prayed devoutly for guidance. God told him to kill two of his companions, the Frazers, and take their dray, thus eliminating the sinful possession of a stolen vehicle from his moral record. Presumably, a dray belonging to the dead is not stolen property in the same way as one belonging to the living. Lynch killed the Frazers, father and son, with a tomahawk. This was the weapon God had assigned to him to help him get through life's little crises, something Lynch was happy to explain in the confession he made before his execution at Berrima jail.

Lynch had trusted God implicitly and obeyed all his instructions; never killing anyone without first resorting to prayer. Sometimes he had left temperance medals and prayers attached to the necks of his victims. He was God's hatchet man.

YOUR CARMA JUST RAN OVER MY DOGMA
— Bumper sticker, Goulburn

Remembering that day at Goulburn jail made me glad to be on the outside, the side where the road runs, and by the time I coasted downhill into Goulburn late that afternoon, I felt lucky. Lucky to have friends in Goulburn, and even luckier that they had a shower and a spare bed.

In fact, my friends had a number of spare beds, spread through a house with over eighty rooms, twenty-seven of them bedrooms. The building used to be an orphanage and if walls could speak, these walls too would have a lot to say.

Catherine had told me that it was not uncommon for former residents to turn up here unannounced, sometimes having taken years to gather the courage together to return to the scene of their atrophied childhood. These visitors recall walking from their dormitories to the ablutions block in bare feet every morning, even in the depths of winter, a season which Goulburn takes seriously.

The orphanage looks out over the site of Kenmore Hospital, an institution which housed the intellectually disabled and the mentally unfit – yet another pile with ghosts. The bleak brick-work of both places says something about attitudes, not entirely dead, to people who couldn't be accommodated by the normal structure of family. They were stored out of sight.

In 1976, the orphanage became the House of Prayer, known colloquially as HOP. At that time the place had been empty for about two years, and had been vandalised and used as Goulburn's lovers' lane. Then a small group of young women decided they wanted to form a community, and moved into the draughty, unloved building where they created something which, many years later, is still alive. The community lives in a contemplative way and offers hospitality to all sorts of people, many of them with special needs.

It is a still place. I was more glad of that than the shower.

The building which houses HOP is owned by the church but the people who live there have no special uniform or status, though they take risks to live simply, making ends meet by hosting groups and retreats. Most of the furniture in the place has come from op-shops and donations.

That very day, Catherine had found a green lounge suite priced at only $45, and this, she told me happily, would be good for the dining room used by visiting groups. The lounge suite was not a thing of great beauty, not by the standards of *Vogue*, nor even by the standards of *Kitsch Weekly*. But the HOP is not so image conscious. It's a haven of sanity.

We sat down to a baked dinner cooked by Ann and read a few words from the prophet Isaiah:

'Truly, you are a God who conceals himself.'

Nobody was running off anywhere. There was a restfulness in that.

The community doesn't make much song and dance when it prays, no effort to impress anyone with clever words or pumped-up emotion. I think that when you've been praying for a long time, you get over that. You don't need a stage, a band and an amplifier. It's better to whisper. Prayer is a form of rest. It's like pillow talk, even if sometimes it's more like sleeping with a partner who won't wear their hearing aid to bed. After a while, it doesn't matter so much what you say in the dark, as long as it's humble and honest and patient, all qualities which have eluded me at different times. Prayer is a form of rest and rest is a form of prayer.

The HOP community prays in the same voice as it talks to visitors. We read a psalm:

'Indeed, you love truth in the heart.
Then in the secret of my heart teach me wisdom'

In 1921, one Australia's more observant characters, Mary Gilmore, returned to Goulburn, where, as Mary Cameron, she had grown up. She spent a good part of the next four years there and discovered that the road was Goulburn's most engaging feature.

From 1908 to 1931, Mary Gilmore edited the Women's Page in the *Australian Worker* and through it exerted an unacknowledged influence on Australian culture in the first half of the twentieth century by introducing her blue-collar readership to a broader sense of life's possibilities, without, at the same time, urging them to buy anything. If it hadn't been for the success of Gilmore's Women's Page in the *Australian Worker*, the *Australian Women's Weekly* might never have taken off to become the ubiquitous *Weekly*, arguably the most formative cultural influence in post-war Australia. Gilmore was its godmother. She also wrote some exquisite poetry, the best of it deceptively slight. She did lots of stuff. She was born in 1865 and died in 1962, so she had time for it. She was a radical, a member of an endangered species.

Gilmore had returned to Goulburn for a respite from the demands of living in Sydney. Her nerves were on edge; she was highly strung and prone to depression. While in Goulburn she wrote:

> *I came home and looked out my window very tired and feeling a little strange in a world I should know so well. There is an ache and an emptiness . . . Life is filled with things as a shelf is filled with empty tins . . . In its continual doing, even the heart itself refuses to remember that it is hungry and starved.*

Mary had packed both her husband, Will, and son, Billy, off to Queensland, where they worked on the land to support her financially while she pursued a literary career. She felt uneasy about that. By the time she got to Goulburn, she hadn't seen Will for eleven years or Billy for eight.

Mary Gilmore viewed life from the first floor, the perfect vantage point for not just observation but also insight. She was slightly above the common sod but not in the clouds.

From 1933 until her death, a period of about thirty years, she would live in a small first-floor flat on Darlinghurst Road in Sydney's Kings Cross, almost directly above the current site of the railway station. From her balcony there, she looked out on one of the busiest streets in town and recorded what she saw: the Depression, World War II and the growth of the local tourist and sex industries all paraded beneath her unflinching gaze. In early 1990, I had been visiting Kings Cross and noticed that Gilmore's flat was on the market. I rang the agent, pretended I was a potential buyer, and had myself shown through. This may have been a little dishonest but I just wanted to see the world from Gilmore's angle, even for a moment. But her balcony had been enclosed and the rooms had been done out in the pastel pinks which were the hideous contribution of the period to interior design. There was no trace of Mary Gilmore's signature clutter, no sign of the sofa buried under books nor of the desk buried under paper. 'Is this the kind of thing you were after?' the agent asked me. I looked at the wall. 'Not really.'

As a younger woman returning to Goulburn, Gilmore had taken a first-floor room at the Imperial Hotel, on the corner of Verner Street and Auburn Street, the name the old Hume Highway trades under when it comes to town. The hotel was directly opposite the site of the house where William Hovell, Hume's companion, had lived out his years. Gilmore's room looked out on the road, which got her thinking and, during a cold winter, she wrote an essay about it, published in 1922 in a collection called *Hound of the Road*:

> There are some people for whom a road never lived. To them it is nothing but a dull dead place of ruts upon an equally dull dead earth . . . People of that kind have no conception of how deep a love a man can have for that which is his only house and land, and what a full book and friend it can be . . . Give a man a road and he has a library which neither comes to an end nor grows cheap and common. I know roads. History lies written in them for those who can read.

Gilmore's observations were nearly always nostalgic. She was fascinated by a plane, a 'Roadman of the Air', which she had watched take off just the day before. The plane carried the name of its manufacturer, a fact which encouraged Gilmore to call to mind the more ironic names that bullock wagons bore in a former age. She remembered one wagon called 'The Red Rose' which had 'the paint burned to a faded brick colour', another called 'The Luck' despite the fact that 'the luck went out when the pleuro struck the bullocks' and another called 'White Rose' even though it was 'up to the hub in mud'. She also knew inventive bullockies, and wrote that day about a team of bullocks comprising Knox and Calvin as the polers, Wesley and Cranmer the middle and Roman and Peter the lead. Such recollections cast doubt on the myth of the unlettered, foul-mouthed bullocky.

Mary Gilmore was always old enough to remember when things were different, and this is a constant theme in her writing. As she got older, the gap between then and now widened. She had childhood memories of travellers on the road beneath her window. Her pioneers were haunted men who wore amulets and saw the country on either side of the road as peopled by supernatural beings. The wilderness was only a few steps from the track and in the wilderness they expected to encounter both God and Satan.

For Gilmore, the road ran through time as well as space:

> *One end of it leads to Melbourne, the other rests in Sydney.*
> *Men made that road in the darker years of this land. It heard*
> *the swing of the lash and the sighs of the broken. It was*
> *cemented with the blood and tears of man. The page is black.*
> *Let us leave it.*

The next morning I cycled past the place where the Imperial has been demolished to make way for a motel, which now has a Thai restaurant on the first floor, roughly where Mary Gilmore used to sit.

Goulburn was bypassed by the new freeway in 1992. The city was afraid of what a future without the road might mean for the economy of the city. As it turned out, the impact of the bypass was less catastrophic than some had feared. In 1995, experts from the School of Geography of the University of New South Wales did a systematic evaluation of life in Goulburn without the road, at least in terms of what it meant to the cash registers. Of the 198 businesses which responded to a survey, it said, sixty-seven experienced a decreased turnover after the bypass was opened, a period which coincided with a recession and a rural slump, both of which may have contributed. The decrease was less than three per cent of Goulburn's GDP. The businesses employed 1,706 people; 58 were laid off because of the bypass, only 13 of whom were full-time workers. A reduction of working hours was more common.

> *In sum, the impacts of the opening of the bypass on the Goulburn economy have been relatively small even though they have not run their full course. The impacts reported in this study are not as serious as those anticipated by the community . . .*

The bypass may not have altered the economy of Goulburn as much as was feared. But it changed the character of the city.

Though Mary Gilmore's Imperial has gone, Goulburn has not been left short of hotels, nor of licensed clubs, most of which dance to the tune of gaming machines. They are abattoirs of the human spirit.

On the road outside town, I came upon the Big Merino, a fifteen-metre-high concrete replica of a sheep, one of the locality's landmarks. To be honest, it looked more a vague likeness than a replica. Real sheep tend not to have retail outlets sitting in their crutch. Nor can visitors usually climb up inside a sheep's head – where in this case they will discover why the Big Merino, standing day and night in all weathers, looks so preternaturally bored. Its eyes are windows which look out over the fibro outskirts of Goulburn. Along with Yass and Albury, Goulburn was one of a number of centres on the Hume which, after Federation, aspired to become the national capital. This end of town could have done with the lift.

I felt sorry for the Big Merino. It is a member of a bizarre fraternity of big objects that sit beside roads in Australia to alert travellers to some source of local pride. The majority of them represent something edible: the big avocado, the big banana, the big pineapple, the big potato, the big orange and the big cheese. Seafood is well represented: the big prawn, the big trout, the big lobster and the big oyster. So are nuts: the big macadamia and the big peanut.

Few of these monoliths have as dreary a post as the Big Merino. It patiently informs passersby that they are in the heart of sheep-grazing country. Inside, the merino contains information for Australia's 20 million humans about the 130 million sheep which provide ten per cent of this country's export revenue. They also provide all of the ugg boots and most of the car-seat covers, but these facts are overlooked. The growth of the sheep industry brought closer settlement and it was this that really ended bushranging along the Hume in New South Wales.

It was only another fifty kilometres home to Gunning. But the wind was against me and playing nasty so I gave away my plan to take the old road over the Cullerin Range. Until 1993, this narrow, winding stretch had been the Hume Highway. It is a favourite haunt of mine. There are still signs along the way advising heavy vehicles to slow to 45 kilometres per hour; it used to be one of the most dangerous parts on the entire trip south from Sydney. In a period of eighteen months before work started on the freeway, twenty-nine people were killed on this part of the road and locals organised public meetings to speed up work on the bypass.

Now the old Hume is the quiet back route between my home and the nearest bank, fifty kilometres away. On top of the Cullerin Range you can find remains of the old road from at least four periods of its history, the earliest dating back to the 1860s when stone bridges were built to take the road across the new railway. In the bush, there are old pieces of road with trees growing in the crevices and potholes.

The highest point on the southern railway line is indicated on the Cullerin Range. The old railway bridges are a reminder that the train still follows its original course. Between Sydney and Melbourne average train speed is still only 55 kilometres per hour, a significant factor in the preference for road over rail. Goods trains have made the same arduous journey through these hills since the line was first laid, while in that time the road has been completely rebuilt.

The road is used by private vehicles, the railway is used by public ones, so the road gets all the money. In the last ten years, for every dollar spent on laying rail in Australia, eight dollars have been spent on highways (and most of the money spent on rail is spent in the suburbs of cities). This is a symptom of something deeper because government spending-decisions simply mirror the interests of voters. Those interests are now less likely to include common property or the development of common assets.

This afternoon, I was glad of the freeway which meant I didn't have to walk my bike over the Cullerin Range. I pushed into the wind. By the time I got to Gunning, I was tired. The town, strung with Christmas lights, was pretty and I was glad to see it.

My neighbours, Kevin and Judy, took me down to the local Chinese restaurant for a celebratory meal. But there was sad news. A local shearer, a young man, had taken his own life. The reasons were complex. They always are. Coming back up the street, the Christmas lights did not look quite so bright.

As I reached the front door, my mobile phone rang for the first time since I'd left Sydney. It was Jenny.

'It's funny,' she said. 'I was imagining you getting home right at this minute.'

'It's been a long ride. I can hardly move.'

Jenny laughed. She had just come home from a session in which she taught dancing to a young man, Chris, who had an acquired brain injury. Today he had moved a few inches.

Two

TWO

Cliff Young, aged sixty-one, was hardly considered a serious threat. In April 1983, he came up from Victoria in a van with a small group of supporters to run in the first Sydney to Melbourne Ultra Marathon. It had taken them three days to drive up because they wanted to see the sights along the Hume. Young ran back in five. One of the supporters was Wally Zueschner, a masseur for the Colac Football Club and a good bit older than Cliff. He was a tough nut. When one of the other competitors told Wally that he needed a break, Wally told him that he could rest when his eyes started to bleed.

Wally's own eyes weren't too good. This had a major bearing on the race. For the first day, Young managed to stay in touch with the field. His running style looked like an uncomfortable shuffle, his feet never far off the ground. He always looked like he was just about finished. But he could go on like that for hours and his shuffle was deceptively fast.

'It's called a low projectory,' said Cliff afterwards. 'I've always run like that. If I lifted me legs up any higher, I'd knock me false teeth out.'

Most of the competitors, including Young, stopped for the first night somewhere around Mittagong. Wally had the alarm clock but had trouble reading it. Instead of waking Cliff at dawn he woke him by mistake in the small hours. Cliff pulled on his shoes and got going. It was dark and before long, Young lost his footing in a pothole and threw out his shoulder, an injury he carried for the rest of the race. After a couple of hours, Young wondered why there was still no daylight, looked at a watch and discovered Wally's error. By the time he got to Goulburn, Cliff was well in front of the field and decided to keep going. This became his strategy for the rest of the event. He hardly stopped. Over the five days and 875 kilometres of the race, Young only slept about fifteen hours. His crew felt it more than he did. One of them was smoking 120 cigarettes a day to cope with the situation.

THE GODDESS IS DANCING
— Bumper sticker, Hume Highway

I came to Gunning to hide, but people kept finding me. One of them pointed out that if I really wanted to escape I would hardly have bought a house by the side of Australia's main street. I saw more of some friends than I had seen of them when we lived in the same city. The reason, I discovered, was not my personal appeal but that of my toilet, located about the distance from the nearest service centre that it takes the typical bladder to move from empty to full. Friends of friends would be just starting to feel uncomfortable when they would see the turnoff to Gunning and ask themselves 'isn't that where so and so got to?' Friends of friends of friends got to hear my theories about the benefits of driving with a full bladder, the main one being that it's impossible to fall asleep behind the wheel with your legs crossed. There should be signs saying 'full bladders save lives' but nobody listens to common sense any more. The only true wisdom left in the world is wasted on bumper stickers.

One of my visitors was Jenny. She came by train, which was just as well as her poor old car would hardly have made it to the station in Melbourne, let alone all the way along the road to Gunning. Luckily, the car was eventually stolen from outside her flat. This saved towing charges.

When I first told Jenny that I was going to cycle the Hume, she said I was crazy. Now I had successfully completed the leg from Sydney to Gunning. But when I told her I was about ready to cycle the remaining 630 kilometres from Gunning to Melbourne, she said I was still crazy – but that this time she would come too. Of course I warmed to the idea at once. The world is a disbelieving place, full of doubters, the worst of them sceptical that I had cycled so far already. I needed a witness. We could do it together in April 2002.

Jenny had her own bike, which may have been worth more than her car but still wasn't worth much. Its best feature was a wire bread-basket which stuck out the front. So Jenny arranged to borrow a swanky road bike from a friend called Eileen. It was a magnificent machine with panniers instead of a bread-basket. Strictly speaking, pannier, which derives from the Latin word for bread, *panis*, is a synonym for bread-basket. In the Roman world, *panis* was the opposite of panic. Panic is a condition, familiar to writers, caused by breadlessness. The useful tag, *panis et penis*, meaning 'bread and circuses', was often used by Roman boys to describe a good night out.

I was jealous of Jenny's panniers because they looked better than mine. Furthermore, Jenny was able to accommodate all her requirements and still zip them up, whereas I had become accustomed to drivers slowing down as they passed me to look at all the newspapers, unread Russian novels and grocery items I had hanging out the top. For the rest of the journey, we were the cause of raised eyebrows. We met people who wanted to know what the woman with the top-of-the-line imported European bike was doing with the fat bloke on the cheap Chinese model. I told them I was her trainer.

Jenny is a dancer. Some of the most important steps of her life have been taken in ballet shoes. When I got to know her, she was teaching dancing to intellectually disabled people. She had invited me to come and visit a session of a group she was part of, called BreakOut, which gathered on a Saturday morning in a tidy hall that had been plugged into the side of a tidy church in a tidy suburb. Outside, traffic moved in an orderly fashion between the great retail outlets which grow alongside Melbourne's major highways. Not far away, parents were dropping off children for their Saturday morning music classes; even the youngest of them carried a violin case or music book and looked like they knew exactly where they were going and what they were doing.

BreakOut belonged to another culture in which, to an outsider, raw energy looked like barely controlled chaos.

'What did you do this week?' Jenny asked the group.

'I farted,' said one dancer.

Everyone laughed.

'I kissed my boyfriend,' said another, a ward of the state.

'I had chicken for my dinner,' said a third. Her mother was sitting in the car outside.

'I went to Southland.'

'I farted.'

'I had ice-cream.'

'I saw my mother.'

'I really farted.'

One of the dancers, Adam, had been coming to BreakOut for a few years. Jenny told me that when he first arrived, he used to sit in a tight ball with his arms bound around his knees, his baseball cap pulled down over his eyes. Little by little, he began to move, a journey which started with his hands as Jenny and the other helpers began to unknot his fingers. It took ages.

Jenny told me that once the body starts to loosen up, the whole person begins to experience freedom. Even I could see this in

Adam, who, at the beginning of this session, was sitting on his own in a corner. Once the music started, he was a different person, his long legs unwinding as he began to stomp his feet more or less in time to the beat. He was different again the next time I visited, when Jenny brought along a roll of bubble wrap and made a road out of it from one end of the hall to the other. The dancers moved along it, delighting in the way the bubbles popped underfoot. Adam laughed the whole way. For me, bubble wrap is the stuff which comes between you and the thing in the package you really want. Here it was too much fun for words. They sang 'follow the bubble wrap road'. Jenny told me afterwards that 'the guys' loved anything tactile.

I'm not much of a dancer. In fact, dancing has always been a source of special dread. When I was a priest, I found myself sitting through more than the average quota of wedding receptions which, as far as I was concerned, were a form of sugared suffering. The problem is that clergy invariably get to sit next to the most difficult relative from either family, the one about whom all others present have had the good sense to stipulate that they would not come if they had to sit near. Often this is an embittered individual who is still burdened by the memory of what the bride's mother said to poor dead Uncle Fred at a similar function thirty years before. Before long you start wishing you were sitting beside poor dead Fred at the heavenly banquet where the good Lord serves white meat to women and red to men.

The other thing that happens is that the priest gets put next to the family's one and only religious fanatic. This person will want to cross-examine the sermon you gave at the church but are already struggling to remember. You tell the waiter to keep your glass full at all costs. With a bit of luck, the waiter will be a born-again Christian who looks at you disapprovingly but is happy to engage with the issues raised by your companion. So you ask the waiter to take your seat while you go around with the bottles. I have actually done this.

It isn't all bad. One evening I took my place, designated simply 'Father', and was having a jolly time in good company. I didn't know anybody but, apart from the bride and groom, the priest seldom does. You just give thanks when you fall into a decent mob. Eventually, however, the happy couple arrived and I realised I was at the wrong reception. It was taking place in one of those complexes where there can be three or four receptions on the same night and you just hope that the newly-wed end up going home with the right bride or groom.

On the occasion in question, I had said to the attendant that I was the priest and she had pointed me to the appropriate place but I had failed to check whose reception this was. So now I made my apologies, wondering where the priest who was meant to be there had got to, and found my way quickly from the Sydney Room to the Melbourne Room, where my table was on the outskirts. Here I had been placed next to the family's deaf relative. She could not understand a word I said and was thus deprived of both my wisdom and wit, a loss with which she was coping admirably. After a time, I remembered something I had forgotten.

'Shit,' I muttered under my breath.

'Mind your language, please, Father,' said the deaf woman smartly. 'You should be setting an example to all these young people.'

I only raise the matter now to illustrate my feelings for dancing. Eventually, at every wedding, all the uneaten rubbery food is taken away to be hosed off the plates. This is the cue for the dancing, an activity about which I felt so awkward that, once the music began, I would suddenly find that the person beside me was fascinating and listen with profound sympathy to the story of poor dead Fred's love for dancing.

'Proper dancing. Not this kind of dancing, Father.'

I would encourage any religious fanatic to discuss the dangers of sodomy. I would talk to anyone about anything. But I would not dance, I would not move.

Yet, for the first time in my life, as I watched Jenny coax Adam onto a roll of bubble wrap on the floor of a church hall, I felt that this was something I could try.

GET OFF MY TAIL
— Bumper sticker, horse float, Hume Highway

History does not deign to record the name of the first person to cycle from Sydney to Melbourne, just as, through the ages, it has turned its nose up at all sorts of people you'd like to meet, such as the first person to ride a pogo stick between the two cities and the first cab driver to con a tourist into going the whole way by taxi.

The first person to drive from Sydney to Melbourne was Herbert Thomson. Born in 1870, Thomson was a pioneer of steam technology. He built the steam engine for a famous merry-go-round which stood for many years at St Kilda on Port Phillip Bay. The merry-go-round travelled the road occasionally, appearing at shows in places such as Benalla and Wangaratta. It is a reminder of the cast of entertainers and bands, carnies and roadies, who live in perpetual motion on the Hume. The merry-go-round was finally relocated to the heart of Canberra's main shopping mall, where it still provides welcome relief from the concrete and chrome which surrounds it.

By 1899, Thomson had built a steam-powered car. The

history of the twentieth century would have been different if
steam-driven cars, which developed initially at a rate compara-
ble to petrol-driven ones, had attracted the same commitment
from industry and investors as the alternative. Thomson
shipped his steam machine to Sydney and exhibited it at the
Easter Show in 1900. Then, to prove its stamina, he decided to
drive it home, taking the long way, via Bathurst and Cowra. He
shared the driving with his cousin, Edward Holmes: the pair
spent fifty-six hours and thirty-six minutes behind the wheel.
On one stretch they were able to outpace a pair of horses. The
car, however, could only carry enough water to last 50 kilometres at a time. But at least they showed it could be done,
despite the lack of a decent road, and a crowd gathered to cheer
their arrival.

The first petrol cars to cover the distance were part of the
Dunlop reliability trials of 1905. In the first of these trials, run in
February 1905, there were twenty-three entrants, including one
woman, Mrs Thompson, from South Australia, described as
'plucky'. Seven finished. Motoring was so novel at the time that
crowds turned out along the way to gawk and wonder. In
Goulburn, the end of the first leg, the cars could hardly get down
the main street for the number of people, especially youngsters,
who wanted to look. In Albury, the mayor organised a public
reception.

Even in 1905, cars were becoming socially complex phenom-
ena. The novelist Miles Franklin, who grew up watching the road,
looked back to that time at the opening of her novel, *Old Blastus
of Bandicoot*:

> It was in those days, so lately fled, when horseless carriages
> were a curiosity beyond the seaboard. Some young bloods had
> made the journey from Sydney to Melbourne in one as the
> most enterprising adventure at command following the
> picturesque performances of the Boer War. . .

She could easily have been describing, among others, the poet Banjo Paterson, one of the motorists in the 1905 reliability trial. Paterson had returned from the Boer War and, since January 1903, had been marking time as editor of the Sydney *Evening News*, a position he described as a 'prosaic billet'. It was no place for a poet, nor even for a 'versifier' as Paterson referred to himself. He was bored to sobs. For a little light relief, he decided to do his own reporting on the reliability trial. For him, it was a novelty. But for the promoters, his participation was a publicity coup. Paterson was the bard of the horse. His name was synonymous with songs of horsemanship and its attendant rituals. He was the perfect recruit to the new craze.

Paterson's account of the journey shows little evidence that he was aware that he was participating in the burial of the culture he loved:

> . . . the only objection to the cars is that they frighten the horses, but the Australian looks upon a race of any sort as a sacred thing.

He was absorbed by the emergence of a new culture and attentive to the language, costume and gestures that came with it:

> One hears of bicycle face. Motor face is the same, but a good deal harder. Concentrated watchfulness is the essence of motor face . . .

If anything, Paterson was infatuated by the new experience.

> When you get a bit of really good road, clear away as far as you can see, smooth gravel for choice and the car is at her best, the engine working with a rhythmic hum but everything else as noiseless as the tomb, and you feel her answer to every least touch of acceleration . . . then one knows for a few brief

moments what motoring really is . . . the car is like an
untiring horse that breasts the hills gallantly and then flies
away again as fresh as ever on each stretch of smooth road.

Paterson had found a new place to channel his restless energy. The car was like a horse, only better. The bush poet would not be the last person for whom the car was less a means of getting somewhere than a means of escaping somewhere else. He hardly notices the places he passes through:

Gunning went by like a flash.

For some years, there was an unofficial competition to break the record for driving the length of the road. It began, in 1909, at twenty-one hours, nineteen minutes. By 1916, it was sixteen hours, fifty-five minutes. In 1923, it was twelve hours, fifty-nine minutes, and then in 1927, it was eleven hours, fifty-four minutes. In 1935, it was down to eight hours, fifty-six minutes. After that, the habit of posting records seemed to dwindle. One reason is that police started enforcing speed limits. Even by today's standards, the record set in 1935 is good going. As the road has improved, the time that most people take to drive from one end to the other has become predictable. The road does most of the work now. You can travel 900 kilometres by land without having been anywhere. The road hides the places it visits, at least from cars. It's different for bikes. A bike is no place to hide on a freeway.

Jenny and I left Gunning on the Tuesday morning after Easter. As we started to gain pace, we overtook Ken Coggan's giant rig, which felt great. I wanted photos. Nobody had to know that the truck was stationary.

After an hour or two, we pulled into a roadside rest stop. The best of these have toilets, drinking water and bins for the disposal of disposable nappies. The Mundoonan rest stop, perched above Hovell Creek, is one of the very best on the Hume. Not only does it have bins but it also has people to come and empty the bins. Mundoonan is a four-star facility, rising to five-star during holiday periods when local groups such as the fire brigade and volunteer emergency service host what is known as a 'driver reviver'. This means that drivers can stop for free tea, coffee and biscuits, and thus not fall asleep at the wheel. It is probably a more reliable strategy than the full-bladder theory. There is also a sausage sizzle, the donations from which help the host organisations.

One Easter I was approached to do a shift as a volunteer on the 'driver reviver'. I felt I'd been around the district long enough to start pulling my weight, so I agreed. It was a cold night but one of the local fire fighters came and lit a fire to cheer us up, a task which he made look easy. I just hoped he was as good at putting them out as he was at lighting them. Before long, we were warming ourselves.

I was rostered on with Kevin, my neighbour, an old hand who told stories of drivers pulling in with no petrol and no money and trying to cadge a few dollars which they promised they would return all the way from Sydney to repay the following week. They generally had a colourful story but their bottom line was always the same. Eventually they'd take to the road again, not knowing how far they would get. The world is full of such people, going nowhere, but somehow they always manage to get there. If they run into the likes of Kevin, at least they can count on a free sausage.

On the night we were reviving drivers, our clientele was better heeled. The person who stayed longest was on one of the shortest journeys. She had just dropped her kids off at their father's place in Goulburn, where they would be spending the rest of the holidays, and was returning on her own to Yass. I got the impression that she was not really desperate for coffee but happy to spend a while in a place that was neither her ex-partner's place nor an empty house. She chatted to a gentleman who had introduced himself to us as a professional golfer. He played the Asian circuit and had just pulled out of the Bangkok Open because of the outbreak of SARS. He loved golf but wasn't going to die for it.

'Take it from me, mate, Asia is deserted.'

Last time I looked, there were three billion people there. I said as much.

'Take it from me, mate. They've all cleared out.'

After they'd signed the visitors' log I took a look and found it made interesting reading. There was an entry from the previous

Friday, Good Friday, in a youthful hand. It admonished those who had organised a sausage sizzle that day without providing a vegetarian option when the author, an observant Catholic, was forbidden to eat meat on Good Friday. She took several lines to point this out, using the kind of 'take it from me' handwriting for which there is never enough room in the space provided. The implication was that the driver reviver was a conspiracy designed to marginalise Catholics and that the organisers could expect a final reckoning. Indeed, there was a final reckoning. By the end of the Easter break, volunteers had made 18,000 cups of tea and coffee, all offered as a gesture of friendship to strangers, but evidently the work of Satan.

Another visitor read the entry soon after I did.

'It's not the Moslems this country needs to worry about,' he said.

When Jenny and I pulled into the Mundoonan rest stop, the driver reviver was not open for business. But there was still an air of fellowship among travellers. A Dutch gentleman walked the length of the carpark to tell Jenny not to worry.

'In Holland, even the queen rides a bike.'

Having delivered himself of this message, he turned around and walked back again.

A couple on the first day of their holidays arrived in a caravan. They had come from Wollongong and were not sure where they were going to end up that night. With a sense of comfortable ceremony, they broke two new plastic mugs out of their packaging and set about preparing the first cuppa of their first vacation in they didn't know how long.

'Since I first took sick,' the woman suggested, allowing us a brief glimpse of some private pain they were towing as well.

The man had plenty to say. Referring to his caravan, he told us he was pulling an '86 Viscount Pop Top', the kind of information you never have to solicit. One of the features of Australian recreational history is that some of our most pedestrian vehicles, so to speak, have the most aristocratic names. In Babyboomalia, the humble family caravan was either a Viscount or a Coronet or a Regal or a Windsor. They generally came fitted with flyscreens so that mosquitoes, once they got in, could be relied upon to stay for dinner. The family caravan was built to facilitate an exquisite form of torture known as the sleepless holiday.

Things are a bit better now. The owner told us that his van would be worth thirty-five grand new – more than I had paid for my house. The caravan did, admittedly, have a few features my house lacked, such as space. On the other hand, I could see my place had advantages as well. It would have been easier to move.

'Thirty-five is entry level. Sixty grand is about what you want for something decent. Where are you heading?'

'Melbourne.'

'How far have you come so far?'

'About five miles.'

'How long will you take?'

'A couple of weeks we think.'

'How long have you been on the road?'

'About an hour.'

'You're going fine.'

'Thanks.'

'Melbourne is caravan capital. All the action in caravan design is happening in Melbourne. You'll want something decent when you get there.'

The beauty of travel is that other people always know exactly what you want.

'I'm not sure I'll be able to tow it with the bike,' I said.

'You'll want a decent vehicle for that, something that starts at fifty grand.'

'It seems like a lot of money for a caravan.'

'Well,' he said, 'you can't take it with you.'

I was going to reply that I thought the whole point of a caravan was that you could take it with you, but then I remembered that his wife had been sick. We left the man in peace to enjoy the comfort of his statistics and headed towards Yass.

An Environmental Impact Study of the effects of the new route around Yass, written before the freeway was built, lurks in the library of the Roads and Traffic Authority in Sydney. While I was reading it, I'd also discovered, nearby, the Post-Completion Evaluation of the project, published in October 1996. It was not hard to see that a Post-Completion Evaluation differs from an Environmental Impact Statement in that it tends to be more lavishly produced and easier to read. Apparently it doesn't matter if people find out about something when it is too late to do anything about it.

The post-completion evaluation of the Yass bypass found that 'the construction of the crossings of Mantons Creek and the Yass River appears to have had little effect on the platypus populations'. You have to take their word for it. The reclusive platypus is found in unlikely and congested places, often close to urban development: perhaps they have discovered that the best place to hide is in a city.

One of the first places that this strange egg-laying mammal

was closely observed was Yass. In 1832, a young British surgeon and naturalist by the name of David Bennett, who'd developed an obsession with the platypus, became the first European to explore its natural habitat. He managed to capture four young platypuses as well as an adult female from their burrows on the Yass River and put the lot in a box. The south road has carried plenty of bizarre cargo, but few consignments have been as out of place as Bennett's. He wanted to get the platypuses to England, where they were supposed to make his name. Sadly, they only made it as far as Goulburn, where the last one died. Bennett paused there long enough to bottle the remains before finding a couple more.

The Hume Highway is still travelled by a menagerie of wildlife which takes its life in its hands when it does. In rhyming slang, the usual phrase for setting out on a road is to 'hit the frog and toad', an expression which is sadly apposite in the case of the Hume. The roadkill on the freeway is extensive, although not as bad as on some of the tributary roads which lead onto it. On one 20-kilometre stretch near Gundagai, four hundred collisions with kangaroos take place in a typical year. These figures are worse during drought when kangaroos come to the edge of the road to find grass which has become scarce elsewhere. In Gunning, there's a running joke that the roos are fed by panel-beaters.

Along the road, there are signs advertising the work of WIRES, the Wildlife Information and Rescue Service, an organisation of volunteers which rescues injured wildlife in all sorts of predicaments, including birds and animals which have been hit by cars. WIRES was formed in 1985 when an injured ibis was found in Hyde Park in the centre of Sydney and nobody had a clue whom to call for help. Now WIRES performs 56,000 rescues a year and claims that 34,000 native animals are killed every day in Australia. Trucks, cars and even bicycles are responsible for their fair share.

One of the volunteers is John Meany, now secretary of the

southern tablelands WIRES group, based in Goulburn, which I had once phoned. John and his wife, Merilyn, had joined WIRES through an advertisement in the local paper, undertaking a weekend's introductory course in the basics of animal rescue. More recently, they had done additional training and now specialised in looking after echidnas, the only other mammal, apart from the platypus, which lays eggs. When we spoke John explained that echidnas have unique needs because they lead an unstructured life and have a fuzzy sense of their territory. A female echidna may dig a burrow, plant her offspring in it and then go away for a week or more. These creatures will wander anywhere without much obvious rhyme or reason and will venture haplessly onto the road without knowing where they are.

John said he dreads being called out to rescue an injured animal from the Hume, especially after dark, because the job means dodging high-speed heavy traffic. The week before we talked, he'd had the unenviable task of separating a surviving wallaby joey from the body of its dead mother. Until he told me, I didn't know that it is important to remove corpses from the road, quite apart from the hazard they may present to traffic: kangaroos are far from endangered and yet another casualty may seem insignificant in the broader scheme of things, but it's the birds which come to feed off the remains of kangaroos that are often rare.

From the Environmental Impact Study for the Yass bypass I'd copied a list of all the landholders whose property had needed to be acquired before the freeway could be built. So it wasn't difficult to locate Mr Graeme Barber, five per cent of whose land had been taken by the road.

Not far from the freeway, Graeme was sitting on the remaining ninety-five per cent, smoking Winfields while he waited for an operation to have both his knees replaced. The physiotherapist

had told him, in his words, that his bones were 'all buggered':
he had worked hard in his life; she could judge that from the
X-rays. He replied that she didn't need X-rays, he could have told
her as much himself.

As a younger man, Graeme had built 120 miles of fencing,
digging all the post holes with a crowbar. The earth was like
rock.

'That's why my bones all got wore out.'

But he learnt the facts about fences.

Graeme and his wife Mary poured tea as they spoke about
their relationship with the Hume. The road has always been part
of life here. Mary said the highway used to be called the Black
Snake because of the number of lives it took when people were
least expecting it.

On one occasion, Graeme recalled, when he was a child, his
mother was driving him to school in an old Chevy. Graeme was
kneeling on the back seat, looking out the rear window:

'Families used to take turns getting the kids to school in these
old cars. Sometimes we used to have to get out and push them.
Anyway, there used to be a terrible bridge over the Yass River. It
was real dangerous. On this day, there was a semi-trailer going
one direction and another one going in the opposite direction.
There wasn't enough room for them both and there were three
people sitting on the back of one of the trailers.'

As the trucks passed each other, one of the passengers was
knocked off, and Graeme saw the person killed. His mother
didn't stop.

She wanted to protect her child from the scene.

'You never forget it. That moment has stayed with me
forever. I'd think of it every month or two. I think it must be
like someone's been raped or something like that. I dare say
they never forget . . . Just like you don't forget your top dog
either. When I was fencing, I had good dogs. But they died off.
Every one.'

Graeme looked at me then and said he'd known that the new road was ready for some of his land when he noticed planes and helicopters doing aerial surveillance.

'They sent a letter saying they'd be going through. That was it.'

After some haggling, the roads department was reasonably just in what they paid to acquire his land.

'In the end, they were fair. But only in the end. We were next door to going to court. They were as cunning as foxes.'

Graeme Barber took more than a passing interest in the progress of the Hume Freeway through what had, until recently, been his land, and he has no doubt that the road itself is a decent piece of engineering.

'They'd got that worked out okay.'

But the fences that came with the road were another story.

'They were absolutely hopeless. The overseer was a Pommy. I don't think he'd ever put up a fence in his life. He didn't have the slightest idea. They must have spent $100,000 to put the flood gates in one of the waterways it went over, Manton Creek. They were cemented in solid. So they acted like a weir! When the creek came up, they were swept away.'

Graeme got a pencil and paper to illustrate his point. Then he said what had happened next:

'The head man came to me and said, "What are we going to do about it?" I told him to run the fence alongside the creek to make the new road stockproof and forget about the flood gate. He said, "I think we'll do it like that, Graeme."'

Graeme drew a diagram for us, illustrating his plan for effectively fencing off a creek that runs under a freeway.

'I think they do it that way everywhere now.'

Graeme isn't sure why the road needed to come through his place at all. The Post-Completion Evaluation observes that 'no records were found of any serious disputes with affected landholders'.

The Evaluation also indicates that the road was realigned to spare one site of pre-historic Aboriginal significance, not far from Mt Mundoonan. Others were fenced off to be protected during construction and still others, 'judged to be of no significance', were destroyed.

Just as Mary was clearing away the cups and saucers, Graeme bent down to retrieve something from the cupboard under his television. It took a while.

'Sorry I'm slow. Me knees are all buggered from fencing.'

Eventually he produced two stone implements once used by Aborigines, showing the right way to hold them, and explained that one was 'for killing' and the other 'for skinning roos'.

'These are not rocks from this area. They were brought in. I'd say they are between ten and twenty thousand years old.'

But he'll never tell anyone where he found them. Not a soul. Not even Mary.

'They might claim the land.'

Not far past Graeme and Mary's place, Jenny and I left the freeway and took the old Hume Highway into Yass. The road changed character immediately. Trees stand close enough to the old road to provide shade. It felt more like an avenue.

'This road feels like it's in retirement,' said Jenny.

Near the turnoff, we rested beside a memorial to one John Stringer, who died in late March 1980 and is remembered by the inscription 'road accident victim'. His anniversary had only been a few weeks earlier, and it had not been forgotten. Near the memorial were some wine casks and an unopened stubby of beer, whose label was yet to fade, which had been left to slake the thirst of the deceased. A tree had been planted behind the memorial, perhaps on an earlier anniversary, and had only just begun to outgrow the stake which had supported it. It was an image of life continuing. The Hume hides evidence of many such small rituals.

I STARTED OUT WITH NOTHING AND STILL HAVE MOST OF IT
— Bumper sticker, Hume Highway

The name Hume means 'of the earth'. Its origins are still evident in words like 'humus', 'exhumation' and 'posthumous'. Humility and humour are thus, when you think about it, earthy qualities. But old Hamilton Hume, who was a man of the land, not of the earth, lacked both of them. Humility is the opposite of inferiority. When the greatest river which he and Hovell chanced upon had its name changed from 'the Hume' to 'the Murray' he complained resentfully, 'but Murray was a soldier and I was only a Cornstalk'.

In 1839, Hamilton Hume bought a property near Yass on which was located Cooma Cottage, where Hume would spend a long time dying. He had only just moved in, when Lady Jane Franklin, regarded as the first woman to travel overland between Sydney and Port Phillip, turned up in the district. She was moving in the opposite direction to that in which Hume and Hovell had journeyed – she was travelling north. A year older than Hume, Jane Franklin was the wife of Sir John Franklin, the governor of Tasmania, a man best known for his tragic attempt in later years to negotiate a North West Passage through the Arctic.

Lady Franklin would eventually be known for her attempts to locate her husband's remains. Already she had shown she was not the retiring type and was inclined, according to the conventional mind of the period, to step beyond the bounds of decorum. She had ideas on which the press loved to pour scorn. She decided, for example, that she was going to do for Tasmania what St Patrick did for Ireland and rid the place of snakes, at least black snakes, by offering a bounty for them.

Maybe Sir John was so relieved that Jane – who has been described by her biographer Penny Russell as 'nervous, anxious, ill and depressed' – had found something to occupy her, that he agreed to such a hare-brained scheme as his wife travelling by road from Melbourne to Sydney in 1838. The road was not considered safe; in places, it scarcely existed. But not only was Jane determined to make the trip, she was determined to do it in style. Her retinue included three gentlemen, two mounted policemen, a full complement of maids and servants, a niece and one large bed which needed to be assembled every night. The servants carried the bed and Jane carried the small notebook in which she recorded her diary. When she arrived in Sydney she was called 'the Queen of Sheba'.

Lady Franklin's anxiety and depression are not immediately obvious in her diary. But when you look twice you find a woman who is intent on harvesting every single detail along the way: every scrap of information, every statistic, every encounter, however trivial. The restless energy absorbed by the pages of her diary is its most revealing feature. It is the work of a woman trying to keep on top of things, to keep them under control by putting words to them.

Hume is the patron of all who take to his road knowing exactly where they are going and why. Franklin is the patroness of the others, often more companionable, who are not too sure why they are on the road in the first place.

Hume doesn't record his impressions of Franklin. Franklin, on the other hand, records her impressions of everyone. At dinner, Hume didn't touch his food and Franklin observed, 'I believe his travelling fatigues have laid the foundation of ill health.' Hume complained that the published account of his expedition had been sourced largely from Hovell and was inaccurate. He 'did not much approve it'. Afterwards, Franklin's companions laughed that she had avoided a *faux pas* by referring to the Murray River as the Hume, the name Hume originally gave it. Hume's sensitivity on this point seems to have been well known. Franklin's companions flattered her tact. 'Did you ever know her at fault?' one of them said; she has no problem recording the compliment along with her inventory of the housing in Yass which, common for the time and place, had twice as many public houses as stores.

The passage of time did not improve Hamilton Hume's frame of mind. He spent years dwelling on Hovell's shortcomings. As an old man, Hume became increasingly grumpy and drank more heavily as he struggled against asthma. His problems with hearing had already been evident on the trip. In later years, however, he became almost entirely deaf. He had no children. He withdrew into an interior wilderness where he nursed his grievances, almost to madness.

Matters came to a head thirty years after the journey. In 1853, Hovell was invited to a dinner in Geelong, a city which was growing rapidly, the city at the furthest point Hume and Hovell had travelled. William Hilton Hovell was not a bad catch as a speaker, a bit like having Remus address the Roman senate. The senate on this occasion assembled at Mack's Hotel.

But there was no Romulus. Hume wasn't there and was far from impressed when he read an account of proceedings in the *Argus*, which, in his questionable assessment, gave Hovell more than his share of credit for the expedition. All Hovell said about the area they had discovered was 'may it live and prosper shall be the prayer of the Parent who looks upon it as his thriving child.'

Hume was touchy on the issue of parenthood and was so outraged by what was reported in the papers that he produced a *Brief Statement of Facts in Connection with an Overland Expedition from Lake George to Port Phillip in 1824–1825*. Neither the statement nor its title are brief. Nor, one suspects, is it entirely factual. Hume got three of the other men who were on the journey, Boyd, Angel and Fitzpatrick, to testify to the accuracy of his claim to have been the real driving force of the expedition. He also got them to endorse his assassination of Hovell's character, a task they undertook with relish. Hume's basic case was that Hovell 'has almost monopolised with the public the fame and credit' and that he, Hume, was being seen by the public 'more as Mr Hovell's companion or assistant'.

Unpleasantries were then batted back and forth. Hovell wrote to Hume to ask if he had implied that he, Hovell, was a coward. Hume confirmed that he may have. Hovell wrote a *Reply to a Brief Statement of Facts* in which he accused Hume of 'a gross perversion of facts and an invention of untruths' based on 'a vulgar and groundless feeling of envy'. Hovell then gave his version of what actually happened; it was incompatible with Hume's.

Hovell said rather snootily that Hume called for support only from his own assigned servants, men who were still evidently under his influence. The exception was Claude Bossawa, whom Hume had grabbed by the neck at one stage of their journey and threatened to throw into the river. Speaking in his own defence, Hovell had no idea what had happened to his servants; Hume has still closely associated with his. This indicated something about their respective personalities.

The feud was still going strong when Hume produced a second edition of his brief statement in 1873; it was published after Hume died. It included endorsements from the explorers Thomas Mitchell and Charles Sturt, both names with which to conjure. Hovell was then in the awkward position of having to argue with the ghost of one of Australia's favourite sons. Nobody ever wins an argument like this. Both Hume and Hovell look like unhappy old men.

Jenny and I climbed a hill to visit Hume's grave in Yass. He is identified there simply as 'an Australian explorer'. It's a pity he never explored a route from bitterness to peace.

Cooma Cottage, the property where Hume marinated in his unhappiness, is now owned by the National Trust and stands beside what was, until ten years ago, the Hume Highway. Hume spent years looking out over the road that was eventually to carry his name. On the day we cycled through the gates, the house was closed to visitors so we rested from the sun under the trees and thought what a tranquil place this might have been, even if it looks like it is being slowly strangled by wisteria. There's a cruel irony in the fate of those who find themselves in peaceful places but are themselves unable to find peace. I should know. I've tried it.

The Cottage is lucky to still exist. In 1985, the executive director of the National Trust wrote to Laurie Brereton, the New South Wales Minister for Roads, pointing out that 'the Department of Main Roads' present proposal provides for a new highway right through the middle of the property!' He wrote that the problem was raised in 1975 but nothing had been done. It would have been ironic for Hume's house to be bulldozed to make way for his highway. But, in the end, another alignment was found and land-scaping was used to make sure that, sitting on his porch, a ghostly Hume would remain undisturbed by the midnight rumblings of his freeway.

Jenny and I sat on the porch ourselves and started talking about our first bikes and how we learnt to ride them. I remembered that

I was taught to ride by the father of a friend of mine when I was about seven or eight. The friend had long been able to use a two-wheeler, a fact which made me feel inferior. I sat on his doorstep and watched him with envy. His father picked up on this and suggested that instead of allowing me to feel left out, it would be better if they taught me how to ride their spare bike so my friend and I could go places together.

We went out the front of their house, which was in a flat street, and Mr Fitzsimons held the luggage rack of the bike while I pedalled. He told me not to think about it, just to pedal. He would hold the luggage rack to make sure I didn't fall off. I could trust him. I felt comfortable enough to give it a go. We went up and down the footpath a few times and, when I looked up, he was always there. Then, at the end of the fourth or fifth length of the street, I looked up, expecting to see Mr Fitzsimons still standing over my shoulder but, instead, he and his son were at the other end of the street, laughing and clapping. I had done it without even knowing.

I told Jenny that this incident has stayed with me as a model of teaching. You support somebody while they need it. When they are able to support themselves, you applaud their achievement and join in their pleasure.

I hadn't been able to tell my parents about being able to ride a two-wheeler, because I thought I'd get into trouble.

Jenny said she had taught herself to ride. As a little girl, she inched up and down the family driveway in Sydney's Auburn, on her brother's dragster, clinging to the fibro wall of the house so that she didn't fall off. Eventually she found that she could balance on two wheels without the house.

'I felt so proud of myself. I did it on my own.'

'You must have been happy.'

'I wasn't really. My brother's bike was blue and I wanted a pink one.'

One of the first trips Jenny had made on her own on a bike

was when she was about six years old and she ran away from home.

'I went to the park which was opposite our school, St Joseph's the Worker. The school didn't have a playground of its own yet so the pupils used to go over and play in this park. Anyway, it was deserted on the weekend when I ran away and I remember it felt like a different place. It was scary without the other kids. I sat on my own for what felt like a couple of hours, really trying to drag out the time. I was being brave. I wanted to make people at home feel sad that I had left and get them really worried. But after a time, I realised it was not so great to be on my own. I was the one who was upset and sad. I think that was the moment in my life when I realised I was never going to survive just on my own. I wanted to be connected to something. So I got back on my bike and went home.'

'Were you in trouble when you got home?'

'They hadn't even noticed I had gone.'

We laughed.

'I don't think I could have been away as long as I thought I was.'

We laughed again at the idea of doing something silly to make a point to others and actually learning something for yourself. We'd both tried it at different times, even as adults. Jenny said that it felt strange to be on the road, away from work. She had this niggling doubt that she should be someplace else but couldn't think where it was. She dug her mobile phone out of its pannier. There were no messages for either of us.

Jenny and I cycled through the town of Yass, pausing at an op-shop so Jenny could get a long-sleeved shirt to protect her arms from sunburn. The problem with op-shopping is that you always find the best bargains at the most inopportune moments. In this case, they had a superb pair of ski boots for a dollar. Given that I don't ski and given that, even if I did, they would take up all the room in our panniers, I decided to leave them for someone else. But I needed to be persuaded. It was dawning on Jenny that, if she hung around with me, she would be spending a lot of time arguing the obvious.

We then went to the supermarket where Jenny searched for and eventually found some small white cotton cleaning gloves.

'What do you want those for?'

'Sunburn.'

'But I've packed some cream for that.'

It was also dawning on Jenny that not only would she be spending a long time arguing the obvious, but I would be spending a long time arguing against it.

The woman in front of us was buying a single potato and it was interesting to watch the solemnity with which this simple purchase was transacted. It was, admittedly, a fine-looking spud. Spuds normally travel in scrums, so the sight of one on its own was strange. The woman at the checkout laid it on the scales with both hands, according it more respect than a trolley full of other stuff. The woman then asked the customer if she wanted a bag for it.

'No,' said the customer. 'Nature has provided it with a jacket of its own.'

The employee smiled approvingly. Then it was my turn. I asked the woman on the cash register if, as well as our own, we could have the plastic bag the previous woman hadn't wanted for her lonely potato.

'What did you want the extra bag for?' asked Jenny as we left.

I hadn't thought of that yet.

We found our way to the Hamilton Hume Motor Inn, an establishment which shares its name but little else with our patron. Once you've passed under its gaudy neon sign, which features a bright yellow image of Hume which adds jaundice to his otherwise choleric appearance, we could forget all about him. We'd had enough of him for one day.

With patience and skill, we managed to get all our gear into the room and then thought we had better bring in the bikes as well for safe keeping. After that, we decided we needed to string out some laundry but we had no string so we draped wet clothing over all the reading lamps, mini fridge and fading prints which had been screwed into the walls. Even that was not enough. So clothes were hung from handlebars and across the bike frames, which at least helped to clean the bikes. By this stage the suite was starting to feel a bit like a suburban garage in the middle of winter when the dryer is broken and a bed has to be made up for some unexpected guests. I unpacked everything except *Anna*

Karenina, who had agreed to come at the last minute and was already wondering why she bothered. There was another woman in my life. We slept peacefully, a gift which often comes by stealth.

The following day, as we were packing, Jenny observed that 'pannier' and 'companion' are words from the same family. A companion is someone with whom you share bread. It can also be a person with whom you share a pannier or even a spare plastic bag for clothes that haven't quite dried.

'I knew it would come in handy,' I said proudly.

A few kilometres out of Yass, where the old road rejoins the freeway once again, you come to a Service Centre where we shared bread, if you can call it that, the following morning. Nearly all the long-distance traffic which once stopped in the centre of Yass and spread its money over dozens of shops, now pulls into this vast concourse. I'd seen it at night, too – as you approach Yass from the south in the dark, their neon signs hover above the landscape. You come over a rise and suddenly, out of the blackness, it looks like aliens have landed and begun to feed.

If you wanted to compose a guide to the great eating houses of the Hume, you might spend more time at the Liberty Cafe, back in the main street of Yass, than at the Service Centre. That was where I should have gone with Jenny this morning, but we had passed it the night before. The Liberty has been there for as long as most people can remember.

When I was travelling from Melbourne to Sydney to be ordained a priest in 1993, I stopped there for dinner with Brother Paul, a member of the Jesuit order who'd grown up in an orphanage where less resilient souls would have learnt to apologise for their existence, something Paul never did. I was happy enough to let him share some of my limelight by acting as chauffeur.

The Liberty Cafe, then as now, offered a traditional menu, with plenty of steaks, hamburgers and fried eggs. On the hot summer's evening in question, Brother Paul and I ordered our meals and waited a long time for the food to arrive. When it did, the thick-shake was warm and runny and the eggs were cold and rubbery. I made this point in no uncertain terms to the man who'd served us, despite the fact that this gentleman appeared to be struggling in the heat. He suggested that, if I preferred the look of my companion's eggs, then perhaps we could just swap plates. Such common sense was not, I believed, an adequate response. I said as much. Brother Paul was unimpressed by my display of authority.

'You know . . .' he said when the man had gone.

'Know what?'

'No one would believe it.'

'Believe what?'

'Believe that you're about to be a priest'.

Since then I've learned that the Liberty is now run by Con Sevros. He doesn't know why it's called the Liberty, but points out that there is a barbershop called the Liberty Salon next door and that the cinema which used to occupy most of the building was once called The Liberty. Con says that teenagers have hung around on the footpath outside since their grandparents came here to the movies.

'You've got to feel sorry for the kids hanging around. There's nothing for them to do. Work is scarce. I tell them to behave themselves. At the same time, you have to respect them. They have to have their place too.'

When he took over the cafe, Con was tempted to pull out all the old booths and replace them with something modern, but he's glad he didn't – the seventies laminex appeals to people. It's no longer ugly; it's novel. He's also pleased that he was able to retain Nick, a staff member who has been working at the Liberty for thirty years. Nick is the very man who served Brother Paul and me ten years ago.

Nick hasn't lost his touch. Last time I was there, he brought us each a cappuccino. Con indicated that some of my coffee had spilt in the saucer. Nick apologised. He swapped Con's cup for mine.

'I have served people as low as the gutter or beneath the gutter,' said Con to me. 'And I have served people as high as the sky. I remember lots of them. Here we serve a lot of the people who get meal vouchers from the St Vincent de Paul, people who arrive in town with absolutely nothing. From an alcoholic to a junky to a hobo. We see all those types. They tend to be moving through. We serve them all.'

Despite the passing parade, most of his customers are local, many of them regulars.

'I am thinking of bringing the menu up to date,' he offered.

'What do you have in mind?'

He smiled broadly as if he was about to share a state secret.

'Salads,' he whispered. He dropped his voice as if he didn't want anyone to hear his plan. 'I am thinking of introducing salads.'

The best part of ten years after my first visit to the Liberty with Brother Paul, the Liberty Cafe still looked exactly the same. As we cycled through the evening before, there were youngsters sitting outside, leaning against the Statue of Liberty etched in the front window. Yass is a long way from New York but the great eating houses of the Hume tend to have names which put them along-side other roads. The Paragon in Goulburn is one, the Niagara in Gundagai is another and Alaysha in Brunswick is yet another.

A few miles from the Liberty, but far from any attempt at novelty, the Yass McDonald's franchise is owned and operated by Karen Rae, who has been working with the organisation since she was a fifteen-year-old crew member. She couldn't easily recall, in all that time, any individual customer nor any incident of human interest involving joe public.

'How many people get to drive a company car at the age of twenty?' she asked. 'And how many people get to study overseas at the age of twenty?'

Karen completed a Degree in Hamburgerology.

'How long did the degree take?'

'It took twelve days.'

'That's pretty quick for a degree.'

'Well, I was away for the fortnight.'

There is a dependent relationship between food franchises and roads. In 1955, one Colonel Harlan Sanders of Kentucky was faced with a problem. He had been running a famous roadside chicken outlet for twenty years and was doing quite nicely, thank you. Unfortunately, in 1955, an interstate highway opened seven miles from his premises and Colonel Sanders' business collapsed, forcing him onto social security, which made him decide that the only future was to make his business travel. Sanders no longer wanted to rely on the road to bring him customers. Instead, he would make sure the chicken could cross the road. By 1960, he had 200 stores on roadsides across his country. By 1963, he had 600. There are now 11,000 all over the world, including one across the way here at the Yass roadside Service Centre.

The McDonald's story is not unlike that of KFC. In 1948, Maurice and Richard McDonald opened a modest burger stall on the legendary Route 66 in San Bernardino in California. Richard and Maurice used to work in props departments in Hollywood; they knew how to make things look real. They did pretty well, offering burgers for fifteen cents, fries for ten cents and milk-shakes for twenty cents, and made their money out of rapid turnover, something that was facilitated by offering a limited range of standardised products. If there had been no Route 66, there would have been no McDonald's. The road brought people who wanted to eat and keep moving.

In the mid-fifties, a pianist called Ray Kroc thought that, just as the McDonald brothers had perfected the art of endlessly cloning the same burger, the McDonald business itself could be endlessly cloned. He believed that such things as juke boxes and cigarette vending machines, even public phones, only encouraged people to needlessly linger, and he brought these thoughts to the McDonalds. It's strange that a man who used to play live in speakeasies should have come to this. The result was that McDonald's got through the fifties without teenagers hanging around. By the sixties, the restaurants were everywhere and customers knew exactly what to expect. But even the most perfect franchise is a bit like Indian whispers – things change along the way. When an official franchise finally opened opposite the first McDonalds brothers' business in San Bernardino, the original went belly up and closed.

There are currently more McDonald's outlets on the Hume Highway than there are towns.

Karen Rae has no doubt that her business depends on the road. If the highway is closed for some reason, which she said happens about half a dozen times a year, then business suffers dramatically. Three-quarters of her trade is from the road.

'If there was no Hume Highway, we wouldn't be here.'

Her busiest day is Good Friday; the second is Boxing Day. The outlet can sell 30,000 burgers on Good Friday, the day when the whole country is on the move.

Karen said that although people might criticise her for what they perceive as taking trade from coffee shops, she is the biggest employer in Yass. She looked proud when she said she has 100 staff, aged between fifteen and forty-five. Seventy-five per cent are under twenty – we could see that – making her a significant youth employer.

'There's always work if you really want it.'

Karen Rae has fond memories of her own childhood, when the family went on holidays in their caravan.

'Mum used to pack us lunch. Sandwiches and fruit. She was wonderful. We used to stop in parks and picnic grounds and eat it. It was great.'

I DRINK RUM BECAUSE I CAN'T SPELL BOURBON
— Bumper sticker, Hume Highway

The road took us over Conroy's Gap towards Bookham. We were entering the homeland of Banjo Paterson, author of 'The Man from Snowy River' and 'Waltzing Matilda'. He also wrote 'Mulga Bill's Bicycle', a lesson to anybody who'd be foolish enough to swap a horse 'that served him many days' for 'a shining new machine'.

Either of us would now gladly have taken his advice. We were already bum-sore and no match for a man who was most comfortable when he was in the saddle or, even better, talking about others who were. Jenny informed me that the inaccessible region of our bodies which was being forced to bear the unaccustomed load is called the perineum. I'm not sure how she knew this; I think it must be used for something in ballet. But I was glad to discover its identity because it always helps when the enemy has a name. Jenny's knee, a casualty of many years of dancing, was also giving trouble.

Conroy's Gap turns up in a number of Paterson's poems including 'Mulga Bill's Bicycle'. The poem which is actually named for Conroy's Gap suggests something of the darker legends that have gathered around this small feature where the road rises sharply and passes briefly through a stone cutting before descending again on the other side. In the poem, Conroy's Gap is a place of menace and foreboding which shelters a disreputable 'wayside inn' known as the 'Shadow of Death':

> *Under the shelter of Conroy's Gap –*
> *Under the shade of that frowning range,*
> *The roughest crowd that ever drew breath –*
> *Thieves and rowdies, uncouth and strange,*
> *Were mustered round at the Shadow of Death.*

There are a number of legends about women disappearing here, some of which may be corruptions of the same story. Cobb and Co coaches stopped on the rise to rest their horses and passengers were allowed to wander into the bush to relieve themselves. There are stories about women never returning from the call of nature and others about women returning from the call to find the coach empty and no trace of their companions.

These days, as we were finding, the freeway makes light of Conroy's Gap. The cutting is wide and the gradient is easy, at least for cars. It is no longer any place for ghosts.

In 1895, Henry Lawson, Australia's poet inebriate, suggested that Paterson change the name of his poem from 'The Story of Conroy's Gap' to 'Conroy's Gap', a change which Paterson accepted; so perhaps the animosity sometimes spoken of between the two writers has been exaggerated.

Paterson was a lawyer and he offered advice to Lawson, a coach painter, about his dealings with publishers. Jenny and I both had experience with compulsive people and agreed that despite their relative social standing, Lawson was the more complex and tragic personality. Paterson looked to us like a reticent man who, even when purporting to write in a personal way, commits virtually nothing of himself to paper. This, in turn, seems to have affected his ability to develop characters: Paterson's creations tend to be two-dimensional. They are often great fun and stick to the imagination like lint but there is seldom much to them.

Both Lawson and Paterson had failed to develop their careers beyond their early success. In this, they were disappointed men, undermined by their own restlessness. Lawson was a victim of his self-destructiveness; Paterson, I thought, was always going someplace else. He was desperate to get involved with both the Boer War and World War I because he was bored. This was also why, in 1905, he became one of the first to drive from Sydney to Melbourne. Boredom is the trade name of a dozen poisons which Paterson never cared to identify.

The two men are hard to get to know for opposite reasons: Paterson because his life scans with deceptive ease; Lawson, whose personality is barely legible under blottings of grog, self-pity, selfishness, depression and isolation, because his life was a chaotic scrawl. Paterson lived in a perfumed world; Lawson's stank. Neither of them were comfortable with reality. They built fictional Australias which have sheltered the imaginations of thousands, although neither Lawson nor Paterson collected much rent. Lawson died destitute; Paterson's estate was worth £225.

The road we were on would intersect with Paterson at Bookham, on the other side of Conroy's Gap. It intersected with Lawson 60 kilometres further along, at Coolac. It touches Paterson's opening chapter and Lawson's final one.

I had promised Jenny that there was a shop at Bookham. Well, there used to be. It turned out that the hamlet had been bypassed only a few months before we arrived; how long before that the small shop had closed down, I can't say. The building was still there, some of the old advertising signs clinging to it faithfully.

Diagonally opposite, the Roads and Traffic Authority had provided a rest stop where we ate tuna and dry biscuits. We noticed that drivers who'd also stopped there didn't seem to pay much attention to each other but, once they saw the bikes, were keen to talk to us.

'How far do you reckon you'll get?' one asked.

'Melbourne,' I said defiantly.

He was already reaching for his wallet.

'What are you raising money for?'

I was tempted to make something up and take his money, but lacked the spark for mischief. We were both feeling a little out of sorts. Jenny was finding the freeway uninspiring. Her knee was sore and there was nowhere in Bookham to find anything that could help.

Bookham used to be called Bogolong. When Banjo Paterson was a kid the place had two pubs, one posted on the road at each entrance to the town to catch travellers from either direction. It also had a picnic races where Paterson encountered a horse called Pardon, now immortalised in the ballad 'Old Pardon, the Son of Reprieve'.

There is a sign off the current freeway indicating Illalong Road, along which it was a short ride to the Illalong property where Andrew Barton Paterson spent the most formative years of his life. His father, who had gone broke on land further north, borrowed money to buy the place. It's wrong to suggest Paterson was born with a silver spoon in his mouth, but he certainly had opportunities Lawson lacked. At the age of ten, he was sent away to Sydney Grammar School, where he dreamed of holidays back at Illalong. He narrowly missed a bursary to university so he became a solicitor the other way, taking articles in the office of a law firm. He may have felt for the unfortunate but was never one of them.

Late in life, Paterson reminisced about his childhood at Illalong, which he described as a 'Wonderland'. By this stage, Paterson was an aristocrat, at least in manner. He chose to overlook the facts that his father had drunk heavily, that his mother was often left to cope on her own and became depressed, that the family sailed so close to the wind financially that Paterson's father was forced to sell the property and take employment as its manager from the new owners. Instead Paterson chose to recall a childhood shared both with the natural world and with a colourful cast of indigent characters ('some with Oxford accents and some foreigners barely able to talk English') which the road brought to their door.

Rose Paterson, his mother, thought of the road not so much as bringing company but the opposite. She wrote to her sister:

> We might as well be on a desert island as here for all we know of the doings of the rest of the world or even of our own family.

Rose's letters include an account of a neighbour travelling to Yass and falling on his horse through a rotting bridge. The road could never be trusted.

Rose welcomed the coming of the railway in 1876. The main Sydney–Melbourne line brushed past Illalong, the point at which, to this day, the railway and the highway part company for a while. The railway line travels further west, through Harden and Wagga, and rejoins the road at Albury. By the time the railway arrived, Cobb and Co had trimmed the trip from Sydney to Melbourne to five days, although their horses were worked hard to keep to schedule. The railway halved the time. Rose was so enthusiastic that she quoted fares in her letters to her sister, Nora: a ticket from Sydney to Melbourne was only £5. Rose longed to be connected to the outside world. Her son's fantasies were about the splendour of isolation and contentment in his own company, about freedom from his own restless anxiety.

The road from Goulburn to Jugiong heads due west. As you approach Jugiong, it starts to turn south again.

'Have you noticed one thing?' Jenny asked.

'What's that?'

'Have you noticed that we are the only people who seem to be doing this?'

I had noticed.

'Why do you think that is?' she asked, rhetorically. I soon gathered that there were a dozen other places where Jenny thought it might be quite pleasant to spend a few days cycling and that the side of a freeway was well down her list, if it was on it at all.

I was starting to wonder what kind of strain this silly adventure was placing on us.

We were relieved to find the turnoff and wind our way down from the freeway towards Jugiong township (population 150), which lies on the banks of the upper Murrumbidgee. We'd progressed 65 kilometres in the day; there had been a lot of wind and plenty of hills. Jenny and I hadn't spoken much until now. Her knee was playing up badly. A lot of the time, I had simply kept my head down apologetically and watched numerous survey marks slip slowly under my front wheel. There were so many that sometimes the shoulder of the road looked like a mosaic and I tried to distract myself by thinking of the road as an embroidered carpet. It didn't help much.

Jenny had perked up and said she kept noticing the number of drink bottles that had been discarded along the way, which got her thinking about what it must be like in the third world to have to walk miles to get water, then lug it miles back home again and then wake up the next day and do the whole thing over again. At least the side of a freeway was better than that.

The proprietor of the motel looked at me, then looked at the bike and started to tell us about an elderly friend of hers who'd recently taken up orienteering.

'It's never too late in life,' she said.

I asked where we might get something to eat.

'There's the pub and the roadhouse. You could try the pub. There wasn't a meal there last night but that doesn't mean anything for tonight. The place has just changed hands. The son has it now. Used to be the father had it.'

There were two people in the hotel when we entered, so we doubled the numbers. The barman was young, and although it was dark inside he wore a hat. Another man appeared and, talking over the bowed heads of the patrons, told the barman to make sure he made an appointment to see the dentist. We presumed this was the newly deposed father.

Before long, the latest edition of the *Jugiong Journal* arrived. The barman put a copy of the journal in front of each of his regulars like a placemat. They didn't have to move.

The Jugiong hotel is yet another which claims to be the oldest in some way, announcing that it has been in the same family since 1845, making theirs the longest licensed dynasty in Australia. So perhaps a generational change from father to son is big news around Jugiong, as much as a royal succession would be elsewhere. It is a fine old building and we learnt that night that for years it had been a landmark on the Hume – all the more so because it stood at the foot of the steepest hill between Razorback and the Murray. After dinner, the barman showed us the old Cobb and Co stables behind the pub, a reminder that this used to be a stage on the long coach haul and that the hill needed fresh horses.

I once lived with an old priest from this part of the world who recalled, as a little boy, being put in charge of a dray and despatched along the road by his father. His father knew the boy was safe because the horses were conditioned never to pass the door of the Jugiong Pub, where he could count on finding his son.

As a priest Charles had gone on to develop an intimate understanding of Greek and Latin; when he died, one of the few remaining bridges to an ancient literature collapsed and I grieved not only him but the loss of his knowledge. He was one of the few people who was at home on both the Hume and the Appian Way.

Charles spent a lifetime teaching at the same school but his message to graduating students was invariably the same – they should go, move on, not hang around school, get a life of their own. He could not imagine a life spent sitting at the same bar.

I dreamt I was pushing a bike up a long steep hill. In the morning, my dream came true. As we were toiling along the old road out of Jugiong, I asked Jenny to remind me to dream of winning the lottery that night.

The proprietor of the motel had told us that the gradient on this road was nine per cent. On the freeway it is now four per cent, so the Jugiong hill is less than half as steep as it used to be. In 1839, Jane Franklin had encountered a couple of travellers on this hill, two women sitting on a fallen tree trunk with no head covering, as a result of which at least one of them, a Scotswoman who'd only been in the colony for a couple of months, was badly sunburnt. She had married just before emigration in order to secure passage to the new country and now she was travelling overland to her new job in Port Phillip. Lady Franklin recorded that the woman's husband was a blacksmith, the contemporary equivalent of a motor mechanic, and there was already plenty of work for him along the road. His sunburnt wife was anxious that grog might be just as plentiful. This woman is unnamed but her presence on the road from Sydney to Melbourne suggests that Lady Franklin may not have been the first woman to travel overland between the two cities, but simply the first whose name has stuck.

At the crest of the hill Jenny and I sat together, and she smiled.

We slid down the other side of the rise, where the freeway brushes past a granite outcrop. Long ago, somebody had painted 'I Luv' in bold white letters and somebody else, in a different hand, afterwards added the name 'Lil', obliterating the object of the first graffitist's affection. Lucky Lil. Some of the world's greatest graffiti has been written for love, as has some of the world's most eloquent poetry. 'I Luv Lil' ranks with the best of either, not necessarily because of its elegance or originality, but more because of its context. Her granite boulder is a stone's throw from yet another roadside memorial, this one to Ian McDonald, whose nickname was 'Gobby'. It simply says, 'Loved by all'. To be loved in the shadow of death is all any of us want. Or so I reckoned and Jenny managed another smile. She still thought the road was ugly, the trucks got on her nerves, her knee was hurting and so was her end. But still she smiled.

At this point the road narrowed, siphoning traffic onto one of the few remaining stretches of single-lane highway between Sydney and Melbourne. The speed limit was reduced and, just to make the point, there was a speed camera permanently installed there. It wasn't very subtle. There were signs the size of football fields letting us know we were about to be photographed, so we waved for the authorities and meekly checked our speed.

This narrow stretch takes you into Coolac, one of the last hamlets on the highway. It will be bypassed eventually. It's been waiting its turn for a long time.

This was where the road intersected with Henry Lawson. By the time he reached adolescence, Henry was almost completely deaf.

Yet, like the ageing Hamilton Hume, he never had a moment's quiet in his life. His mind produced a kind of chaotic racket over which he could scarcely hear the whisperings of his own soul. Yet when he could, the sound was sweet. The best of his stories understand the worst about people.

Even Lawson's most ardent fans – and I, as Jenny who was grimly enduring an unsolicited lecture on the subject can tell you, am one – find the man frustrating. As far as I can tell, he only ever made one serious attempt to get off the grog. That was in 1899. The prose piece that came out of it, 'The Boozers' Home', is riddled with self-pity. In his fiction, however, Lawson could show a grip on reality which eluded him elsewhere. Lawson was in and out of jail and mental hospitals. He made little provision for his children and none for his wife, Bertha, who had mental illness of her own. He was incapable of relationships of any depth, used his associates shamelessly, attempted suicide at least once and drank every penny that came his way. By the end, which was not long in coming, there was very little of him left. His firmly held social views were sold up the river as he became more and more prepared to jump on any political bandwagon, including imperialism and militarism, which would sell copy. Banjo Paterson said that Lawson's publishers were prepared to pay good money just to stop him from hanging around the office.

In his later years, one place where Lawson could find sanctuary was in Coolac.

A branch line used to run from Cootamundra to Gundagai, so Lawson came to Coolac by train. The road wasn't much to write home about, which would hardly have troubled Lawson as he hated cars and saw them as symptoms of a degenerate society. By 1920, Lawson was pretty degenerate himself. Some well-wishers thought that time away from the big smoke might help, so his publishers gave him an advance of £25 and a copy of a dictionary in the fond hope that he might return to writing. He was entrusted to the care of Andy McManus, who owned the store in

Coolac and whose family lived in a residence at the back. Unfortunately, the pub (still standing) was right next door.

Something about this desperate figure touched Grace McManus, Andy's daughter. She called him 'Uncle 'Arry' and got him walking in the hills that overlook the town in the belief that exercise might calm his spirit. When Lawson returned prematurely to Sydney, she wrote him affectionate letters and asked him to come back to Coolac, which he did on at least one occasion. She paid his fare, sending him money which he called 'the necessary'. Grace was the last person to trust Henry. Sadly, he used Grace as well and spent her money on grog.

In the final two years of his life, Lawson fantasised about Coolac. He regularly broke promises to return there because he was on a bender, but he kept thinking about it. Coolac represented the dream of a sober life, one in which he was able to connect with people.

On 2 September 1922 Lawson died alone and destitute in Sydney. Ten thousand people came to his funeral. They loved Lawson's myth but, like the man himself, found reality less palatable.

We rested outside the Coolac store, looking at the heavy cast-iron camp ovens for sale in the window. This was one business on the Hume that seemed indifferent to the road: cow vaccines and chocolate bars sat side by side in the refrigerator, but no motor products. A man was waiting with his young son for the bus to Cootamundra: the baby was sucking on a dummy and the man was sucking on a cigarette. When the baby dropped its soother on the ground, the man moved his cigarette to the side of his mouth, put the dummy in the other side and sucked the dirt off it. Then he returned it to the baby.

'Don't worry, mate,' he said to the child. 'If it kills you, it'll kill me first.'

Before long the owner of the store came out and introduced himself to us as Carberry. We exchanged the usual small talk about how long he had been here and how far we were going and how the grocery side of his business had died the day they opened the big supermarket in Cootamundra, 40 kilometres away, so that now he banked on selling farm supplies. Work on the bypass was scheduled to start in the next year or so. We asked if he served tea or coffee and he said he didn't.

Carberry became suddenly more animated when we asked about Henry Lawson. He knew the McManus family and could remember his own father talking about Lawson.

'He came here to sober up. Dad said he used to go walking in the hills. Lawson thought there was gold up there and that people had approached the hills from the wrong side. Dad thought that maybe he had an intuition.'

Two of Carberry's McManus friends are buried in the local cemetery now. He told us to pay them a visit on the way out.

'The McManus family used to have the general store adjoining the pub. They didn't tolerate Lawson's excesses. Probably did him a bit of good.'

He then asked if we were still interested in a cuppa, took us into his own kitchen and told us to make ourselves at home.

Leaving Coolac, we paid our respects to Grace McManus. Then, before long, I had a puncture in my rear tyre. The only reason I mention such a commonplace occurrence is that for us it was not so common. This was the only puncture that either of us experienced on the entire length of the road. The road makers could use that in their publicity. I'd been on rides where I seemed to spend longer fixing punctures than I did in the saddle which is, admittedly, how the perineum likes to travel. But 400 kilometres from Sydney, I was so surprised by my first blowout that I felt indignant for a moment.

'Don't worry,' I told Jenny after inspecting the damage. 'It's only flat at the bottom.'

I was well equipped. All I had to do was unpack the left pannier, which contained such essential tools as the corkscrew, can opener and *Anna Karenina*. But, to my confusion, no bike equipment. It had to be in the other pannier, buried under a steadily growing collection of souvenirs. With some relief I found the small bundle of implements which included a universal bike spanner which I showed proudly to Jenny. I had planned well.

I think I may even have given it a modest twirl in celebration of the display of manly mechanical skill she was about to enjoy. A truckie honked and I waved cheerfully.

The spanner was indeed a universal spanner. But my bike had come from a different universe. For half an hour it showed no sign whatever of being able to comprehend the meaning of what the spanner was trying to do. The whole situation left us with a difficult cosmological problem about the existence of parallel universes and also, more worryingly, with a flat tyre on the shoulder of the Hume. The pages of *Anna Karenina* flapped impotently in the backdraft of passing traffic.

I had no choice but to walk to the next sign of civilisation, the famous Dog on the Tuckerbox. Jenny was being a good bloke. She could have ridden ahead and had a leisurely afternoon tea while I caught up, but she walked with me. I warned her that the Dog on the Tuckerbox was a famous tourist trap and the last place people would want to help. It existed to give visitors a taste of the real Australia in less than fifteen minutes, long enough to make them glad they could retreat to the safety of their air-conditioned buses. Not the kind of place that flows with the milk of human kindness. Jenny said that we'd see. I said that we didn't need to see when I already knew.

Sure enough, people could not have been more helpful.

The proprietors of two service stations consulted each other on our behalf and eventually a spanner was produced which fitted only one size of nut, but that size happened to be the one we wanted. It came from the same narrow universe as my bike.

In the meantime, I came to feel sorry for the Dog which sits on its Tuckerbox in all weathers. The statue, a memorial to Australia's pioneers, is meant to be a major drawcard but soon people began photographing *us*, commenting in several languages on what we were doing. It was hard to believe that a punctured tyre could be so fascinating. Some even got out of their buses again to see what was happening.

'They must be on the most boring tour in the universe,' I said.

We smiled sweetly. I felt like a busker. Eventually, a man came forward with his daughter, breaking the invisible cordon which forms around any performer, and told us he had the perfect tool for what we were doing. It was back in Cleveland.

The Dog looked on. He owes his existence to one of the more scatological parts of Australian folklore. In the early days of inter-colonial transport, the creek at this point, Five Mile Creek, was a popular camping ground for bullock teams. Indeed, next to the Dog are the ruins of a roadside inn built in 1851 by one Joseph Carberry, possibly a relative of the storekeeper of Coolac.

Bullock teams usually included a dog, a primitive but still effec-tive security system. There arose a story about one team of bullocks which got bogged at Five Mile Creek, where the driver took out his frustrations on his dog. The dog, a master of non-violent industrial action, took revenge on the driver, and his efforts were duly noted in song: 'A dog shat in the tucker box, Five miles from Gundagai.' This was sanitised for circulation beyond the world of the bullocky, which was known for its limited but intense vocabulary. It took the form, 'the dog sat on the tuckerbox'.

The image of the Dog sitting patiently is sometimes seen as one of dumb fidelity: a creature waiting to be fed by its master. It is, in fact, an image of resistance. The figure is part of a memorial to the nation's pioneers, unveiled at the onset of the summer of 1932. The myth of the pioneers was one of rugged individualism and free enterprise, tempered on occasions by a network of strategic alliances known as mateship. This is not quite what Frank Rusconi's statue of the Dog, unveiled in the middle of the Great Depression, represents. It stands for the refusal to be bullied by the boss.

The words chosen to accompany the statue were written by a radical left-wing intellectual, Brian Fitzpatrick, who won a competition which earned him the privilege. Fitzpatrick was in some ways a paper warrior and never did much apart from express his views with great vehemence. But he was an outed socialist in a conservative nation who campaigned long and hard for civil liberties and the abolition of censorship. He liked to conduct business in the front bar: that liminal place in male Australian culture which is neither home nor the road.

Fitzpatrick was an admirer of Lawson's but wary of the kind of hollow nationalism which turns somebody like Lawson into a saint. He said that 'no community can produce a literature able to maintain its place with the world's best while it is still at grips with its environment', thinking which is evident in his inscription. The Dog on the Tuckerbox has become a cliché but the words that come with it are seldom mentioned. They speak of the Australian environment as a difficult lover:

> Earth's self upholds this monument,
> To conquerors who won her when
> Wooing was dangerous and now
> Are gathered to her again.

Three

Cliff Young ran in a pair of long johns over the top of which he wore plastic pants with holes cut into them for ventilation. He kept his legs covered because he had skin cancer and didn't want people to see them. He didn't change his clothes for the entire journey. He ate out of saucepans, standing up by the side of the road. He drank out of jam jars. He kept going.

He got to Yass, 300 kilometres south of Sydney. Another sixty to Jugiong where school children stood at the foot of the hill. A wave of media interest was building and, with every new town, the crowds were bigger. Forty more to Gundagai where Cliff's crew went looking for fresh shoes for him. Trucks were starting to slow down respectfully and steer wide as they went past. Young had now become Cliff, part of the coterie of celebrities recognisable by their first names alone. He trundled through Tarcutta and Holbrook.

When Cliff Young got to Albury he was just about exhausted. He agreed to have a sleep. He didn't realise that a competitor from Western Australia, Joe Record, had been running without a break for the last twenty-four hours in an attempt to overhaul him. Record was a friend of Cliff's. He was known as 'Gentleman Joe'. At midnight, Record knocked on the door of Young's van to let Cliff know that he had been caught. That was a mistake. Cliff got straight out of bed and started running again. He caught Record within 500 metres. Before long, Record withdrew. He had spent himself in the effort to tag Young. Cliff led the rest of the way to Melbourne.

In one interview along his run to Melbourne, Cliff Young was filmed as he was eating tinned fruit from a can. A representative of the canning company raced up the Hume from Melbourne to get Cliff's signature on a bit of paper. Before the race was over, the company was already running full-page advertisements which pictured Cliff feasting from their tins. He was paid $500 and a year's supply of fruit. You could get away with that in 1983. You still can if your starlet is hungry enough.

IT'S A JINGLE OUT THERE
— Bumper sticker, Hume Highway

The Hume Highway links Sydney and Melbourne. But it touches every corner of the country. You can list the Prime Ministers whose memory is attached to it in some way.

The most celebrated encounter of the road with prime-ministership occurred on a Saturday night in 1942. The country was at war. Around midnight, a car pulled up outside the Niagara Cafe in Gundagai and from the car there emerged not one, not two, but no fewer than three Prime Ministers. John Curtin was the incumbent at the time. Artie Fadden had been ousted by Curtin the previous October after a little more than six weeks in the job. As in the story of the flood, Fadden reigned for forty days and nights. He and his vanquisher, Curtin, must have made jovial companions on the road. With them was Ben Chifley, who would replace Curtin after he had died in office. Finally, there was a lesser being called O'Sullivan, the only person in the car who was never Prime Minister. Doubtless he did most of the driving.

We speak of a set of prime numbers and a side of prime beef but I'm not sure of the appropriate collective noun for a group of prime ministers. A party of prime ministers sounds a bit festive. A herd of prime ministers makes it seem like people listen to them. A crush? A strain? A lobby? An order?

Let's call them a stand.

A stand of prime ministers found itself outside the locked door of the cafe. They were on a very important mission and were not going to leave until they had accomplished what they had come here to achieve. Nothing would come between them and the object to which they had committed themselves at this moment.

They wanted something to eat.

It says something about Australia at the time that, under threat from invasion, the entire national leadership was in one car, travelling lonely roads. It says even more that senior members of the war cabinet, hunting in packs, were happy to knock on the doors of strangers. But they were hungry. That explains everything.

John Curtin did a number of significant things in his life. One of them, for example, was to recall an Australian army from the Middle East in order to defend Australia itself, much to the confusion of Sir Winston Churchill who thought that an Australian army had no business doing any such thing. But if you visit the Niagara Cafe you will find that, whatever you may have thought before, the most important thing Curtin ever did was to turn up here in the middle of the night in the middle of a war and eat.

The man who got out of bed and opened the door was Jack Castrisson, who pulled an apron on over his pyjamas and served his notable guests. They were grateful and he was canny, complaining to them about how wartime rationing was making it difficult to look after people such as themselves who travelled the Hume. By the end of the meal, his monthly tea ration had been increased from 28 lb to 100 lb. Rationing was always a touchy subject in the land of plenty. In 1949, Artie Fadden got his own back on his Labor adversaries, Curtin and Chifley, when he persuaded Menzies, the conservative leader, to promise an end to petrol rationing. This contributed to Menzies' victory and marked the beginning of a new chapter in the life of the Hume as, post-war, freight started to make the transition from rail to road.

The crockery on which Curtin and companions were served sits in the window of the Niagara to this day. As does the teapot from which the PM strained his share of the ration. They may not be the very ones, of course. There could well have been some confusion after the place was damaged by fire in the seventies. But, on the other hand, they may just be authentic. It's a fine thing to think of three prime ministers putting their differences aside to drink from the same teapot.

The Niagara Cafe got its name because, at the turn of the twentieth century, the original owners once ran a cafe beside Niagara Falls. They brought the name with them to a dry place.

'I guess it was hard when they got here,' said Jenny. 'Hard to accept they were someplace else, I mean.'

'I guess so.'

'You know, I think I'll enjoy the ride a lot more when I stop wishing the Hume was a little leafy lane in the countryside. I'll just try to accept it for what it is. With all the trucks and all the noise. It'll be easier.'

'It's hardly the most romantic road in the world, is it?' I conceded.

'It's not the Champs Elysées.'

We laughed.

'So why did you come?' I asked.

'I came for you. Not for the road.'

'Well, that sounds romantic to me.'

We chinked our coffee cups, the very ones from which a stand of prime ministers either did or did not drink.

'It's hardly champagne,' I said.

'Just accept it for what it is,' said Jenny. 'You'll enjoy it more.'

MUM'S BUS
— Bumper sticker, Hume Highway

DAD'S BUSTED
— added underneath

The road which leads off the Hume from Yass to Canberra is the
Barton Highway, named after the first prime minister. There is a
bridge north of Albury named after Billy Hughes, prime minister
during World War I, although it's not clear if it bears his name
because he opened it, paid for it, slept under it or, at different
times, did all three. Gough Whitlam, the pompous Labor chief of
the early seventies, has his picture in more cafes on the Hume
than any other prime minister, although none of them is the kind
of place he has ever tended to frequent. Whitlam had an idea that
regional cities could be twinned with each other and made
centres of development. He thought that Albury–Wodonga, the
cities which lie on either side of the Murray, could be named
Whitlamabad. The suggestion is unlikely ever to be adopted,
especially since Albury was the place where, in December 1944,
at a meeting in a department store aptly known as Mates,
R.G. Menzies, Australia's longest-serving prime-minister, assembled the conservative party which he drove for many years.

Whitlam's successor, Malcolm Fraser, committed the Federal

Government to redeveloping the Hume for the bicentenary of European settlement in 1988, a job which is still not finished. Menzies' successor, Harold Holt, once represented the electorate of Fawkner on the Hume in Melbourne. Bob Hawke represented the area around Sydney Road, the name given to the Hume as it edges slowly into Melbourne through a landscape of cafes, pawn-shops and bridal boutiques. Hawke's successor, Paul Keating, fared badly in the election of 1996. As his political fortunes waned, he toyed with concrete proposals which might appeal to voters, such as incorporating the Hume into a massive 4,000 kilo-metre four-lane freeway from Cairns to Adelaide. Eight months after defeating Keating, John Howard unveiled the statue of the surgeon and war hero Weary Dunlop at Benalla. Howard praised Dunlop as a doctor who cared for all comers with equal concern, regardless of who they were or the circumstances in which they came. This was not a health policy which Howard was inclined to implement himself. Photos of the unveiling of the Dog on the Tuckerbox in 1932 show a bystander holding up an umbrella to keep the sun off the prime ministerial head of Joseph Lyons.

McEwen was born on the road, Scullin is buried on it, Deakin's father earned his living off it, Watson spent his retirement trying to improve it. The moral is clear. If you want to run this country, the best place to start is the Hume. With a bit of effort and an occasional realignment of the facts, you can attach every prime minister to it. The ones not mentioned above either fought or did deals with the ones who are. The Hume may link two cities but it goes everywhere.

The road is a great leveller. For a couple of minutes, it can turn any truckie who manages to get through to a talk-back radio station on his mobile phone into the leader of the nation. On the other hand, it can turn a prime minister into just another tired and hungry motorist who wants to get home.

The road has no respect for persons or status. Nor, I used to think, did I. But one of the things that surprised me most when I stopped working as a priest was that I missed my title. I used to be called Father. Then I became plain Mister. I caught myself out one day trawling the internet looking for on-line universities where I could buy a doctorate for under a hundred dollars, a small price to pay to put Doctor in front of my name without having to do any work. It would have been cheaper than starting my own religion. By the time I had scrolled down to the section where they asked if I wanted to pay half as much again to have my doctorate presented on 'reproduction parchment' which would be 'more impressive to family and clients', even I had begun to realise that I was grieving for something. I didn't know what to call myself. The hardest thing was waiting for someone to call me. Only other people can give you your name.

Different parts of the Hume have been given names by drivers who have developed a relationship with the road.

On one occasion, I was introduced to Emil Pich who had driven buses up and down the Hume Highway since the 1980s. He'd seen a lot of changes. Everybody has. This is the most common experience of the road. It's not what it was; it has always been a reminder of something that was there before. For Emil, who had taken over 100,000 passengers between Sydney and Melbourne for Firefly Express, the road represents a large part of a life's work.

Firefly is one of two or three survivors on a road which is littered with the memory of failed buslines. Emil was driving passengers from one end to the other when he used to come home to three small kids; by the time we met, the kids had their own careers and Emil had been divorced for ten years, since not long after he began working nights.

'You have to have an understanding partner when you're away so much.'

Emil was doing two return trips a week from Sydney to Melbourne, every week of the year. A small number of passengers had lodged in his memory. There was a period, for example, when he had a passenger who lived 100 kilometres on the other side of Melbourne who worked during the week in Sydney. The man had been a prime mover in a prestige car company in Geelong but following the collapse of Pyramid, Geelong's resident building society, the economy of the local area had suffered and prestige cars were not in much demand. The man was lucky to find a job in Sydney. Every Friday night, he'd catch the bus to Melbourne and then get a train to Geelong. Every Sunday night, he'd get the bus back to Sydney. He was spending two nights a week with Emil and one with his wife. After eighteen months of nodding as he got on and off, he came to life one night and told Emil that he had learnt more as a nobody on a bus than as a somebody in a board room. Emil assumed he'd found another job; he didn't see him again.

Emil Pich refers to the Hume Highway as Sesame Street.

'That's the name the truckies use all the time. I think it's because the highway was where all the boys come to play with their toys.'

Gradually, phrase by phrase, Emil introduced a code. There are two Hume Highways, one that runs between official signs and is measured in kilometres and another which has created a modest patois of its own, a vocabulary familiar to those who fish their living out of it. This is a road not measured in numbers but owned with clever, well-rubbed turns of phrase.

Wagga Hill, coming in to Tarcutta, is sometimes known as Aeroplane Hill. This is not because it's so steep. This is because, years ago, truckies could only pick up one radio station from the hill and that station was always playing advertisements for Aeroplane Jelly. Truckies had to suffer the same jingle over and over.

At least three places have got their names from the fact that they have been common places for the highway patrol to be lurking.

'The steep downhill part from Glenrowan to Wangaratta was always called Revenue Hill. The area just outside Coolac was called Money Money. The tree in the median strip in the middle of the old road at Jugiong was called The Money Tree.'

Emil produced a long list from memory. Gasoline Alley, the Shit Pit, the Keyhole, Viscount Corner, Suicide Corner, Champagne Corner, Hot Dog, Steps and Stairs, Clayton's Divide. Each place got its name for a reason; few of them are still on the Hume. Curiously, the new freeway has not generated an argot to anything like the same extent as the old road. It is too bland. The result is the same as the loss of language in any context: loss of identity. Drivers never had title but they used to own the road. Now they just work on it. There isn't much poetry left.

'The Road to Gundagai' is a song about anything other than the Hume Highway. It was originally going to be called *The Road to Bundaberg* but Jack O'Hagan wanted to write a song about a river and the Burnett, on which Bundaberg is built, presented problems for his melody. The song needed something that would have the same rhythm as 'Mississippi', so O'Hagan got out the map of Australia and discovered the Murrumbidgee. The name was perfect. Then O'Hagan traced his finger along the river and found Gundagai.

It was easier than getting there by push-bike.

Gundagai has an affinity with poets, if not, at first glance, with poetry. The main street, formerly part of the Hume, is called Sheridan Street. Sheridan's interminable comedies of manners must have been popular at the time the place was being established, although it is not easy to see any obvious connection between his eighteenth-century drawing rooms and here. The town also has streets dedicated to those two reputable travel writers, Homer and Virgil. You can climb your way up to the nearby lookout on Mt Parnassus. The forebears of the Castrissons and the Loukissases, the past and present owners of the Niagara Cafe, regarded Mt Parnassus in Greeece as the source of music and poetry. There are enough aerials on Mt Parnassus in Gundagai to suggest the muses are still churning it out.

We found a room at a motel called The Poet's Recall where every room honoured a man or woman of letters. The ones down-stairs seemed to be named mainly after English writers and the ones upstairs after Australians. We took a room upstairs, not for patriotic reasons but because the room had a bath. It was named after Jack O'Hagan. Judging from the bath, Jack was no giant.

You wouldn't guess from the sign honouring him on the door of our room, but Jack O'Hagan did more to make the name of Gundagai famous than anyone else. Yet he achieved this years before he ever set foot in the place. O'Hagan was born miles away, in Victoria. But he wrote songs. Hundreds and hundreds of songs. One of them was 'The Road to Gundagai'.

According to Mel Morrow, who, along with David Mitchell, wrote a stage show called *Jack O'Hagan's Humdingers*, the song-writer had a knack of picking up any tune that had become popular in America and writing an Australian version of it. Morrow says his tunes were 'a bit like fairy floss'; they have a marked affinity with advertising jingles. Indeed, O'Hagan wrote scores of tunes for radio advertisements and a raft of morale-boosting songs during World War II. He produced them in an unending stream between World War I and around 1960 when the muse left him. In legend, the original Mt Parnassus had two peaks: one dedicated to the muses and the other to Bacchus. O'Hagan stopped trying to climb one peak and camped on the lower one. In other words, like Henry Lawson, he hit the bottle.

O'Hagan did make one attempt at a comeback, thinking he would write Australia's national anthem but the result, 'God Bless

Australia', is, if anything, worse than the anthem we got. Eventually, O'Hagan reached sobriety and, like many, found that sobriety was a full-time job. By the time he died in 1987 at the age of eighty-eight he'd been quiet for some time. Yet in his heyday, says Morrow, he 'was a one-man tinpan alley'.

O'Hagan may have borrowed his style but he applied it to local situations as he churned out songs about Australian celebrities, towns and places, including places on the Hume. 'Things are crook in Tallarook' is one of his numbers, as is 'Let's take a trip to Melbourne'. The name of Gundagai appealed to him enormously. One of his best known wartime songs, 'When a boy from Alabama meets a girl from Gundagai', glosses over the tensions that were created when American soldiers dated Australian girls while the Australian boys were off fighting.

'The Road to Gundagai' is an earlier song. It was written in 1920; the famous version was recorded by Paul Dawson in 1922. It marries the bush ballads of the Lawson and Paterson era to the imported melodies of popular American music.

In telling the story of someone, anyone, who wants to go home along an old but familiar road to an old but familiar house and find their parents and childhood friends waiting for their return, the song reflects the homesickness of the generation that went to World War I. The track winds back in time as much as place. The lyrics show a longing to return to innocence, to a place where it's always sunny and the Murrumbidgee burbles happily along. Naturally, the prodigal son or daughter promises never to leave again. In its context, the song caught on as few others ever have. Like all popular music, it is essentially unthreatening and the audience will always feel superior to it. But like all great hymns, it allows the public expression of private feeling.

sex@myplace.now.ok
— Bumper sticker, Hume Highway

Jerome Kern, who along with Isaiah Berlin and Cole Porter, had a strong influence on Jack O'Hagan, had never seen the Mississippi River when *Showboat* hit the boards in 1927. It didn't stop him writing 'Ol' Man River'.

Like most of the rivers in Australia, our Murrumbidgee has diminished. Livingstone called the Zambezi 'God's Highway' and once upon a time, even in Australia, rivers were highways. Now there is hardly anything left in the way of heavy inland shipping on waterways such as the Murrumbidgee. Col Doolan, who has been building roads all his life and was the engineer responsible for developing and managing the contract for the Bookham bypass, once told me that the biggest challenge in construction used to be getting the road safely across a river, but now the challenge is to get the river safely under the road.

In its early history, Gundagai was destroyed at least twice by flood. In June 1852 the town experienced a nightmare when the Murrumbidgee rose to heights the settlers had not seen before. They clung to the roofs of their houses and let their livestock take their chances. The lucky ones spent days on end clinging to the tops of trees, listening to the screams of the less fortunate. By the time the waters subsided, the number of dead was at least seventy-five – probably higher, as the area was host to numerous itinerants, mostly *en route* to or from the gold fields, for whom nobody thought to go looking. An anonymous survivor wrote a graphic account of the shameless looting that followed the tragedy.

Not everyone behaved badly. The writer herself had been rescued by a Wiradjuri man known as Jackey who had a bark canoe which was far better suited to the eddies and currents of the flood than the boats the Europeans tried to manoeuvre. Another Wiradjuri man, Yarri, sometimes called Warri, also rescued dozens of settlers, after which a grateful town presented the two Aborigines with commemorative breastplates. These breastplates can now be inspected in Gundagai's historical museum where they are housed along with Phar Lap's saddle cloth, a model T Ford, a shirt worn by a gentleman called Kiley about whom Banjo Paterson wrote a poem, and an 'old fashioned shack' of the type to which the track in O'Hagan's song was winding back.

Most of Gundagai was rebuilt on higher ground after the flood. A decent bridge across the Murrumbidgee was also thought to be a good idea. The result was the Prince Alfred Bridge, named after Queen Victoria's second son, the first member of the royal family to visit Australia, a fact which may explain why schools and hospitals in this country carry his name. Alfred never came near Gundagai on his visit but that wasn't going to stop a proud town paying homage.

Jenny and I dismounted here and discovered that the oldest parts of the Prince Alfred Bridge date back to 1867. Looking at the metal truss structure, it was hard for us to believe that this bridge was part of the main Sydney to Melbourne road until as late as 1977.

The Prince Alfred Bridge, balancing on stilts over the Murrumbidgee flood plain, is, for my money, despite being closed to traffic, the most exquisite unnatural feature on the Hume. It is the best part of a kilometre in length and boasts of being the oldest bridge still standing across either the Murrumbidgee, Murray or Lachlan rivers, but its real attraction is the way it relates to the river and plain underneath. It seems to be cut from the same raw ingredients as the world around it. It's a pity we were not allowed to ride on it, although the splintered beams would have eaten our tyres.

When you cross the river at Gundagai, you use a different bridge. In 1932, the New South Wales Department of Main Roads was already musing in public about the cost of maintaining the Prince Alfred Bridge and making it more serviceable. A bypass was envisaged even then.

The new bridge is called the Sheahan Bridge. It is straight and narrow and does the job it is paid to do, even if it sometimes creates a bottleneck as traffic approaching from either side has to form a single file to cross. When a group, usually of truck drivers, wants to blockade the highway these days, this is the place they choose.

The Sheahan Bridge can boast of impressive statistics in its own right: it is 1,144 metres long, making it the second-longest bridge in New South Wales (the Sydney Harbour Bridge being five metres longer). It's a mystery that the builders didn't stretch it out a bit more, just to take the distinction away from Sydney. Unlike the Prince Alfred, the new one has a perfectly formed platform. It doesn't talk back to traffic the way the old bridge did. It was a necessity, of course. But it ain't pretty. A number of locals had wanted it named after Yarri, the Aboriginal hero of the floods of 1852.

Before leaving town, Jenny and I visited Yarri's grave. Afterwards, nearby, we came upon the grave of the bushranger Captain Moonlite, Andrew George Scott, whose epitaph suggested that he was like a 'rough hewn stone' whom 'kindness and charity could have shaped . . . to better ends'.

Moonlite was a celebrity criminal who got caught up in a script of his own devising and was half surprised when real people ended up really dead. Unlike other bushrangers, his problem was not that he couldn't express himself but that it wasn't himself he was expressing, but some overblown substitute.

A plaque informed us that in 1995 he had reached his final resting place here in the Gundagai cemetery when his remains were brought from Rookwood cemetery in Sydney.

Jenny and I cycled down to the Gundagai public library. One of the staff there told us that even after all that time, local feeling had been stirred: on the day in 1995 that Scott was re-buried, the police mounted an all-night vigil at the grave of Constable Webb-Bowen, whom Moonlite had killed on the road to Gundagai and whose neighbour he had suddenly become.

We left the library together and walked across the footpath on the Sheahan Bridge, because the bridge doesn't leave much room for a cyclist to share the road, and made our way into the Riverina, where the land is bounded by rivers, the Murrumbidgee and the Murray.

The sun was out, there was a light breeze and we were soon in good spirits. We stopped for morning tea at the Tumblong Hotel, one of the diminishing number of pubs which still shade the road. In its early days, the road south had kept any number of licensed premises in business. In 1839, Jane Franklin observed that many broken bottles already littered the side of this section of road. They 'shewed the prevalence of drunkenness.' Later, in the 1860s, one of the arguments advanced in favour of building the southern railway would be that it was possible to control the availability of alcohol on trains. But as early as 1847, the firebrand preacher and republican, John Dunmore Lang, urged the extension of the line to Goulburn on the grounds that rail would 'greatly promote the moral welfare and advancement of the colony'. The highways, by way of contrast, had 'low public houses by the wayside' which were 'nests of deprivation and dissipations' frequented by 'bullock drivers'.

The Tumblong Hotel, however, was still open for business and, though it was not exactly crowded at 11 a.m., there were one or two patrons in attendance. They did not look to us like bullock drivers.

The first thing that caught my eye was a hole in the ceiling with the words 'Bill's bullet hole' next to it. I asked what its significance was.

'Why don't you ask Bill?' said the barman. 'He's right here.'

Bill had the paper open in front of him and half a glass of beer at his side. He was slow to stir from this important work for the sake of a story he had told before, so the barman supplied most of the details. Bill listened, nodding in appreciation of his own exploits, watching us hear that, about twenty years previously, a policeman had entered the bar and taken a shot at Bill. There was no indication as to why this had happened. It was just a fact. The bullet entered the roof.

'Bastard of a shot, he was,' added Bill.

Bill's bullet became the stuff of local legend, so much so that when the place was renovated the hole we were all gazing at now had been rebored so that the story would not be lost. The incident had taken place in another part of the building.

'He was a bastard of a shot,' repeated Bill dolefully, sounding sorry that the policeman had missed him.

There was a short silence, during which Jenny and I looked from the peripatetic hole to each other. Then I thought of Jane Franklin's roadside bottles, and asked the publican how a place like this managed to stay in business, when it had no visible means of support other than the road and most people have woken up to the dangers of driving under the influence. Jenny delicately suggested that there didn't appear to be anything more to Tumblong than the tavern. The publican said, in reply, that there was still quite a strong community in the area.

'It's a family pub. All the farmers and their families come in on a Friday night to eat. That's our big night.'

He flourished a copy of the *Gundagai Independent*, the local paper, which carried news of a 'back to Tumblong day' which had taken place in the local hall the previous Saturday. People had come from Sydney, Melbourne and all points in between. Two hundred of them returned on Sunday for lunch around the Tumblong Tavern.

'It was a great weekend,' says the barman. 'It was a reminder of how much this place means to people.'

He folded up the paper and put it back on the bar. From the front page glared the story of an eleven-year-old, travelling with her family from Melbourne, who'd been killed three days earlier in a road accident, at precisely this point on the Hume at precisely this hour of the morning. Her parents and two sisters had also been badly injured. For some reason, a four-wheel-drive driven by a 23-year-old had crossed onto the wrong side of the road. In a split second, lives were turned inside out.

We read the paper quietly.

'Yeah,' interrupted the barman. 'I was the first on the scene.'

He says nothing more.

'It was a real bastard,' concludes Bill for him.

If I had half a brain
I'd have half a chance
— Bumper sticker, Hume Highway

We slogged on, working our way up a few hills and eventually coming upon a feature known as Wagga Hill. It was a full-length feature, a nasty rise which led to the junction of the Sturt and Hume highways. The Sturt Highway leads inland to the City of Wagga Wagga and eventually to Adelaide. Its name celebrates the man who first followed the Murrumbidgee westwards in 1830. In so doing, he inevitably reached the point at which the Murrumbidgee meets the Murray but failed to realise that the Murray had already been called the Hume. So a relatively minor government official pinched the honour of being identified with Australia's main drain. Hume coped as best he could, which was not very well. He respected Sturt. They'd paired up to explore western New South Wales together in 1828, and reached the Darling. Hume found Sturt's melancholy, even depressive, temperament easier to bear than Hovell's nervous humour. They covered miles of wilderness in silence, one going deaf, the other blind. Even in our sweatiest hour, there were couples Jenny and I were glad not to be. Sturt, who belonged to a group of

Australian explorers whose mental baggage is as interesting as any material achievement to which they may lay claim, was possessed by a desire to set foot in the centre of the continent before anyone else. Sturt went blind trying to see what none had seen before. Hume, to be fair to him, was not as starry-eyed as that. He would have been just as happy with the road as the river. Besides, the road is in better shape.

Jane Franklin observed piles of trees at the foot of Wagga Hill, discarded there by carriage drivers who were in the habit of felling timber to attach to their rear axles to slow their vehicles as they descended. It was a throwaway society and nobody was going to be silly enough to cart the timber back up to the top for re-use. We had enough trouble getting ourselves up.

I fixed my gaze on the surface of the road immediately beneath my wheels, making patterns from the endless runes carved by surveyors at one time or another. There's no point in looking too far into a difficult future.

'You know,' said Jenny suddenly. 'There are two ways of looking at the world.'

'What are they?'

'There's a concave way and there's a convex way.'

'What do you mean?'

'The concave way is pessimistic. It thinks that every time things are going well and you're in a part of life which feels like gliding downhill, then an uphill part lies ahead as punishment.'

'And the convex?'

'It thinks that every uphill push is a prelude to an easy glide which will soon be your due.'

'I think my mind's concave,' I said after a while.

'I think you might be right.'

We got to the top of that hill and glided down again, waving for another speed camera.

'Whereas,' said Jenny deciding to enjoy herself, 'I think I've well and truly earnt this easy part already.'

Philosophy has often made use of the image of a road. It is the universal metaphor and can be used to illustrate anything. The information superhighway is one philosophical image; the road to hell is another. Zeno of Elea, who lived in Greece before Plato, said that it was logically impossible to get to the end of any road because, to do so, you have to pass through a point halfway along and, to get *there*, you will have had to pass through a point halfway to the halfway mark and so on. As you keep going, there will always be a point halfway between where you are now and the end of the road.

The place halfway between Sydney and Melbourne is called Tarcutta and, despite these logical objections, we got there. Tarcutta, home of the Halfway Motel and the Halfway Cafe, is unashamed of the fact that most of the people in town at any time are on their way to someplace else and are only halfway to where they want to be. For the convexed, the optimists, the journey is half done. For the concaved, the pessimists, half of it still lies ahead.

There wasn't a lot for a couple to explore late on a Friday after-noon midway on the road we were bound upon. We left our bikes tethered at the Halfway Motel and went out looking for some-thing to eat. The door of a small weatherboard church was ajar so we decided to look inside and found, to our surprise, that Mass was about to begin. There were two other worshippers, another couple, kneeling with their backs so perfectly aligned that I wondered if they were in some kind of yoga class. They didn't even seem to breathe. Perhaps they were statues. A bell indicated that Mass was starting and they stood. Statues can move too, it

seemed, and Tarcutta is exactly the kind of place where they are
likely to do so.

The priest said Mass in a choreographed manner, his every
action carefully rehearsed. The responses of the other pair of worshippers never missed a beat as, for half an hour or more, a
stylised ritual unfolded.

When I was working as a Catholic priest, I found it hard to
understand this style of Mass. I could probably still list a dozen
reasons why such formality was the wrong way to be going about
things. The whole point of Christianity is that God became
human and so the gap between humanity and divinity is a mere
chink, a small gap that you can whisper through. It is not a cavern
that you have to yell across. People should feel free in church to
be themselves.

For a congregation of four, this priest had all the trappings and
was more elaborately dressed than any priest I had seen for ages.
Nevertheless, I found the Mass comforting. It had a timelessness.
This does not only mean that the priest was in no hurry, but also
that he was perfectly happy to repeat exactly what he had done
yesterday, and the day before that and what some other priest had
done years before. He did not feel any need to impose his own
personality on the ritual. There was no cheery 'good morning'
and no light banter with the congregation. I have often found that
a little human warmth helps people relate to God, but on this
occasion I began to glimpse something else. The man was leaving
himself out of it and lending himself to a higher function. Late in
the afternoon on the Friday in the week after Easter, I found that
sustaining. That and the fact that he could be bothered, even
when most of the sedans pacing endlessly up and down the
highway outside had as many people in them as his church.

Throughout Mass, the trucks too kept rumbling past, loaded
up with all sorts of consumables. Maybe that was what I was

responding to. The trucks are symptoms of a frenetic culture. They never stop. They never arrive, because as soon as they reach the end of the road they turn around and come back the other way. The only difference between a truck and a caged animal wearing a track around its enclosure is the scale. On every truck is stuff that will be inventoried, invoiced, paid for, used and then thrown away, creating space for more stuff to follow the same route. In the circumstances, this simple Mass was like a rock beside the river. It was happy to let the world thunder past outside. It wasn't budging.

Afterwards, we spoke briefly with the priest, who told us affably that, every morning, he rode a push-bike for 20 kilometres through the hills around these parts. He was nearly knocked off his bike once by a police car which was chasing some sinner in a hurry.

'Do you miss saying Mass?' Jenny asked me later.

I didn't really. I felt safer on a road where I had to take responsibility for my own life . . . To be honest, the vow that undid me as a priest was the vow of obedience. People find this hard to believe. It wasn't that I found obedience too difficult. I found it too easy. I became compliant; my life was dedicated to gaining the affirmation of those around me, especially superiors, as I became dependent on the support of the institution. This is ironic because the purpose of a vow of obedience is to set a person free, the same as a vow of poverty or chastity or stability or anything else. I was abusing the vow of obedience by using it to make up a sense of purpose which I otherwise lacked. I was bludging off it.

Most people thought I was doing a terrific job, but underneath a calm exterior, my life was starting to crumble.

You can only live like this for so long before you start causing as much pain to people you love as to yourself. There comes a point at which you can no longer recognise yourself in the things you are starting to say or do.

I was also anxious about whether or not I really believed in God. I wondered if, for me, faith had become part of the uniform and if I believed because it had become my job. After all, I was being paid to believe and you don't bite the hand that feeds you, even if the hand is invisible.

Once I took off the uniform, I found, to my disquiet, that I still did believe. In fact, it was easier to pray when I didn't have to talk about it all the time. I have tried at different periods in my life to stop believing in God but it's never worked. I have always failed miserably in my quest for disbelief. A friend of mine describes his own predicament by saying he is a lapsed agnostic but in my case I have never managed to believe in myself as an agnostic in the first place. For me, the alternative to believing in God is to believe in myself in some kind of absolute way, a loneliness too horrendous to contemplate. I can't live in a space that small.

'I don't miss being a priest,' I replied plainly.

The more I thought about it, the more I wondered what kind of price the priest we had spoken to was paying to give himself up to a timeless ritual. It is a brave and foolish thing to do. But I was glad he did it and also glad that a small unadorned weatherboard church could hold its ground, mostly empty, alongside a road which was cluttered with speed limits, load limits and signposts. The road is burdened, day and night, with the imagined needs of a compulsive society. A church is a blank on the map. I need them. I need them empty, a space that can't be filled.

As we were leaving the church, I recalled the opening words of Dante's *Divine Comedy*, a work which sets out from a place called 'halfway' on a road without direction:

> *Midway through this life we're bound upon*
> *I woke to find myself in a dark wood,*
> *Where the right road was wholly lost and gone.*

We crossed the road to the Halfway Cafe and took a seat in the window which looked out romantically over a truck parking bay.

'Do you miss ballet?' I asked Jenny.

'Yes I do.'

From when she was eight until she was well into her twenties, Jenny cycled off every Saturday morning, first to learn and then, as time went by, to teach ballet. Her ballet shoes were always in the bread-basket attached to the front of her bike. It was the highlight of her week, the thing she lived for.

'I just loved it. I honestly think that was when I became myself.'

'Why?'

'When I was dancing, I was living totally in one moment. I think that's what it was. I wasn't worried about home or school or exams or anything. I was just dancing. It was the time each week when I could just enjoy being myself. Myself right now. Then, at the end of the Saturday morning, I put my shoes back in my bread-basket and cycled home again to what I thought was reality.'

When I was getting to know Jenny, she showed me the programs of performances she had been in as a girl and later as a teenager. She didn't need photos. The programs triggered detailed memories of who had been there and where they had sat and what the music was like and who made her costumes. I was sorry I had missed those performances. By the time I met her, Jenny had returned from five years in England and had discovered that the intellectually disabled responded in a special way to the invitation to dance.

'I found that those people just knew how to fill the present moment. They filled the present moment until it was ready to burst. They were natural dancers.'

I had confessed that I was not a dancer. It wasn't just that my body was like a wet tent which would neither fold where it was supposed to nor ever fit back into any space it had come out of. That was not a real problem. I have seen old people lost in a dance when they can only move a few inches here and there. They were still dancing. My problem was that my mind was always in half a dozen places and half a dozen time zones. Joan Rivers said that if God had wanted her to bend over, he would have put diamonds on the floor. My difficulty was that I never knew what I wanted God to have put on the floor.

The Halfway Cafe has a niche in many stories of the Hume. It was on these premises in September 1961 that the celebrated Australian poet Les Murray wrote one of the poems which first established his reputation. Murray was hitchhiking from Sydney to Melbourne at the time, sleeping under trees along the way. He was a month short of his twenty-third birthday and, already becoming familiar with the demands of living with mental illness, was feeling lost and restless.

Back in 1961 he had got a lift which left him at Tarcutta and then he had time to wait for another. In the interval, he composed 'The Burning Truck'. It's never easy to say what a poem is actually about, any more than it's easy to say what Mass is about. Murray's poem works with a disarmingly simple image. A truck catches fire, the driver jumps out, but the vehicle manages to keep going:

> *And all of us who knew our place and prayers*
> *clutched our verandah-rails and window-sills,*
> *begging that truck beneath our teeth to halt . . .*

The truck consumes itself but does not stop. It attracts followers:

> *And as they followed, cheering, on it crept,*
> *windshield melting now, canopy-frame a cage*
> *torn by gorillas of flame, and it kept on*
> *over the tramlines, past the church, on past*

the last lit windows, and then out of the world
with its disciples

'I was exalted and crazy at the time,' Murray once told me, 'in the manic phase I guess of a depressive breakdown. I'd dropped out of university, sold all my possessions, cut adrift and had been living in Sydney as a street kid. I'd published a few poems . . . I was just beginning to convert a dream of being a poet into an attempt to realise the dream. My head was full of violence and war imagery – I was a little boy during World War II –'

Eventually, Les got a lift out of Tarcutta. The driver was not heading south but west, along the Sturt Highway:

'. . . the next lift went to Narranderra, which made sense to me since I wasn't in a hurry and had all of Oz before me to explore. That next lift delighted me, in fact, with my first vision of inland plains. Flat land! To a hillbilly kid!'

Murray finally reached Melbourne with 'The Burning Truck' among the limited number of possessions he had:

'I polished it up . . . the next day and . . . sold it to Vin Buckley, then poetry editor of *The Bulletin*, for £5. That modest amount kept me fed for a week.'

After that, Murray tried his luck selling door to door. Not poetry. Other stuff.

'Welcome to the Halfway Cafe,' I said to Jenny with undue formality.

'I wonder if they have half serves?' she replied. She'd been quietly looking at the menu.

Sure enough, it said that the pasta dishes came in two sizes.

'How small is the small spaghetti?' we asked.

'Very bloody small. We don't have any.'

We chose something else and, while we were waiting, absorbed all the evidence of truckie culture in the place. You could buy scale models of all sorts of trucks, the kind of thing that an absent father might take home to a boy. There were also laminated newspaper clippings about the town. One told of a time when, at the age of twenty-one, Tony Roche came home to Tarcutta after having taken on the world at tennis. He was accorded the greatest honour available when, for ninety minutes, the road was closed. Five hundred people came to applaud; one of the residents had lent an open-topped car for the occasion and two tennis rackets were strapped to the front grille.

From all this memorabilia, we could see that this town and the transport industry have lived together for a long time. One picture from the winter of 1956 showed the Hume Highway closed for almost a fortnight owing to heavy rain and flooding. Four hundred trucks, said the story, had been stranded in Tarcutta when a section of about a hundred metres, at a place called Little Billabong just south of town, was washed away. Tarcutta responded by providing breakfast each day in the Memorial Hall and social activities in the evenings. When the road finally dried out, the drivers passed the hat around and raised £1,000 for the Tarcutta hospital.

The road means life to a town like this.

It also is lined with countless reminders of death. Across the highway from the cafe, immediately opposite the War Memorial Hall, we came upon another memorial, the National Truckdrivers Memorial, established in 1994 to remember truckies who have died at work on Australian roads. The monument, made of house bricks with black granite plaques attached to them, is touching in its simplicity, all the more so at night when headlights occasionally play across the polished stone. The phrases used in the inscription resemble those found on war memorials:

This memorial stands at Tarcutta to recognise the contribution

of the trucking men and women to this nation . . . This
vocation demands many a high price – in the loneliness of
the long haul, missed family events and, in some cases, the
ultimate sacrifice . . .

The individual inscriptions on the memorial, however succinct, gave us a strong impression of the personalities of the dead. Most of the drivers were young and are remembered by the nicknames which have been inscribed alongside their span of years: Crapper was thirty-one, Gentle Giant was twenty-six and Commo was twenty-two. There are plenty of others. Perhaps some men were imprisoned by the expectations that come with a nickname, especially ones such as Mongrel or Muscles or Killer or the Menace. On the other hand, nicknames are signs of belonging and marks of affection, reminders that the small figures in the cabs of rigs have a greater presence in the world than the trucks which dwarf them.

We were struck by the number of children, presumably travelling with their dads during schools holidays or something like that, who are commemorated on the memorial. They, too, have nicknames: 'Little trucker' was only three. We could find only two names of women drivers on the entire wall. One was Elizabeth Kenney, known as Cheeky Breed, who died in 1983 at the age of thirty-five. The other was Glenda Bitcom who died on St Valentine's day in 1989. She was twenty-three.

When we got back to the motel, Jenny couldn't find her wallet. Before long, it seemed that the whole of Tarcutta was engaged in the search to find it. I rang the priest, who was quite happy to come around with a torch, but nothing came to light either inside or outside the church. We told him where we were staying and he wrote down our room number. We rang the police and then started the dreary task of cancelling credit cards, deciding to take a risk and do nothing about Jenny's library card. Anyone, we decided, who would drive 400 kilometres to Melbourne to steal a book was the kind of reader who needed to be encouraged.

In the morning, the priest called to say the wallet had been discovered in daylight. It had spent the night unmolested in the grounds of the church. I told Jenny that it was a sign of real poverty when your wallet had to sleep under a tree. The priest told us that he'd been confused because the name in the wallet was not mine.

'No,' I said, 'it's Jenny's name.'

'But you only gave me one room number at the motel.'

I realised then that we were being rebuked either for our accommodation arrangements when we were unwed or, maybe even worse, for being wed without Jenny changing her name. I was on the verge of putting the man's mind at rest by telling him that I had slept with the horses in the stables. Or that I had sat up all night reading *Anna Karenina*. But you can't lie to a priest.

'Don't worry, Father,' I said. 'At least we're riding separate bikes.'

DEATH IS THE MANUFACTURER'S RECALL NOTICE
— Bumper sticker, Hume Highway

Now, somewhere in the back of my mind I wondered if I was acting my age. I asked myself how many forty-year-olds travel interstate on cheap push-bikes instead of in planes or company cars.

'At least we're not on roller skates,' answered Jenny.

I also wondered how many people would get so close to the halfway point of their lives before they embarked on their first intimate relationship, doing so in full view of the nation's transport industry.

'They don't care,' said Jenny. 'They probably think we're doing this to try and get divorced.'

I was a novice again and sometimes I didn't know where I was. Yet when I was a priest I had written and preached about relationships and imparted my wisdom to couples getting married. I was glad I had done all those things before I knew anything about the topic, as it would have been much more difficult once I did. It's a lot easier to speak about a relationship when you are dealing with the idea in the abstract. I think this is why they ask priests to be celibate. It makes giving sermons a lot easier. I tried giving Jenny a sermon once or twice. Believe me, it just doesn't work. I didn't even bother taking up a collection afterwards.

For me, when I think about it, religious life was a flat road with numerous twists and turns. You could be going anywhere, depending on what you were asked to do, but the road itself was basically at the same emotional level. One of the hardest sacrifices of Catholic priesthood is, I suspect, the blandness of the private life. I didn't think this at the time I was in the service. I thought my heart was getting a reasonable workout when it was really pretty sluggish. Perhaps that was just me.

Life with a partner, on the other hand, is a straight road with numerous hills and valleys. You have an idea of where you are going together but getting there can be sometimes hard work, other times sheer exhilaration. The ups and downs give the heart a decent workout such that you sweat more but you also feel more alive. Your perineum might get sore occasionally but the heart feels great.

I would have told all this to Jenny on the road except that I'd learned the futility of preaching to a partner. There's no guide-book for the inexperienced as they enter the land of intimacy but I was helped by one-word wisdom. I would not forget that when I had asked Ken Coggan, the truckie who'd been on the Hume for over thirty years, what had kept his marriage alive even longer, he immediately said, 'Honesty.' That was it. He had nothing else to say on the subject. There was no fine print. Yet in my imagination I heard him drop that word again, over and over, for months. It was the right word in the right ear and I took it as a challenge as much as an answer. Maybe this is why I believe in bumper stickers.

It's a mystery how your partner is revealed to you in a thousand small stories, the telling of which can never be scheduled.

If Jenny and I had asked each other what we did when we left school, Jenny might have said that she went off overseas and I would have said that I went off to the Jesuit novitiate which was in some ways a bit like overseas. But we didn't ask that question. Instead, as we left Tarcutta, facing a long haul to Holbrook, we started making an inventory of the trucks that passed us. We saw a prefabricated house on the move, followed by three fibreglass swimming pools stacked inside each other, followed by a load of eight new cars, all of which prompted us to consider why one house would need three pools and so many cars. We then saw three truckloads of photocopy paper followed by an old tram on the back of a lorry.

The tram would have passed without comment except that its destination indicator still displayed the name of Marzahan, which Jenny recognised as a place in East Germany, the kind of area, we later discovered, where the dictator Erich Honeker liked to build model housing for workers. It was strange enough to find a tram from behind the old Iron Curtain being piggy-backed down the Hume, but the sight brought to mind, for Jenny, the day in 1983 when, aged nineteen, she went through Checkpoint Charlie and found herself in East Berlin. As a tourist going through the Berlin Wall, she had to change a certain amount of money, about ten or twelve dollars, which could not be changed back on return.

After trying all day, Jenny found it was impossible to spend the money. There was nothing to buy. She found a big department store but it was virtually empty. She spent the evening in a bar, talking to locals, where she lost track of the time and almost missed the midnight curfew at Checkpoint Charlie. As she went running out the door at five to midnight, one of the young women in the bar said to her, 'You are so lucky you can go where you want.' Jenny gave the woman the money she hadn't spent. 'You are so lucky you can move freely,' the woman repeated. Her face and those words have stuck with Jenny for twenty years.

It was 70 kilometres from Tarcutta to Holbrook, further than we had attempted in a single day before, but there was no place to stay in between. By now my legs were cranky and Jenny's knees had stopped dropping subtle hints in favour of more blatant protests.

Possibly it was consciousness of our own frailty that made us even more aware than before of the unending sequence of roadside memorials along the way.

By mid-morning, we had come to a place identified as Marian Hills Shrine where we dismounted and went for a stroll around the paddocks, dodging sheep droppings. There wasn't a soul in sight. High on a hill, somebody had welded two vast steel girders together in the shape of a cross. It wasn't exactly the Christ of Rio de Janeiro, but it had a commanding position over the road. The message of this cross was unmistakable: it projected certainty and strength.

People have often put religion on hilltops, sometimes to be closer to God but more often to be above the people beneath. It's the wrong place. As far as I was concerned, the plain crosses used by the grieving for most roadside memorials had a lot more to say than those two heavy girders, however much I admired the brawn of the people who got them up there. Not content with that, they had then put a wire fence around the cross. The wind whistled over the wire as sheep rubbed up against it.

'It feels like a place of sacrifice,' said Jenny.

But you don't need to build altars to make sacrifice. Sacrifice is part of life. It comes standard on all but the cheapest models.

We got back on our bikes and pushed on.

On the road beneath Marian Hills, one memorial said nothing more than 'Mum and Dad' but seemed more articulate than the two huge girders. A more elaborate site further along honoured a thirty-three-year-old truck driver, Tony Forsyth, 'Chooky the Trucker', who'd been killed a couple of years before.

By the time we stopped for lunch, it seemed like we had seen nothing other than memorials for hours.

A few yards from the parking bay where we unpacked our tinned tuna and biscuits, there was another one. A sign at the back of it invited people to call a number 'if needed', presumably if anything was amiss with the shrine. There wasn't. It was beautifully maintained. There were some plastic pipes for flowers, a couple of cans of Jack Daniels and a lunch box, weighed down with stones, which appeared to contain letters. We didn't open it. I took down the phone number and resolved that, when we got home from our ride, I would give Bill a call to say how touched we were by what he had built for his son, David.

'Has anything happened to it?' he asked anxiously when I did.

Nothing had. In our whole journey we saw no evidence of any vandalism to any roadside memorial.

Bill, who lived in Wodonga, explained that David was his youngest child, a plumber who had trained as Bill's apprentice. Father and son had continued to work together after David had completed his apprenticeship and were obviously very close. At one stage, David had gone to Tumut, up in the mountains, for work. Around two-thirty on a quiet Friday afternoon, he and a friend were making their way home. David was the passenger. Three-quarters of an hour after they set out from Tumut, they were on the Hume where it appears that the driver fell asleep behind the wheel. Tragedy can be mundane.

At five forty-five that evening, Bill had just stepped in after nine holes of golf and was having his first beer in the clubhouse. Bill has spent a long time living with that moment.

'It was one experience I will never forget.'

He wonders why it took the police three hours to notify him, by which stage David had been airlifted to Canberra, where he was put onto life support but died the next day. He was twenty-eight. Bill has often wished that the driver talked more with him and his family.

'There are things I would have liked to know. Like why he fell asleep so soon into the trip. I guess he had a lot of guilt feelings.'

He has also wondered about the young woman who was driving the car with which David and his friend collided.

'We have spoken with her but lost contact since. She was critically injured. I didn't like her chances. She was facing a miserable life, maybe as a paraplegic. I really don't know.'

Bill says that the roadside memorial has a significance beyond words for him and his family.

'He died in the Canberra hospital but that is where he is. Do you know what I mean? That is where he is. We like to stop and remember and talk to him. Sometimes we sit down and have a drink with him. Occasionally a mate will leave a can of Jack Daniels for him.'

'It's been tough for the family. Even talking about it feels like opening old wounds. It's nearly impossible to cope with it. I can't cope with it even now. It's just something to have a place when we stop to put a couple of flowers down. It's good to have a place. It's something.'

Every cross on the side of the road, and there are many, tells a similar yet unique story. Each year, 1.2 million people around the world die in road accidents, a cause of death which continues to rise on the list of most prevalent killers, only ranking behind heart disease and depression. The third world has twenty per cent of the world's cars but eighty per cent of the road fatalities, a statistic which indicates that, on top of every other advantage, the first world has more to spend on roads.

The highway itself is indifferent to who you are or even what you are. The roadkill we noticed that day included birds, possums, kangaroos, one cat, one wombat, one echidna and one tortoise, all mere creatures. Humans, however, suffer differently. We remember. David's cross bears the words, 'In our hearts forever.'

Saturday afternoon always has a certain feel for me; I often associate it with loneliness. Either that or with being the priest at a wedding, which was, for me, a honeyed form of loneliness. If I am going to be lonely, I'd rather be on my own. It's easier than in a crowd. This particular Saturday, pushing a bike towards the promise of a shower, reminded me of dozens of other Saturdays. The afternoon sun cast long shadows and the air, suddenly losing its warmth, had the melancholy feel of autumn. Somebody, probably returning from the mountains to our east, had tied several large fish to a sign indicating the turnoff to Tumbarumba.

'Maybe the winter is so cold around here, the fishermen know they can come back for them in spring,' I suggested.

'After they've been smoked in diesel fumes,' said Jenny.

The day passed in small exchanges. I didn't feel melancholy but rather peaceful. For the first time on the trip, I stopped counting kilometres.

We talked about other journeys. When Jenny finished Year 11 at school, she and her friend, Antoinette, decided to cycle around Tasmania. Up till then, Jenny had always gone to ballet on her brother's dragster but now, for the first time in her life, Jenny had a new bike, as did Antoinette. The two went on training runs before finally packing their shiny new machines onto a plane and taking off into the unknown.

'We spent hours planning everything, right down to the food we were taking. We had a box of Nutra Grain with Grant Kenny on it. He was our token male.'

Their parents were provided with detailed information about where they expected to stay each night. The pair were travelling in that brief interval between the invention of speech and the invention of the mobile phone when people had to think ahead about how they might be able to stay in touch with each other. As time goes by, people have less and less to say but more and more ways to say it. I have seen a bride take a call at her own wedding reception table while her father was making his speech. She didn't seem too worried about missing the moment because she had to clarify the arrangements for the cars.

'It doesn't matter,' I heard her say later. 'The speech will be on the video.'

Jenny and Antoinette expected to discover a wilderness in Tasmania, which was why they took the trouble to leave a detailed itinerary, in case anything happened. In fact, when they got there, they found that the island was full of cyclists. There was hardly enough room on some of the roads to fit them all.

'We thought we'd be the first people to come up with the idea of cycling around Tasmania. It was such a let-down. Everyone was doing it. And on the first day we encountered nothing but hills which all the other cyclists seemed to take in their stride.'

We hadn't come across anyone else cycling the Hume. I pointed this out.

'I know. It feels like we've got it to ourselves. Even with all the heavy traffic. We are the only people here for no good reason.'

Eventually we came into Holbrook, a long, narrow town. The road tends to stretch communities out like this.

Close to the centre, near the school, is a pedestrian crossing which used to be controlled by a famous woman, one of the great army of lollipop wardens all over the country whose mission is to get children safely across the road. This officer became an identity among regular travellers on the Hume. Despite her small stature, she would wait until a truck was approaching before stepping solemnly into the middle of the crossing and holding up her sign, sometimes thrusting out her other hand for added emphasis. The trucks obeyed her. She gave quite a performance as she held back the forces of evil. A friend of mine who, when driving from Melbourne to Sydney, used to time his departure to make sure he reached Holbrook when school was coming out. He didn't want to miss the show.

The Riverina Hotel in Holbrook, where Jenny and I ate that night, is one of many places on the road which provide evidence of the affectionate connection between the Hume and sport. In September 1933, the New South Wales cricket team, which included the likes of Kippax, McCabe, Oldfield and Bradman, came to town to take the field against Holbrook and districts, a somewhat less impressive outfit. It was quite an occasion and was marked by a dinner where the visitors all signed a commemorative menu which now sits behind glass on the wall of the Riverina Hotel, protected from stray tomato sauce. The cricketers' menu had included *Lamb aux Oldfield* and *Consommé a la Bradman*. To this day, Australian cricketers prefer to order in French, the language they use to address their adversaries on the field.

If the road has had a flirtatious relationship with sport, it has had a passionate involvement with war. There are dozens of war memorials on the Hume, some of them hard to find, but there was no escaping the large submarine on the side of the road as we came into Holbrook. It sat in a park, 400 kilometres from the nearest port. Like most things in town, we soon found out, it had come on the back of a truck.

Holbrook wasn't always Holbrook. The settlement began in the 1830s; its identity started to gain a fixed shape in 1840 when John Christopher Pabst took over the licence of the Woolpack Inn. Pabst was German, so the watering hole became known as 'the Germans' and, as the town grew, it assumed the name of Germanton.

It did perfectly well under that title from 1858 to 1915, when there arose the small matter of World War I. The British royal family was German and decided to change their name. Looking around for the equivalent of a royal family, the best we could find in Australia was German Sausage. Overnight, it turned into Devon but didn't taste or smell any better.

If German Sausage needed a new name, then so too did Germanton. A quick look in the atlas revealed the disappointing fact that there was already a place called Devon. Frankfurt had also been taken. It was too early to start calling places Bradman. The burghers had a problem.

At that point, Lieutenant Norman Holbrook surfaced. Holbrook was the young commander of a small submarine which, in December 1914, slipped into the Dardanelles to torpedo a Turkish battleship, the *Messudiyeh*. He negotiated minefields and dangerous waters and pulled off a feat of daring. In so doing, he kept a basic B-class submarine submerged for up to nine hours at once: it had been designed to stay under water for only two hours. Holbrook brought the whole crew of fifteen safely home in the nick of time, as their air supply was on the turn. When they opened the hatch, the vessel smelt like a lunch box of devon sandwiches on a hot day.

Holbrook got the Victoria Cross, the empire got a hero and, on the other side of the world, a small farming community got the bloke it needed to provide a name for their inland town. Holbrook was touched by the gesture. He made several visits from his native England to the place which had chosen his name from all other war heroes and, after he died, his widow, Gundula, donated his medals to the town.

In 1995, HMAS *Otway* was being prepared for the scrap heap. I remember the *Otway*. It used to anchor in Sydney, adjacent to the park in which we practised cricket. I was the kind of player who was lucky to hit anything, even when Mr Foster let me have a swing at a ball which had come to a standstill in the middle of the wicket owing to potholes in the asphalt surface.

The cricket pitches of my childhood looked like poorly maintained sections of road. I used to stand in my position in the field and dream of stowing away on HMAS *Otway* and escaping into another life. The strange thing is that, had I done so, I would have finished up in Holbrook anyway. In the end, all roads lead to the same place.

Once again it was Gundula Holbrook, the lieutenant's widow, who made a donation – $100,000 towards the cost of relocating the decommissioned *Otway* to the side of the road in her husband's town. Other people chipped in smaller amounts. The result was the purchase of the upper part of the outer skin of the *Otway*, the part that would normally surface above the water. It is almost 100 metres long and looks like something out of Jules Verne, a machine which has surfaced from the centre of the earth and is waiting to return there, just as soon as the children climbing on it get off its back.

The next day we pedalled on through Woomargama and Mullen-gandra, communities where the biggest things in town are the signposts spelling out their names, and stopped at lunchtime in Bowna, pronounced Boner. Bowna was removed to its current location in the 1930s when the Hume Weir was flooded, and that when it moved it had brought the road with it.

There is a single building there, a store, with a single petrol bowser out the front. I had driven past it dozens of times and always assumed the store had long since closed down. It looked dowdy, a bit like the scene for a road movie set in the 1940s. When Jenny and I stopped, however, the store proved not only to be still functioning, but open on a Sunday.

Inside, Jeff Lewrie was cutting his fingernails with a bowie knife. Barbara Lewrie was cooking his lunch: the smell of cauli-flower wafted through the premises. From time to time, Barbara came into the shop to get something she needed for the meal. It was difficult, in fact, to know where their residence ended and the shop began. Every time Barbara came into the store, Jeff lifted his hat, scratched his head in bewilderment and squinted through bullet-proof glasses.

The Lewries have the distinction of being the last people to operate the kind of business which once grew like grass along the Hume and any other highway. This is the local shop with a petrol pump planted out the front. The one in Bowna is the last of its race. It only survives, the Lewries explained to us, because they needed 'a bit of an interest'. Their post office agency has been taken from them because it was so quiet. They'd be lucky now if four or five cars called through in a day. Albury, 30 kilometres further south, is too close. Locals used to go there once a week. Now they go every day.

'They've been ruined by air-conditioning in their cars,' said Barbara. 'Utterly ruined.'

Jeff agreed.

'We worked that much out,' he said. 'The cars are too comfortable. Air-conditioning has buggered us right up. Thank Christ the drivers still have to stop for a piddle sometime.'

He inspected our bikes.

'You know that the bicycle is the most efficient means of transport there is,' he said. 'That is, measured in terms of how much extra food you need to do the distance.'

He told me that I could travel forever on what I've managed to put aside.

'In my time, a bike cost fifteen or twenty quid. That was an entire month's wages. Now you can drive down to Albury and get one for half a week's wages or even less. A day's wages.'

Driving to Albury sounded like a crime.

Lewrie had recently bought a small bike computer and attached it to the horse and buggy which he still takes out on the Hume.

'It even tells me how many calories the horse has used so I can work out how much oats to give it.'

We spent the afternoon covering the remaining miles to Albury. On the way, Jenny's mother, Coralie, pulled over. She happened to be on her way back to Melbourne.

We arranged a rendezvous in town and met up at an Albury cafe, a venue so far from Bowna in everything but distance that it might as well have been part of a parallel universe. It was made of the same matter: but here, corrugated iron had been used to create chic cafe furniture. We offloaded some of our excess luggage into Coralie's car, including *Anna Karenina*, although it was still in the back of my mind that I should be reading quietly under some roadside tree in the heat of the day after a leisurely morning's ride. Reluctantly, I now accepted my relationship with Anna was in crisis and I let her go.

The unit next to us that night was occupied by a long, narrow stretch of highwayman who pulled up in a ute. He was in his early twenties, had a pack of cigarettes tucked up in the short sleeve of his T-shirt and was master of a ute, the one-tonne pick-up truck which has become an icon of a certain type of Australian masculinity. He was only staying overnight but took half an hour to unload his entire cargo into his unit. The back window of the ute was emblazoned with stickers which proclaimed the man's irresistible appeal to women and his innumerable sexual conquests. Yet the man himself, travelling alone, seemed rather shy. Some people get their cars to articulate things they are unable to say themselves. We talked for a while before he bent over to remove a black vinyl cover which wrapped around the front grille of his vehicle. It looked like something to stop the engine sucking in insects.

'What's that?' I asked.

'It's called a car bra. It comes off at night.'

'Same as a real bra,' I suggested.

'My oath,' he said, kissing his ute lightly on the windscreen to remove a bit of dirt.

For some people, the ute is not a vehicle. It is an organ of sex.

IFUCANREADTHISUR2FKNCLOSE
— Bumper sticker, Hume Highway

Roads tend to be associated with quests. Bridges often turn up in riddles. Think of the story of Robin Hood and Little John at the bridge. There was only room for one of them at a time. The riddle was: Which one? The correct answer was: Both of them if they both headed in the same direction. Before he could arrive at the correct solution, Little John had to learn that life's riddles are not all solved by brawn.

Don Quixote promised his faithful companion, Sancho Panza, the throne of an island kingdom. Sancho is a better friend than Don Quixote deserves. In the story, some of the people who prey on the knight errant decide to play a hoax on poor Sancho and carry him off, with mock solemnity, to a village which they convince him is an island and he is its Lord. Surprisingly, Sancho turns out to be quite a good ruler. His subjects present him with a number of riddles to which he responds with common sense, developed in part from his love of proverbs and aphorisms, many of which he confuses and misquotes.

Even in their corrupted form, Sancho's aphorisms serve him

well. He was the first traveller propelled by bumper stickers. He was also driven by love. He says of his famous companion:

> *a child might persuade him that it is night at noonday; and for this simplicity I love him as the core of my heart, and I can't bring myself to leave him, let him do ever such foolish things.*

The Murray has long posed riddles of its own. Hume and Hovell, the first Europeans to stumble across the river, had problems getting from one side to the other. They reached the northern bank on 16 November 1824. Hovell thought that the river looked dangerous and wanted to take the Governor's advice that, if they found a river they couldn't cross, they should follow it downstream rather than get their feet wet. Nevertheless, Hovell's journal for Saturday 20 November indicates that he had taken charge of improvising a boat to get them over. He says that, apart from *his* tarpaulin and the valuable lessons *he* learnt while shipwrecked during his naval career, the expedition would have been sunk.

Hume's *Brief Statement of Facts* of 1853 gives a different version of events. The main witness Hume calls for the prosecution is Thomas Boyd, one of the assigned convicts who made up the expedition. It had taken almost thirty years for the other members of the party, the servants, to be given a name and a voice. By that stage, Hume was looking for supporters. He quotes Boyd at length:

> *. . . Mr Hume and I got ready a tarpaulin punt, and swum across with the lines . . . Mr Hume never had any assistance, nor to my knowledge any suggestion from Mr Hovell in those matters; he took no share nor part in them. During the time we were engaged in making the punt, Mr Hovell sat under the shade of a tree; it was a hot day.*

Hovell replied that, indeed, he had sat under the tree but only to repair the tarpaulin which others had allowed to fall into a ruinous condition. The argument about who did what, who helped whom, who went to water and who owned and cared for the one and only tarpaulin they had in their possession continued to the grave.

So did the argument about who named the river: Hovell wrote in his diary,

This I named Hume's River, he being the first that saw it.

He happily concedes that Hume made the discovery. But Hovell is the one giving out names, a role which, since the Book of Genesis, has been the sign of a privileged position with regard to creation. It meant that Hovell was the boss, the one with real authority, a point which was lost on neither Hume nor Hovell.

In 1853, Hume wrote his riposte:

I named it the 'Hume' in compliment to my father.

So Thomas Boyd was the first European to cross the river.

He was a strong swimmer, a skill that had been significant in getting the party across the Murrumbidgee as well. After the expedition of 1824, Boyd married, had a tribe of children and settled in Tumut, where he lived for the best part of sixty years. He drove a bullock train and made countless journeys up and down the route which he had pioneered, bringing settlers into the high country. His swimming ability is recorded as having saved lives during a flood in the area. Boyd enjoyed a period of prosperity and owned land. Then his fortunes waned again; he died in poverty in a bark hut in July 1884.

Remarkably, though, Thomas Boyd had been present in Albury the year before his death when the Sydney to Melbourne train line was finally joined. He was one of the guests of honour at the opening. It's hard to underestimate the emotional significance of rail in nineteenth-century Australia. The tracks were more than items of infrastructure: they were seen as binding far-flung places together. They also bound the country in the sense that they showed how the land was finally being brought into captivity. Rail signalled as nothing else before or since that the place belonged to the settlers. It tamed the land. The road has never stirred hearts in quite the same way.

On 14 June 1883, one thousand gentlemen, including many dignitaries, sat under electric light, itself a wonder, to hear how the journey from Sydney to Melbourne could now be completed in just twenty-four hours. The menu for the five-course banquet was printed in French and 200 waiters had been recruited from Sydney and Melbourne to serve the meal. The Governor of New South Wales, Lord Loftus, was fulsome in praise of 'the auspicious event of the union of the two colonies by the iron rail, or, as it may more gracefully be termed, the fond embrace of the child by the mother.' Thomas Boyd, long a pardoned convict, was introduced to him. Boyd was aged eighty-five. God knows what he thought. He had been a simple man.

Just because Sancho speaks the language of bumper stickers, it doesn't mean what he says is simple. His relationship with Don Quixote is profound: a lover can often accept and cherish parts of their beloved which the beloved has built elaborate fantasies to disguise. Jenny was like that with me. One sad thing about the knight of doleful countenance, as the don was known, is that he fantasises about the ladies for whom he will undertake deeds of chivalry. Yet they don't exist. All the time, Sancho is by his side. The reality is much more beautiful than the fantasy, only less glamorous. The real is more ideal than the ideal. Don Quixote can't see this; his imagination has been strait-jacketed by the popular culture of his time, namely junk novels about knights and chivalry, the contemporary equivalent of glossy magazines. For him, madness was alienation from reality. It was because he was mad that he left home and took to the road. Bitumen, leaving the priesthood, a sore bum, snoring and Jenny were all part of my real world, one I was coming with pain and wonder to love. Priesthood, for me, was an ideal, an unreal hiding place, a place not to rest but to lie.

One of the riddles Sancho has to solve in his kingdom concerns a bridge across a river. On one side of the bridge is a courthouse and a gallows. In the courthouse, there are four judges, positioned to administer an unusual law which required anyone who passed over the bridge to state their destination and their reason for going there. Those who answered truthfully were allowed to pass unhindered. Those who lied were put to death on the gallows which were located conveniently nearby.

Once, however, a certain traveller announced under oath that he was crossing the bridge because he was going to die on the gallows which he could see on the other side. This created a quandary. If the man was telling the truth and intended to die on the gallows, then he was, by that very fact, required to go free. But if he was lying and was not going to die on the gallows then, obviously, he would die on the gallows. If he is hanged, he would have been truthful and justice would have been defeated. If he is allowed to go free, then he was lying and justice would again have been defeated. How was justice to be served?

The courtiers tell Sancho they have approached him because of his incisive mind. He corrects them, tells them he is a blockhead, then says that the obvious thing to do is to let the man go free. The reason is that it is always better to do good than to do evil and that in cases of doubt, leniency and mercy are to be preferred. It is a disarming answer. He defeats the riddle by reminding his listeners that life is not an intellectual exercise; justice is not an abstract notion. If you can find the person inside the riddle, it isn't a game any more.

For complicated but irrational reasons, the two colonies built their rail networks on separate gauges. There are many travellers still alive who remember the absurd spectacle of a train full of passengers being woken at Albury in the middle of the night to change onto a fresh train, one that had been built for the wider or smaller gauge used in the state to which they were heading. The myth of Australian egalitarianism is sometimes sourced to the fact that, in a beach culture, we grew accustomed to seeing each other in our bathers. Nobody is an emperor without their clothes. It's easy to overlook the no less chastening effect of seeing each other in our pyjamas. This happened every night of the year on the Albury platform as a trainload of wayfarers struggled out of the sleeping compartments of one train and went in search of another. The train was never popular with honeymooners.

In 1895, the distinguished tourist Mark Twain invited readers to 'think of the paralysis of intellect that gave that idea birth'.

Yet the situation persisted until 1962 when the Southern Aurora finally came into service on a single line between Sydney and Melbourne.

But crossing the Murray posed still further riddles. The river formed the border of two colonies which, until they were feder-ated in 1901, looked after their own interests. In the nineteenth century, you had to go through customs as you passed from Victoria to New South Wales and vice versa. The dues collected on either side of the river were charged in the name of the same queen yet, strangely, the level of tariff varied depending on whether or not you were taking stuff one way or the other. It was confusing and there was plenty of work for bean counters. Indeed, in 1899, the tariff on beans entering Victoria was almost three shillings for 100 lb. If you took them the other direction, there was no tax. Tea was taxed in both directions. But there was never any tariff on coffee, a commodity too important to muck around with.

George Broadbent's 1929 motoring guide spells out the expectations placed on drivers who crossed this state line. Every motorist entering New South Wales from another state 'must report at the first police station and obtain a "sticker" to be affixed to the windscreen at the bottom left-hand corner.' On the other hand, 'New South Wales motorists entering Victoria are merely required to report at the first police station over the border.' It was an era in which there were either not many cars or too many police.

The man who first promoted the idea of long distance motoring as a pastime in Australia was actually a cyclist. George Broadbent was born near Geelong in Victoria in 1863, a year before Banjo Paterson. When Paterson was gently poking fun at the likes of Mulga Bill who rode push-bikes, Broadbent had already helped form an association of serious cyclists, the League of Victorian Wheelmen, founded in 1893.

Broadbent didn't see the car as a rival to the bike. In 1903, he became one of the founding members of the Royal Automobile Club of Victoria and lobbied for improvements to roads as he set about creating guidebooks to show people how to use them. He was a pioneer of that ubiquitous publication, the street directory, which, until recently, had a home in every car. In 1929, he published his guidebook for motorists travelling between Sydney and Melbourne 'with maps and detailed description of Road – mileage, hotels, garages etc.'

Driving was still young enough in 1929 for Broadbent to refer to the journey as 'the Grand Overland Tour'. He recommends five days for the trip so that 'the tourist has ample time for sightseeing' but acknowledges that it can be done faster: 'a motorist on record bent solely has compassed the 565 miles under 12 hours.'

The small book tells a lot about the road and its users in the year that it was first called the Hume Highway. He says that the condition of the road changes so much 'even from month to month' that it is difficult for a guide to be entirely reliable and advises that no motorist should take to the Hume without 'water-proofs, dust-cloths and rugs' as well as 'a full tool-kit' and 'chains, or at least a length of rope, for use on greasy surfaces'. Similarly, 'it is good practice to carry a spare tin, or even a case of petrol, because the fuel tank might develop a leak at any time and the petrol be lost unawares.' A trip on the Hume was a major under-taking. After all, the road was not sealed until 1940.

ELVIS IS STUCK IN TRAFFIC
— Bumper sticker, Albury

On Monday morning, we picked up a copy of Albury's paper, the *Border Mail*, where it was reported that a rally was going to be held on the following weekend to support the building of an internal bypass in Albury. An internal bypass is a freeway which has been proposed to run through the built up areas of the city, masked by noise deadeners and vegetation. The external bypass is a freeway which has been proposed to pick up traffic south of the river and takes it on a route well to the east of the city before rejoining the existing Hume Highway somewhere to the north. The proposed external model would cover about 40 kilometres from Barnawatha to Bowna. Traffic on this route would be lucky to see the lights of Albury in the distance, especially during the day when all the lights are off.

The article in the paper was headed 'Road Rally to break deadlock'. Some readers would have been surprised to hear that there was a deadlock. At that stage, it was thought that a decision in favour of an external route had finally been made. But people have thought that the issue has been resolved on numerous occasions. They have always been wrong.

In 1985, the Wodonga bypass was opened to traffic and this left Albury on its own in desperate need. Every day, about 40,000 vehicles cross the Lincoln Causeway, currently the only river crossing by road. They have to negotiate fourteen sets of traffic lights to get from one end of Albury to the other. In 1992, the Federal Government said it supported the external route; in 1996 the two relevant state governments decided to endorse the internal route. By then, the natives were restless. In 1998, the federal government announced once and for all that an internal bypass would be built. The front page of the *Border Mail* had then proclaimed 'It's Final'.

That was when Tom Jensen pricked up his ears. He couldn't see why anyone would want to put a freeway through the middle of his living room when it belonged outside. He was worried, it seemed, about toxic fumes and, in the event of a major trucking accident, the risk of chemical spillage. He was also concerned about noise and inconvenience and cost. He became active in a group named Save Our City, and joined forces with Claire Douglas. Claire is a dietician. Tom is a physicist. Neither of them ever imagined that they would commit a large part of their lives to the cause of a road. Nor could they identify the precise moment at which an interest became a concern and then became a passion. In their minds, the route of the freeway was an issue of identity, for both them and their communities.

'At the end of the day, the road is a piece of apparatus,' Douglas told me. 'But it is also about how you define yourself, about your core values.'

The fight over the course of the road has been bloody. Supporters of the 'internal' route have been concerned about the loss of business to Albury if the road went away. With an 'external' bypass, getting to Albury would require a more significant detour than that required to reach any of the other towns which created the Hume. This side was also believed that the local economy was spending too long gummed up in traffic and needed the internal route to speed up travel within the area, not just through the area. Potential investors in an area always want to see infrastructure.

Supporters of the external route have held that a centre this size has its own economy, which would grow if the heavy traffic was taken away and the place became easier to live in. Furthermore, we were told, an arterial route with the number of exits and interchanges required in a short distance to serve the local economy would be almost as slow and as dangerous as the current arrangement. Investors would be bringing not just their money but also their families and they wouldn't stay long if the air was poisonous.

This complicated debate had been going on for thirty years or more.

And the strife had been triggered at one level by the division between Federal and State responsibilities.

'It got to the point where people would ask each other if they were internal or external supporters,' said Claire Douglas. 'I can tell you exactly where every family I know stands on the matter. There are people, even family members, who will never talk to each other again over this issue.'

On 21 February 2001, the deputy prime minister and minister for transport, John Anderson, announced a compromise which would see the federal goverment pay for both an external freeway as well as a new river crossing and the first 6 kilometres of an arterial road through Albury, asking the state government to complete the remaining 13 kilometres. The state government refused to come to the party. The *Border Mail* wasn't happy:

> The 'decision' made by Mr Anderson yesterday was
> half-baked and promises absolutely nothing for

> *Albury-Wodonga and the wider region . . . There are no*
> *winners from yesterday.*

The paper indicated there would be a clear loser. It predicted that Anderson's party, the Nationals, would lose the local seat at the election due later that year and that the whole mess will have to be sorted out by an incoming Labor government. 'The Coalition will not be in government after November.'

In fact, the conservative Coalition was still firmly in government after November. It had won an election fought largely over border control, in the context of which the border traffic between New South Wales and Victoria had paled into insignificance. A few hundred desperate asylum seekers in leaky boats had provoked a national crisis. The military was mobilised to make sure they did not invade.

On 7 December 2002, the front page of the *Border Mail* blazoned a single word: 'Internal.' No explanation was required. Beneath was a picture of the prime minister, John Howard, shaking hands warmly with the two local federal members. In the end, John Howard persuaded his deputy, John Anderson, to back down. There wasn't a border Mr Howard could not control.

Four

From Kalkallo, on the fringe of Melbourne, the roads were lined with well-wishers. TV cameras followed Cliff Young's every move, even when he slipped into the bush to answer the call of nature. On Monday, 2 May 1983, the front page of the paper announced 'a warrior shuffles to fame'. It said, 'Cliff Young is a shuffling advertisement for the wonders of vegetarian life and perhaps even of bachelorhood.' In the city centre, a busker called Bert the Tune-maker did a couple of dummy runs past the waiting crowd and was cheered. He looked old enough to be the man of the moment. Bert told a reporter that, in fact, he would not be able to emulate Cliff's feat.

'I've got a double hernia. I'm deaf in one ear and I'm three-quarters blind in my right eye.'

TV reporters asked Cliff what he was going to do when he got there.

'I'm going to go to the toilet first.'

Cliff said that he'd been waving to people non-stop for three days. He was finding the waving more tiring than the running.

At 1.35 a.m. on Tuesday, 3 May, Young crossed the finishing line. There were 5,000 people in the shopping centre to welcome him. These were the days before it was normal for people to shop in the middle of the night; the place had to be kept open. Cliff had taken almost two days off the record for a run from Sydney to Melbourne; all six competitors to finish the race broke the previous record. Cliff announced that he would split the prize money with the others. He had entered the event because he was hard up for cash. But he did not agree with the philosophy of 'winner takes all'.

Everyone wanted a piece of Cliff. As he approached the finish, a stranger offered him money to change into a T-shirt endorsing the stranger's business. A gumboot maker said they'd give Cliff ten years' supply of gumboots. They got a lot of coverage but were as good as their word. They gave him three pairs.

Cliff's mother had been brought up from the farm to welcome him. Cliff said later that, when he was in real pain in the dead of the night, he had decided that he was prepared to die rather than forfeit the lead.

'My only concern was that it would upset Mum. She worries.'

As the crowd at Doncaster became excited, Mary said simply, 'Well done, son.' She then told reporters, 'I hope he forgets all about it when he gets home.'

MY OTHER CAR IS A PICASSO
— Bumper sticker, Parliament House, Canberra

Our own border crossing took about five minutes. It would have been quicker except for the fact that we stopped to speak with a group of older people who were embarking upon a four-day cycle ride through some of the historic towns nearby. They asked us if we wanted to join them.

'No thanks. Too many hills.'

We were looking forward to the fact that the Hume Freeway south of Wodonga and heading for Melbourne is as flat as an old joke. We cycled under a gantry which displays the speed of every car entering the freeway. We didn't register. But we had the breeze at our backs and were soon wondering why we ever thought this trip would be such a big deal.

We pulled into a rest stop and met a man named Ken. He was on his way back from Corryong, on the upper Murray, where he'd spent the previous three days at the Man From Snowy River Festival.

Ken might not have told us any of this had we been in a car, but the law of the Hume is that the smaller your vehicle the more conspicuous you become. The most invisible people drive the biggest rigs, whereas bikes invite conversation. They are a bit like babies in that regard.

Ken was driving a 1965 Nissan Cedric station wagon and had slept in the back of it for the weekend, presumably leaving the tailgate open so he could fit. When he got back into the small car, we saw that Ken held his beard close to his chest so it wouldn't catch in the door.

Once upon a time, it was more common for people to just pull over for the night by the side of the road, like Ken. A friend of mine recalls a family holiday on the Hume sometime in the fifties. The children had been looking forward to it for weeks and, when the big day came round, were over-excited. As a result, their behaviour was atrocious. They fought and screamed all day in the back seat. By nightfall, their father had had enough and announced they were going home in the morning. They pleaded but he was adamant. They went to bed sulking.

Sure enough, next day, Dad was as good as his word. They packed their tents away, and Dad turned the car around and started heading back along the road. The children were silent in disbelief. It wasn't until lunchtime that they realised they hadn't seen this part of the Hume before.

As it turned out, their father had got up in the night, when they were all asleep, and already turned the car around so it faced the other direction – then, when he astonished them by doing a U-turn in the morning, they thought they were going back home, though they were actually still going forwards. Dad just wanted some peace and quiet.

We stopped next at Chiltern, which advertised itself as a 'peaceful vision of the past'. The main street, Conness Street, was a tight thoroughfare where shops stretched out their awnings to the road – a narrow passage which used to be part of the Hume. One of Chiltern's signs boasted the oldest grapevine in the southern hemisphere, planted in 1846. It now had a trunk like a tree. In the old days, trucks were always knocking branches off it.

Further along Conness Street we came to Stephens Motor Garage, which had begun life as a wheelwright and blacksmith in the days of horse and buggy. Gordon Stephens was still selling petrol there, amidst his passion for automotive memorabilia, especially petrol pumps – there were eighty-eight of them in the workshop. He told us that he used to let people wander in off the street free of charge and look around them.

'Now I've put a couple of bucks on it. It keeps out the free-loaders.'

We paid $3.50 each.

'I've never heard anyone say they didn't get their money's worth.'

The place was full of old motoring gadgets and gimmicks. There was one of those inflatable tigers which, when I was a kid, were put around by the Esso company because their motto was 'Put a tiger in your tank'. There were old uniforms, complete with caps, which used to be worn by driveway attendants in the days when somebody else put the tiger in the tank for you.

'The badges on those caps are bringing in extraordinary money now,' said Gordon.

Gordon, a mechanic, is sixty-six; his son was running the garage these days while Gordon restored unloved mechanical items. There was nothing in the place to rival his collection of petrol pumps.

'I used to have one hundred. I decided to sell twenty. I've got eight to go.'

There were price tags on some of them showing they were not cheap – between $2,000 and $5,000.

'Who buys bowsers?'

'You shouldn't really call them bowsers.'

Gordon explained to us that Bowser, like Biro and Hoover, was actually a brand name which has come to substitute for the product itself.

'A Bowser is actually a very rare brand. The Bowsers were all imported from the United States and they stopped making them in the 1930s.'

Gordon didn't have a Bowser. He did have a Wayne, though. And a Gilbert and Barker. He said that pump design was originally an art form, the reason being that there was once, especially in the United States, such a large number of places to refuel on the side of the road that pump design became instrumental in attracting trade. The oil magnate Rockefeller believed that anybody who lived next to a main road could put a pump out the front of their place and sell his product. It was only the look of the pump that would get a motorist to stop at one place rather than another.

'Not like these days. All the pumps look the same.'

Long after service stations in cities had developed driveways to get cars off the road while they were refuelling, an idea which took on in the United States around World War I, rural areas continued to plant pumps right on the edge of highways. The original pumps had an important feature. Generally, they first filled a glass reservoir on top of the pump and then used gravity to let this petrol go down into the tank of the car. This meant that buyers could see exactly how much petrol they were getting.

'So who buys them?'

'Collectors.'

'But why collect petrol pumps?'

No answer. I guess if I couldn't work that out for myself then no explanation was going to help.

'Look, you can buy a painting for $3,000 and what have you got? It's just a bit of canvas with paint on it. But a pump is a real work of art. It's there forever and it increases in value. It's an investment as well as art. People come in here and look at the old pumps and they mean nothing to them. For me, they are part of history as well as art.'

I BELIEVE IN DRAGONS AND GOOD MEN AND OTHER CREATURES OF FANTASY
— Bumper sticker, Hume Highway

We had wanted to see Lake View House, also in Chiltern, the childhood home of Henry Handel Richardson – one of those stubborn craftspeople whose slow, grinding work did more to shape Australian culture than a rack of celebrities. Henry Handel was born Ethel Florence in 1870. She became Henry because, in those days, you had to be a bloke to cut the mustard. It was the only domestic chore to which they attended. She became Handel because it was a name that opened doors.

Henry or Ethel, who was known to her intimates as Ettie, was born in Melbourne in 1870 and lived in Chiltern for about fifteen months between July 1876 and October 1877. This brief period counted for a lot in the development of her inner resources. The house and the district figure prominently in her book *Ultima Thule*, the third part of *The Fortunes of Richard Mahony*.

This trilogy is based closely on the lives of the author's parents. Ettie's father, Walter Richardson, was a doctor who specialised in midwifery and what were spoken of in his advertisements as 'diseases of women'.

The first thing that greeted us on our arrival at Lake View House was a display of nineteenth-century obstetric equipment, including a cabinet full of bakelite cervical dilators, the kind of devices which make even a bloke squirm. Nearby was a birthing chair of the same period, which looked like an instrument of torture. There were other blunt instruments, the exact purpose of which we were happy not to know.

'You'd think twice before getting pregnant,' said Jenny.

'I didn't know we were thinking of that at all,' I replied.

Walter Richardson was not a man to think before anything. Like others in this story, his life was destroyed by his own restlessness. He could never be still. In Chiltern, his mind, which had long been nibbling at the edges of his personality, finally decided to eat itself.

Ettie had no option but to sit at the table and watch. He died eighteen months after the family left Chiltern, 'a gentle broken creature who might have been a stranger'. Ettie would spend far longer working on the trilogy which attempted to come to terms with this man than she had actually spent with him. At one level, she gave her life to trying to understand her father.

Ettie left Australia in 1888 at the age of eighteen and only ever returned for a few months in 1912, her purpose being to refresh her memory of the places she had lived in and now wanted to write about, including Chiltern. *The Fortunes of Richard Mahony* is a passionate engagement with Australian landscape and culture, written by someone who was absent from the country in the years she was working on it. Built over almost twenty years, it is a work of memory. It shares this quality with a list of Australian books such as George Johnston's *My Brother Jack* and Tim Winton's *Cloudstreet*, works about home which could never have been written at home. Joyce's *Ulysses* is in the same category. The traveller writes about home; those who never really leave home write travel books.

Lake View House is the central location of the work which is central to Henry Handel Richardson's reputation, *Ultima Thule*. The house is haunted by the presence of an unhappy father:

> *He had always been in flight. – But from what? Who were his pursuers? From what shadows did he run? . . . Himself, he was the hunter and the hunted: the merciless in pursuit and the panting prey.*

The property, owned by the National Trust, was not normally open on Monday but the manager, Pat O'Connor, was expecting a group which hadn't arrived so she was happy to talk to us. Meeting Pat was lucky. She had moved to the area from Sydney about twenty years before and had been a volunteer at Lake View House for about nine years; she knew the house and Henry Handel Richardson inside out and had feeling for them both, yet she admitted she was having difficulty getting other people to show much interest in the house and its story.

'The locals aren't that concerned.'

Pat believed that, in the language of today, Walter Richardson had a bi-polar disorder.

'He could never stick at anything. They were always moving and every time they moved, they lost money.'

His manner was also authoritarian.

'They moved here from a large house in Hawthorn. Mary his wife wanted to store some of their furniture because she knew it wouldn't fit in this small place. But he insisted. He was like that. In the end, a lot of the furniture she had collected from Europe had to be left out in the weather and was ruined.'

The family, it seemed, was destined for financial difficulty. Mary, at least, was willing to turn her hand to anything and eventually became a postmistress in order to keep bread on the table.

We were shown a desk which, much later, Ethel Richardson's husband had bought for her and which had travelled with her from place to place. Her husband, George Robertson, was a scholar of German literature. The couple used to host dinner parties in England and, according to Pat O'Connor, one such party brought together Agatha Christie, H.G. Wells and George Bernard Shaw. Only Ethel's publisher had known the real identity of Henry Handel Richardson and that the pseudonym was that of a woman. At the time of this gathering, *Australia Felix*, the first part of the trilogy, had been released. Both Wells and Shaw had read it and voiced strong opinions which provoked Ethel to say that she was also familiar with the work. This raised eyebrows because it had only been published that week, so Ethel had to cover her tracks and quickly explain that she had seen it in proofs at her husband's publisher.

Shaw said that he had found a mistake in the book where the author had said that it had not rained for five years. He said that there was no place in the world where it did not rain every three weeks. H.G. Wells had found a mistake as well. The author had said that it was forty miles to the nearest doctor. This was absurd. He could imagine, it seemed, both a time machine and an invasion from Mars but he could not conceive of a world where there wasn't a village every two or three miles. Ethel Richardson could feel her anger rising. It was all she could do to control herself and deny Agatha Christie the makings of a literary murder mystery.

She shouldn't have worried. Nothing gives a reader as much pleasure as finding a mistake in a book. That's why I have included so many in this one.

My other car is a bike
— Bumper sticker, Hume Highway

Wangaratta is the only place on the Hume to honour a cyclist. Signs on the approaches to town let the visitor know that Wang, as it is invariably known, is the home of Dean Woods. Woods won medals on his push-bike at the Olympic Games in Los Angeles, in 1984, Seoul in 1988 and Atlanta in 1996.

The only medal I ever got on my push-bike was a St Christopher's medal. St Christopher used to be the patron saint of travellers but was dropped from the ministry for no better reason than that he had never existed. I believe the portfolio is currently shared by St Nicholas and St Anthony of Padua. St Nicholas is appropriate because he gave us the idea of giving gifts at Christmas, the time when everyone is on the road. He is also, for obvious reasons, the patron saint of pawnbrokers. It's a wonder he is not the patron of shopping centres, credit cards and broken toys as well. St Anthony is the saint who helps you find things, which is, when you think about it, the basic purpose of travel. It must be said that St Anthony does seem more responsive when you are trying to find something small, such as a place to park the car, than something major, such as a life partner. That kind of work often gets referred to St Jude, who deals with hopeless cases.

The heavenly cabinet is a carefully chosen team. The patron of road builders, as well as bricklayers and stonemasons, is St Stephen. He was stoned to death which may be why he is also the patron saint of migraine sufferers. St Vitus, the patron saint of comedians, was also martyred.

Dean Woods has come back to earth from Olympian heights. On the side of the former Hume Highway he now runs a bike shop which has strollers sitting demurely out the front. You can hire bikes from him if you want to take in some of the surrounding countryside at a leisurely pace, and customers are provided with maps which suggest ways they can go and places they can see. Woods calls his bike-hire business 'Gourmet Trails'. The Hume Highway does not rate as a gourmet trail.

'It's really too busy for leisure riding,' says Woods. 'And too monotonous.'

Despite the way it appeared both to Dean and to us, there is a constant trickle of bike traffic on the Hume. One time, when I was driving on my own to Melbourne, I encountered a man called Rob who had pulled over just north of Wangaratta. He didn't look like a typical long-distance cyclist. He had left Sydney the previous Sunday with three litres of water, the clothes on his back, the manuscript of his book and some artwork. Other than those possessions he had nothing and certainly no money. It was now Friday afternoon and Rob was on his way to Bendigo to see his mother, who had just turned seventy-one: it was fourteen years since he'd spent Christmas with her.

Rob had recently been living in a room in Kings Cross in Sydney, was having trouble making the rent and was also in strife with his neighbours. One day, he found a bike. So he decided to leave town and visit his mother, sleeping at night by the side of the road. Around Yass, he found another bike dumped by the freeway which looked better than the one he had.

'So I did a quick upgrade.'

Rob's knuckles and calves were blue with sunburn.

Rob gave me his mum's address and asked me to write to her to say that he was on his way and that he loved her. That night I did as he'd asked, feeling a bit awkward about it – but surely, at the rate he was going, he'd have reached Bendigo before the mail.

That's assuming both he and his bike made the distance.

'This is a character-building exercise for me,' he'd said. 'I wanted to prove to my mother that I love her enough to ride like that. I've got ambition too. I want to make a movie in the next four or five years. Plus I've invented a video game. I wanna tell her about them.'

He had no money for a camera.

'The next best thing is a diary. I've been writing heaps. I opinionate everything. I just have to. I opinionate all the time.'

Rob had been collecting business cards from cafes and other places and getting the owners to sign them as proof that he had done the trip.

'My numerologist told me that I knew somebody who was destined to be famous. I asked him who. He said it was me.'

Other people cycle the same road for different reasons. In the late seventies, Dorothy Johnson, a writer, was part of a crowd that cycled from Melbourne to Canberra to protest against nuclear weapons. They slept in scout halls and the like. Dorothy had a frail old bike and recalls being overtaken by an athletic rider on the latest machine who had joined the protest simply because it would be a good training run. He almost went home when he discovered what it was all about, but he needed the workout.

In late October 2003, Samuel Johnson, an actor, left Sydney to ride to Melbourne on a unicycle. He made a few detours to round the journey out to 1,000 kilometres and averaged 37 kilometres a day. Johnson wanted to raise money to support young people with cancer. He had imagined the trip for a long time: his older sister had cancer when she was twelve. I presume he chose a unicycle because it halves your chances of getting a puncture.

At any given time, somebody will be doing something strange on the Hume to raise money for some good purpose. No sooner was Samuel Johnson reaching his destination than Dean Jones, a former international cricketer, was leaving Sydney to walk to Melbourne to raise money for the Bone Marrow Institute to help people with leukaemia. He was accompanied by his wife Jane and various well-wishers. They estimated the trip would take thirty-one days, not much longer than it took me to cycle.

At the beginning of August 2002, a man sitting high in the saddle of a pennyfarthing rode along the Hume past Gunning, having come from Uluru and heading towards Sydney. This was John McDermott, who described himself as a pennyfarthingologist. John had spent thirteen years in the police service before deciding to move to a career in rehabilitation. At the age of thirty-five, he was in the third year of a four-year course in occupational therapy and was doing the ride in his semester break.

John was inspired to undertake such a difficult journey because a friend of his, aged thirty-three, had multiple sclerosis and was confined to a wheelchair. John chose to begin at Uluru, in the centre of Australia, because he wanted to draw attention to the centre of the problem of MS, namely that its causes are not properly understood. The idea of the pennyfarthing was to highlight the difficulties people with MS face, especially with mobility. A pennyfarthing is an awkward beast to manoeuvre. The rider can't even stand up on the pedals to relieve the pressure on his bum. For the first two days of the ride, John was in agony, his only relief being paw-paw ointment applied liberally to the perineum. He had to get off and push the bike up hills. It took forty-one days to get from Uluru to Sydney.

John was accompanied on the trip by a support driver, David Penberthy, whom I also met that day outside Gunning.

'He is a very patient man. I averaged about 13 kilometres per hour at the start of the trip so we made that a distance marker.' David drove 13 kilometres ahead and waited for John to catch up.

'I would eventually arrive,' said John, 'and have a ten-minute break and then cycle again. He would overtake me and drive ahead another 13 kilometres and wait for about one hour for me to arrive. All the way from Uluru.'

In total, David would have done this about 250 times.

With the help of family, friends and supporters, John met all the costs of the expedition out of his own pocket. People were urged to ring a special number on the side of the van David was driving and make a donation for research into multiple sclerosis. John hoped to raise $100,000 and literally worked his butt off. But in spite of a lot of media attention, he only raised a small fraction of his target.

'But one woman pulled over out of the blue and gave me $100. That lifted my spirits for a while.'

Although Dean Wood's Olympic success was mainly on the track, he used to train on the roads around Wang. By the time he was eighteen, he had won an Olympic gold medal. 'I think that initially cycling just gave me freedom. I didn't have to depend on Mum and Dad to take me places. By the time I was fifteen or sixteen I knew I had ability.'

Occasionally Dean would race in Melbourne on the weekend and ride the 240 kilometres back to Wang on the following Monday. He used to cover the ground in six or six and a half hours, depending on the wind.

'It was frightening in the days before the dual carriageway. There was a white line on the side of the road and then just dirt. I guess I was lucky that I never had an accident.'

These days, running a bicycle business, the only cycling Dean does is around the local shops with his six-year-old daughter.

'That has its own challenges too, I might say.'

I SLEEP WITH MY TEDDY BECAUSE
I KNOW WHERE HE'S BEEN
— Bumper sticker, Wangaratta

We found a room in a motel which looked like a nursing home but was run like a boarding school. Nevertheless, the place did bring us closer together. This was because the bed sagged in the middle.

There are several things that a man leaving the Catholic priesthood is not well prepared to cope with. One is automatic teller machines. At first I loved them because it was so easy to get money. It just came spewing out. Then I discovered that every time you took money from an ATM, it was deducted from your account. They didn't just give it to you. I couldn't believe it. I was not used to such petty behaviour, especially when the banks seemed to make such huge profits.

The other thing new to me was sharing a bed. When Jenny and I first teamed up, I spent a long time lying in bed at night like a tin soldier, terrified that if I moved I would wake her up. I put my arms by my side and played statues, trying to get through the night without turning over. It was bad enough, I thought, for Jenny to have to put up with the sleeping machine which, when not buried by day deep in my pannier, keeps me breathing till dawn and, more importantly, dampens my snoring. Before the invention of these machines, jowly men died in their sleep and their partners simply rolled over, thankful for a break from the noise. But despite its effectiveness, the machine is hardly the most glamorous item of intimate apparel. Earlier in the trip I had been able to quieten the sound it makes by resting my copy of *Anna Karenina* on top of it. All those unread pages made excellent sound insulation. But foolishly I had sent the book south with Jenny's mother.

Now the bed was making matters worse by rolling us into each other. I held onto the edge of the mattress, desperate to let Jenny sleep in peace. It felt like holding onto the edge of a cliff or a lifeboat. I thought that if I let go, disaster would follow.

But sometime in the night, I must have fallen asleep and relinquished my grip. When I woke up, I found I was tangled up with Jenny. It took me a few minutes to work out which arm and which leg belonged to which person. The funny thing was, Jenny didn't seem to mind. We were dancing.

That morning, we were getting ready to leave when an old-timer came up to us and, without a word, knelt in front of my bike. I thought he was performing an act of worship, but before long he stood slowly and told us not to mind him but he just needed to check if our wheels were 26-inch or 27-inch. He was interested in such things. He got around on a 1944 Malvern Star which he had bought when it was new.

'It still does me. I can still find parts for it when I need them.'

He looked at the frame of my bike.

'You know that thing was made by communists,' he said and then vanished as suddenly as he had appeared.

On the way out of town, we passed the cathedral in which

the grim rocker, Nick Cave, had sung as a choir boy. The cathedral was still there even if Nick wasn't.

I began looking out for a particular roadhouse which has a place in my memory. I had only ever set foot in it once and I have never been able to locate it with any certainty since. Sometimes I wonder if it really existed. Maybe it was part of a dream. I was certainly less than half awake when I was there.

At the age of twenty, I had just made a life-time commitment to the Jesuit order and pronounced perpetual vows of poverty, chastity and obedience. Travelling to Melbourne by bus was an expression of poverty, although, after fifteen hours in a tight squeeze, it also become an expression of chastity. You could spend the night sitting across the narrow aisle from some attractive young stranger and, by the morning, all you could think about was finding a shower. Long-distance bus travel produces all the effects of drunkenness without the need of alcohol.

On Wednesday, 17 February 1982, my ticket (which I still have) tells me, I was on a Deluxe Coaches service that left Sydney at 8.45 p.m. On the way to Central Station, from where the bus pulled out, I had been allowed to drop in briefly to my family and say goodbye – I was leaving Sydney, where I had grown up, and was moving to Melbourne, where I would start theological studies and, with that, a new life. I was no longer a novice but now a fully fledged member of the order. I was proud of that. It was a big trip, my first lap of the Hume.

At dawn, the bus pulled into Wangaratta. I was thirsty and wanted to buy an orange juice. But I was tortured by the thought that such an outlandish purchase for my own benefit might be a breach of the vow of poverty I had just taken. We had each been given ten dollars for emergencies but I presumed that meant the 'loss, damage, death or accident' described in the small-print disclaimer on the ticket. I didn't know what to do and would have been happy to drink water, except for the fact that the tap in the bathroom had been clogged with toilet paper, perhaps by a passenger who, in the middle of the night, mistook the dripping plumbing for his own.

I raised my concern with my travelling companion, Phong, who had also just taken vows. Phong's group of Vietnamese boat people had left his country in a leaky vessel in the late seventies with an inventory of possessions which amounted to, in an expression we were only too happy to teach him, bugger all. He'd survived pirates and God knows what else. This trip in a bus was a paltry affair by comparison. He couldn't see my problem. He went and bought the orange juice for me.

I took the drink outside and looked up and down the Hume. I felt that somehow I was being stretched like a rubber-band along the entire length of the road and was about to snap. I still feel that sometimes: that I belong at one end of this road but I don't know which one. This is one of the reasons why I live in the middle of it, a bit like a donkey stuck between two piles of hay. At the time, however, I had a painful feeling of being alone. It was a brittle feeling, as if a small stone tossed up casually by any passing car would break me into a thousand worthless fragments, just like a windscreen.

I seldom feel that these days but I won't forget the time when I did. I have never been able to find that place again. Maybe that's a blessing. It has probably been refurbished as a computer store or drive-through nursery.

The road joins two cities. It also keeps them apart. By the time we reached the freeway again, Jenny and I were talking about all the places we had gone on our own and all the places we had cycled alone. Jenny had lived for five years in England and cycled everywhere, even under London's cheerless winter skies. The problem with feeling alone on a bike is that you are so exposed. It's easier to be lonely in private.

We rode into Glenrowan.

In June 1880, the outlaw Ned Kelly did the same thing.

Kelly's story winds around the highway like a vine. His life maps the road as it moves north from Melbourne. The son of an alcoholic Irishman and former convict, Red Kelly, he grew up at Beveridge on the outskirts of Melbourne. Always in search of a fresh start, which meant escaping both grog and police surveillance, the family moved 80 kilometres north to Avenel. Ned was twelve when Red died. He assumed the mantle of the man of the house. Later, he built for his mother, Ellen, a home at Eleven Mile Creek, not far from Lake William Hovell. One of Kelly's most daring bank robberies, in December 1878, took place at Euroa. By this stage, he was in flight from the murder or assassination of police at Stringybark Creek. Yet he put on a good show for his hostages, many of whom held him in high regard for the rest of their lives and proved to be awkward witnesses at his trial.

The alignment of the current Hume Freeway was altered to preserve an old grainstore, built partly below ground level, where

Ned Kelly was said to have held his hostages. The police who pursued him were stationed in Benalla and Wangaratta, the two towns frequented by his invisible band of collaborators. He made his final stand at Glenrowan. It was all on the road.

Nevertheless, it was the railway more than the road which figured in the tragic side of the Kelly story. The railway was built during the years of Kelly's career and had a marked impact on the north of Victoria. The hotel where Kelly made his last stand in Glenrowan only existed because the owner, Ann Jones, one of nature's battlers, had gone out of business in Wangaratta when the advent of the railway robbed her roadside refreshment rooms of business.

The railway stirred Kelly. He chose Glenrowan in which to surface after months on the run because he and his gang, Joe Byrne, Steve Hart and Dan Kelly, planned to derail a train and blow up the railway, thus isolating the area and facilitating the eventual declaration of some kind of home rule. It was a terrorist scheme, a detail which is often overlooked by Kelly adherents.

In 1880, the Sydney Road ran through Glenrowan on the western side of the railway. Now, it doesn't run through it at all, but, by the time Glenrowan was bypassed in 1988, it had found its way onto the other side of the tracks. By then, the entire town had inched closer to the site of Australia's most famous siege. In 1880, most of the town was over a kilometre from the location of Ann Jones' hotel. Now, it can't get close enough.

The plantation in the middle of the freeway was widened just north of Euroa to preserve the grainstore in which Ned Kelly is believed to have held hostages. According to Bill Peyton, the place was never signposted and it was difficult for visitors to stop there. Traffic thundered past on either side. Eventually, despite the effort that had been made to change the alignment of the road, a truck crashed into the building and demolished it anyway.

'It's just a pile of rubble now.'

Bill Peyton is an engineer. He knows every stone on the Hume Freeway in central Victoria. He put them there.

Despite appearances, the Hume Freeway in Victoria is made of stone. In that respect, it is a descendant of the Appian Way. Peyton had technology at his disposal which the Romans could not have dreamed of as they cobbled their road together, but the Hume in Victoria is, nonetheless, made from the same earth as that through which it passes. It is distinct in this respect from the road in New South Wales. The two state authorities have built the road in different ways. They look much the same, do the same job and have the same name. But, technologically speaking, they are chalk and cheese. In lay terms, one is made of cement and one is made of stone.

Bill Peyton joined the Country Roads Board, now called VicRoads, at the age of twenty-one in 1962. For eighteen years between 1976 and 1994, he occupied senior management positions on the Hume, most notably as project manager for the reconstruction. During those years the road was almost completely rebuilt. When Bill started work on the road it meandered from Melbourne to the Murray, passing through Seymour, Avenel, Longwood, Euroa, Violet Town, Benalla, Winton, Glenrowan, Wangaratta, Bowser, Springhurst, Chiltern, Barnawatha and Wodonga. Not one of those towns remains on the road. They have all been bypassed.

The last place to disappear was Wangaratta. It vanished in April 1994. The day of the opening was emotional for Bill and a big event in the life of the city. The council organised a street carnival on the ground which had just been won back from the trucks. There was a sense that the town had been liberated. For those who were already homesick for noise, the council organised bands. Couples who had not heard each other speak for years could now understand what their partners were saying. This put a lot of stress on marriages.

For Peyton, the opening of the Wangaratta bypass was the end of a job. Once the road left Melbourne, there was not a single house on Victoria's main street.

Nobody knows the specifications of the road as well as Bill Peyton. There are 294 kilometres of it in Victoria, including fifty-six bridges. The whole lot, in the dollars of the day, cost $700 million. Twenty-five million cubic metres of earth were moved to make room for it. Half a million trees were planted to beautify or disguise it. Each lane is 3.7 metres wide, with a 3-metre stopping lane on the left, a 1.2-metre median shoulder and a 2-metre outer verge. The plantation between the north and south carriageways varies between 19.4 and 25.4 metres in width. This means that the total width of the road is over 50 metres, more than two and a half times that of the Appian Way. But it is less than a metre deep: it has a lower base of sedimentary rock of less than 300 milli-metres, topped by a sub-base of crushed rocked of about 200 millimetres, topped by a base course of finer-grade crushed rock of another 200 millimetres. Bitumen goes over the top like icing on a cake.

Bill started work on the Hume after the Wallan–Broadford section of the road had already been opened. The pavement, or surface, of that section, which was meant to be a show-piece, failed soon after traffic started using it in 1974. It was an embar-rassing debacle.

'It was manufactured out of a crust rock called Greenstone which turned to mud under moisture, partly because that type of rock did not allow water to escape.'

This experience changed both the way the road was built and the type of material that was used to build it. A method was developed to make the pavement permeable, so that water could move through it and be carried away through subsoil drains. Geologists moved up and down the corridor looking for suitable rock to use on the road. Special quarries were licensed for the purpose.

'In New South Wales they used concrete. In Victoria, we used unbound flexible crushed rock pavements, with a final bitumen surface, and no cementitious material.'

A large part of Bill's job involved working out the best place to put the road. This was easier said than done and involved negotiating some troublesome natural terrain, especially around Euroa. It also entailed meeting with communities, an aspect of his work which he relished.

'I enjoyed the rush of confronting often hostile audiences in the public meetings held along the Hume corridor. They often involved as many as 150 people. I really got quite a buzz out of those meetings, to be honest. I enjoyed the thrust and parry. There were always people baying for our blood.'

By the time the contract to build the road on a particular alignment was actually drawn up, the hardest part of the job was frequently already done.

'If you get the plan wrong, it costs a fortune. It cost us $40 million to move the Goulburn Valley Highway, where I am now working, about 40 metres because Aboriginal bones were discovered on the route. We should have been more careful in the first place.'

Some of the most emotional meetings to negotiate the path of the Hume took place in Glenrowan.

'The town was just developing its Ned Kelly precinct and a lot of money had been invested in that. It relied on having access to through-traffic. Towns of more than 3,000 people, such as Benalla, were never going to be very adversely affected. But Glenrowan has about 400 people and was much more vulnerable to the economic impact of a bypass.'

The whole of the Hume Highway between the outskirts of Melbourne and close to the New South Wales border basks in the

Kelly legend. It's everywhere. Towns such as Euroa and Benalla have Kelly Country Motors and Kelly Country Meats, but *they* have other attractions besides. Glenrowan only has the Kelly story. It seems that everything that ever happened there happened on 29 June 1880. The place is so crowded with reminders of that one day that there isn't much room for anything else ever to happen. In Glenrowan, every day is 29 June 1880. Even 9 April 2002, the day we rode into town.

Ned's Burger House, Kelly's Cookhouse Cafe, Kelly Country Motel and Ned Kelly's Bar were all open for business. Kate's Cottage did, admittedly, break the routine. It was named after Ned's sister.

Kelly said he feared death 'as little as a cup of tea'. If he visited Glenrowan today, he may have feared tea more. The place is drowning in tea. And coffee. The Kelly Cookhouse had umbrellas outside, provided by a coffee company. They promoted espresso, caffe latte and cappuccino, beverages which may not have been popular with the Kelly Gang but which have found favour among the film-makers and artists who never seem to tire of the tale.

Jenny and I settled ourselves at a table in Dad and Dave's Billy Tea Rooms. The Dad and Dave stories of farming life 'on our selection' really originate in Queensland, but, after a while, one part of olde worlde Australia is as good as another. The menu, however, did pay tribute to the local lad. It included Ned Kelly Scones, Ned Kelly Shearer's Damper, Ned Kelly Pikelets, the Gourmet Ned Kelly Open Sandwich, the Chef's Pride Ned Kelly Sandwich, a Great Australian Ned Kelly Salad, Kelly's steak pie, peas, chips and gravy, Ned Kelly Billy Tea, Ned Kelly Saddlebag Coffee and, for afters, Ned Kelly's olde fashioned nut sundae. The establishment was taking the micky out of the very legend that feeds it.

Ned Kelly's last supper, before he was hanged, had been lamb and peas. But his favourite dish was the one thing not on offer today.

NO REASONABLE OFFER REFUSED
— On garbage truck, Hume Highway

I have a soft spot for Benalla. There's a great second-hand bookshop on the side of the road which always has two or three copies of *Anna Karenina* in stock. I bought one and told Jenny, to her surprise, that I realised I did need it after all.

'I can ring your mother and ask where my bookmark is so I know where to pick up from,' I said.

'I think you'll find it's still near the beginning,' she replied.

I was learning that Jenny and I live by different purchasing policies. I tend to be a junk meister who finds empty spaces threatening and needs to fill them. Jenny is the opposite. She finds clutter disconcerting and likes to get rid of it, tending to buy stuff only when she needs to, an absurd idea which would bankrupt the economy if it ever became popular. Luckily, there is little prospect of that. Our respective panniers told the story. My rear axle was working a lot harder than hers.

A friend who knew Jenny during the five years she was living in London told me once, in a stage whisper, that Jenny would always put her heart before her pocket. I had already worked this out because she would hardly have been hanging around with me if it was any different. There was something about her approach which I found comforting: her attitude to possessions gave me more security than the possessions would have themselves. I had spent a lot of my life prospecting in op-shops and used to wonder where all their stuff came from. At last, in Jenny, I had met the source.

As we were leaving Wangaratta, she had told me about her life in London. Because of the nature of her job there, she was often short of money. Many days, she had to walk to work, often through bad weather, because she didn't have money for the bus. It was just the way things were. Eventually, somebody gave her a rickety old bike which she got into working order. She used it to get around more quickly and to arrive where she was going with drier feet. She also started running creative-dance sessions for children to supplement her income, riding off to the classes with a portable CD player perched precariously in the basket at the front of her bike, hoping it would work when she arrived. I would have found that kind of life nerve-racking. I never leave the house unless there's money in my pocket.

'The more stuff you have,' said Jenny, 'the more stuff you end up throwing out. You only have to look at all the junk on the side of the road to realise that.'

Travelling at a slow speed magnifies everything on the road and you see the rubbish. You can work out how many kilometres it takes to eat the typical fast-food meal-deal combo as the wrapping is discarded course by course. At one point, we found a cassette of a lecture on the theme of happy families on the shoulder of the highway. It had the owner's name and address on it so that evening I posted it back to her explaining, untruthfully, that I was in the process of returning every item of rubbish on the Hume Highway to its rightful owner, a task that would take several lifetimes. A while later, I would get an apologetic email from the woman concerned. She said the tape must have been there for years. She and her husband were divorced now and she was loving life but felt the same way I did about thoughtless people. She had been married to one. Come to think of it, it must have been him who threw the litter out the window. He was like that. Treated her the same way. I was sorry I asked.

It's amazing what gets offloaded on the side of the road. Between us, Jenny and I managed to pick up almost five dollars in loose change on the journey, which we put aside for luck. If we ever need it for any serious purpose, we'll know that our luck has just about run out. We saw where somebody had discarded a double mattress. And somewhere else an old washing machine. Disposable nappies. An umbrella. A raincoat. Lots of shoes, always on their own, never with their partner. We found a pair of cyclist's gloves, still in their wrapper, and also a spanner, but picked up neither. I was making an honest attempt to limit my baggage by restricting it to useless items.

One hot January, a fire jumped a fence and took to the nature strip in the centre of the freeway near Gunning. It quickly wasted the vegetation so that, from a distance, the strip now looked like a river. This was because, once the grass was gone, it brought to light the hundreds of empty drink bottles lying there. They shimmered in the sun.

In early spring, you notice trees in blossom on the side of a road, especially along its older sections. They are mostly apple and plum trees and occasionally peach trees. They have all grown from half-eaten fruit which has landed in a comfortable place and made the most of its luck. Only a tiny percentage of the fruit which is tossed from car windows ends up growing. You have to admire the determination of those trees that do make it. But very little rubbish grows into anything useful. Most of it either rusts or rots. Just about all of it is evidence of a culture which has plenty, which is choking on its own excess.

'THERE IS NO ROAD TO PEACE.
PEACE IS THE ROAD' — GANDHI
— Bumper sticker, Hume Highway

The Hume Highway has never carried an army to battle. Nor has it seen an exodus from war, invasion, famine or disease. No road in Australia ever has. But there are literally dozens of places on the Hume where we saw war remembered and its human cost given reverence. Benalla is home to one of the most telling, an image of two doctors, one known and one unknown, helping sick prisoners of war.

Louis Laumen's monument to Weary Dunlop, surgeon and soldier, stands in a rose garden, a few steps from the site in Benalla where Major Mitchell camped in 1836 on his return from the discovery of the fertile farming country he dubbed 'Australia Felix'. Dunlop is one of those figures who suggest that, once in a blue moon, a dehumanising situation will uncover humane qualities. He was a native of the area. Ten thousand people, mostly locals, turned out in November 1996 on the day before Armistice Day, to see the Prime Minister unveil the statue of a man they knew.

Edward Dunlop was always called Weary. He was taken prisoner by the Japanese in Java in 1942 because he chose to stay with the men he was caring for, and from there he was sent with them to work on the notorious Thai–Burma railway. For the three and a half years he was in captivity, he was subject to unimaginable pressures, both mental and physical. In many respects he was preserved by the steeliness in his character which was seldom able to admit feeling pain. He kept a diary which was also lucky to survive. In July 1943, he wrote:

> ... the incongruity of things struck me – that men with comparative peace, comfort and security at home should be obliged to go to war and to suffer hunger, hardships and privation along a grim road leading to such a miserable death in a little quagmire in the jungle.

Weary had something to live for or, at least, someone. It is a tribute to both Weary and his fiancée, Helen Ferguson, that together they were later able to bear the burden of expectation created when their relationship itself was practically Weary's only source of hope. Thinking this as Jenny and I stood before Weary's statue that day, I knew I was speculating, of course, about matters which were scarcely my business. But it's never been easy for people who have left prison yet are still captive. One of Dunlop's companions remarked that London after World War II became 'full of men who wouldn't go home'. Weary himself baulked at the last moment at the idea of going home to Melbourne and went to Sydney to lie on Bondi Beach before being reunited with Helen, from whom he had, by then, been absent for seven years. He wondered if he was the same person as before and pondered the adage that 'hope deferred grows sour, like apples in the loft'.

Weary's untold achievement was his sanity. His post-war life was every bit as remarkable as his life during the war, not least because of his lack of bitterness towards the people who'd inflicted suffering both on himself and those dear to him. His diaries during the war include entries such as this:

> *. . . a searing hate arises in me whenever I see a Nip.*
> *Disgusting , deplorable, hateful troop of men – apes. It is*
> *a bitter lesson to all of us not to surrender to these beasts while*
> *there is still life in one's body.*

Forty years later, when he came to write an introduction to the diaries, Dunlop reflected on a Buddhist belief that 'all men are equal in the face of suffering and death'. He hints that the beginning of a change in him was, towards the end of the war, finding himself confronted by a trainload of Japanese soldiers 'in wretched condition'. After the war, he worked extensively in Asia, work that 'has left me with the conviction that all the races of mankind bear some special mark of God's tenderness, some unique contribution to human kind'. He was sitting by Helen's bedside when she died in 1988.

In some ways, the Hume Highway is one long war memorial. Its fortunes have clearly been affected by war. Significant sections were built by returned soldiers, especially during the Great Depression of the 1930s when work was created on road projects, some of which, east of Goulburn, are still in partial use. Conversely, war slowed the development of the road when revenue from taxes levied on cars and petrol decreased and personnel were diverted to war projects. By 1943, one-third of the staff of Victoria's Country Roads Board was in uniform.

For much of its history, the Hume has commemorated war in modest, understated ways. Over 1,400 memorials were erected in Australia after the First World War, most of them the articulation of small communities speechless with grief. These memorials say a lot to those of us who read them, because, for the most part, they offer little or no explanation of what happened to those who fought. Those we saw rarely carried even as much explanation as a Christian cross. They also tended to be purely commemorative:

obelisks and statues and so on. After World War II, partly owing to tax concessions, more practical memorials were built: halls, swimming pools, schools and hospitals. The Hume has a few of those including the swimming pool in Yass and the Memorial Hall we'd seen in Tarcutta.

But the less pragmatic memorials are more moving. The Hume has its fair share. The names on them are the names of locals.

Until the 1970s, the war memorial in Gundagai stood at the end of the wooden bridge which still carried all the interstate freight. It was a stubborn reminder to the traffic that lurched past that there was a local community in this town and, in another hour, when the traffic was miles away, the relatives of those whose names were engraved in stone would still be here, as they would in another week, month or year. As traffic became heavier, the memorial might have found a more convenient location and the steep gradient on that corner, notorious among truckies, could have been improved. But it never happened.

The memorials become part of the natural landscape of towns. Travellers just have to work around them.

The memorial in Gunning stands just four steps from the old highway – outside the post office, the building in which many of those whose names are engraved in stone went to enlist. One hundred and one people went from Gunning to fight overseas in World War I. Thirty-two were killed in action. That level of carnage was common in small communities. If, before the freeway bypassed the town, the road had needed to be widened, it would have been the focus of a battle between those on the move and those staying put.

Even as it is, the obelisk, made from the same stubborn granite that dominates the landscape of the area, says something about the gap between those in motion and those at rest in our town. On Anzac Day, 25 April 2003, the guest speaker was Frank Chattaway, a man who had distinguished himself during long years of service as the principal of Goulburn High School. Frank had been on the HMAS *Perth* in 1942 when it was sunk in Sunda Strait, after which he spent the rest of the war in horrifying conditions as a prisoner, an experience about which he spoke that day without rancour or resentment. His tone was as straight as a staffroom announcement.

In the middle of Frank's brief speech, a car which had found its way into town from the freeway in search of petrol went past loaded up for the holidays. The children in the back seat all stared at the assembly as if it was something on TV, then one of them let go of an ice-cream wrapper. The wind took it. By the time it landed beside the wreaths on the memorial, the car was well on its way and Frank was nearly finished. The whole incident took a few seconds.

When parts of the Hume were named after war heroes, you often needed local knowledge to appreciate the fact. There has never been anything around either Tubb's Hill or Maygar's Hill, both in Victoria, not far from Euroa, to let you know that these places were both named after winners of the Victoria Cross, the highest military award for bravery available to Australians. It is awarded by a foreign monarch.

Colonel Les Maygar, who grew up in Ruffy, a small community not far off the highway, won his VC in the Boer War. Major Fred Tubb was awarded the same honour for his efforts on Gallipoli in 1915 during the battle of Lone Pine, a tragic offensive which yielded Australia seven VCs, so, if nothing else, we could console ourselves that we died brave. Among the decorated was Alex Burton, twenty-two, also from Euroa. As far as I know, Euroa is the only small community in Australia to have nurtured three winners of the Victoria Cross.

On 16 December 1934, three English oaks were planted on the Hume Highway outside Euroa Primary School, in honour of Maygar, Tubb and Burton, a ceremony in which the families of the deceased were given positions of honour. On the same day, the Victorian governor dedicated two hills on the highway, one each to Tubb and Maygar. Burton's roots were in the town, not in adjacent farming communities, so the new bridge over Seven Creeks at Euroa, also on the highway, was named after him. It had replaced a bridge known as 'Hemley's rattle' because it had so many loose planks.

The people who gave Tubb's Hill and Maygar's Hill their names knew both the hills and the men they were named after. In a sense, it became easier to imagine them fighting to defend those hills than in an assault on places on the other side of the world with such colourless names as 'Hill 60' and 'Hill 971'. The same applies to Burton's Bridge. Until the burial of the unknown soldier in the Australian War Memorial in November 1993, the remains of only one soldier who died in World War I had been repatriated to Australia. The creation of war memorials after World War I was about bringing the dead back home. They were expressions of intimacy.

This is true even of larger monuments, such as the imposing memorial in Albury. It had looked down on us from its hill over-looking the town, with its back to the setting sun as we cycled through. Before the Hume was re-routed, all Melbourne-bound traffic passed through Albury under its reproving glare. It was the first monument anywhere in the world to be floodlit and, when it was opened, Lord Stonehaven declared that he knew of nothing to equal it. For all that, the monument carries the simple message, 'Albury District War Memorial, 1914–1919'. Nothing else. It was erected by people who were still personally traumatised. They had nothing to say. They just needed to say it loud.

War affects the highway differently now. It reflects the way in which the remembrance of war is moving from the personal to the public sphere and, with that, from a description of something unspeakable to something about which you can never say enough. As fewer and fewer Australians actually know somebody who fought in World War I or World War II, the commemoration of war has changed from a quiet remembrance of other people to an unrestrained endorsement of ourselves. As ideology comes to replace history, there are fewer and fewer faces to go with the stories. They have been replaced by a lather of clichés, most of which are as much about filling a void in the narcissistic present as lending dignity to the past. People seem now to believe that in looking at the Anzacs they are looking at themselves. They aren't. The dead deserve more respect than to be used to make ourselves feel larger.

The Hume gives evidence of this creeping Anzacism. About a quarter of the road is now part of Remembrance Drive, a name which has been given to the route from the obelisk in Macquarie Place in Sydney to the Australian War Memorial in Canberra. Despite the fact that much of that route is now a freeway, it is presented as a memorial avenue, a living tribute to those who fought in war. It includes half a dozen or more rest areas dedicated to men who won the Victoria Cross. They honour men who had nothing to do with that locality but who have become national identities, their stories public property. In most cases, the signage points out that their gallantry was an inspiration to their colleagues. They are now an inspiration to the casual motorist. The high drama of the stories, not to mention their tragedy, is in sharp relief to the monotony of the road they garnish. The original versions of such avenues were created during and after World War I. Seymour planted one on the road to Trawool, which was renamed Anzac Avenue, in July 1917. There was a tree for each soldier from the district and families sometimes had picnics beneath the tree planted for their son.

This is true, to some extent, of the striking war memorial in Goulburn which, in 1925, partly through the efforts of Mary Gilmore, came to be built above the town on Rocky Hill, rather than beside the road. It celebrates such flesh and blood people as Bill Punch, a local Aborigine, who enlisted to defend the interests of a nation in which he was not counted as a citizen. Indeed, he had been the only survivor of a massacre in 1880 in which the rest of his family had been killed in retaliation for the supposed theft of livestock. When a neighbour rode over to the scene of carnage, he found a baby still alive, trying to suckle from his dead mother's breast. That baby was Punch. He served on the western front and died of pneumonia in 1917 after having been wounded twice. God knows what he thought he was fighting for.

There are now large replicas of the Goulburn War Memorial at both main entrances to the city and its image is used in tourist promotions. It was built to preserve the identity of people who were known in the community. It is now used to create an identity for the town.

The Hume nearly did carry an army to war. When Jane Franklin was passing through the area near Benalla in 1839, she thought she was in a combat zone and was afraid of being attacked by natives. Franklin, however, enjoyed anxiety. She des-cribed the district as an 'eternal forest' and made detailed notes about the living conditions of the small police force that was stationed along the way. Franklin was well aware of what had happened to the Faithfull Brothers, sometimes known as Faithful, twelve months, to the week, before her tour.

The fate of the drovers employed by George and William Pitt Faithfull sent shivers through the colony and occasioned a debate in the House of Commons about the difficulty of policing the south road. The Sydney press milked it for all it was worth, fuelling fear of open insurrection on 'that dreary road' to Port Phillip. In the context, Franklin's version is quite restrained. She does, however, refer to a 'black campaign', something that implies a war of guerrilla resistance to white settlement.

In April 1838, the Faithfull brothers were bringing stock overland from Goulburn, where they had heard about rich pastures to the south. It was only two years since Mitchell had been through the area: the overlanders followed hard on the heels of the explorer. In early 1838, George Faithfull had established a station on the Ovens called Wangaratta, a name that now covers a small city. Moving further south in the autumn, George sent a group on ahead. On the morning of 11 April, that group was camped on Broken River, the site of present day Benalla. As they were packing up prior to moving on, they were suddenly attacked.

Depending on whose account you believe, between seven and fourteen men were killed. Their sheep were scattered. Not much of material value was taken.

Two issues have been hotly debated ever since. The first is whether or not the attack was, indeed, part of an organised resistance to European settlement. The second is the extent, if any, of European reprisals.

After the massacre, settlers pressured the government for a greater level of protection. They were prepared to take matters into their own hands, a situation which would have been perilous for the remnant of the Aboriginal population.

Thankfully, Governor Gipps, fairly new to his job, declined the suggestion that he should go to war against the Aborigines. But he did create a Border Police, which was in reality a militia, and established military posts for them along the emerging route to Port Phillip. It was the closest thing to an avenging army that the road ever hosted.

Five

Suddenly, Cliff Young was everywhere. A local production of the *Mikado* put Nanki Poo into gumboots. A cartoon showed the new prime minister, Bob Hawke, thinking about fixing the economy and saying, 'It's a hard road to hoe but if Cliff Young can do it, so can I.' The *Coffs Harbour Advocate* said, 'his great victory has done more for senior citizens than any increase in the pension could.' *Queensland Country Life* said that 'Cliff Young is the kind of man that Henry Lawson wrote about . . . he has re-opened a chapter of Australia's past when men could be toughened in mind and body by the bush and the sweat of hard work.' The *Sunday Telegraph* called him 'Don Quixote of the highways'. A writer in the *South West News Pictorial* compared his determination to that of Christ.

People were obsessed with Young's diet. He'd been a vegetarian for twelve years because his conscience had rebelled against killing animals. The front page of the *Sun*, Melbourne's biggest paper, was devoted to a picture of Cliff eating eggs. 'This is his third plate.' It was the main news of the day. A writer in *The Land Magazine*, said that the example of Cliff's eating habits should be used to improve the food available to other travellers along the Hume from the take-away places that sold only junk food. 'This is even more obvious on public holidays when bread is stale and attractive, salad-filled sandwiches are hard to find'. Fruit and vegetable traders reported increased sales of potatoes. In England, sellers said that Cliff had convinced people to put pumpkin on their tables and not just feed it to livestock.

Cliff wanted to go home. He didn't understand why nobody had paid him this much attention when, a couple of years before, he had jogged twenty-six miles to get to a neighbour's funeral or when he ran six miles for a haircut.

'They'll find somebody else to write about and I'll go back and relax in the bush.'

On the night of his victory in 1983, Martin Noonan took Cliff Young back to his place to rest. Cliff had six infected toes and had lost three toenails. But his blood pressure was 120/70.

'I still have the ECG they did on him the next day. It was perfect.'

Two days later, Noonan and Cliff were out jogging in the Dandenongs.

'People would pull over from nowhere just to shake his hand,' says Noonan. 'It happened all the time. You have no idea how he touched people.'

Noonan says that Cliff taught him the difference between a simpleton and a simple man.

'He was a simple man.'

The wind was at our backs. We were sailing. Jenny pulled ahead of me and gained ground, gradually pulling away. I felt like a donkey chasing a carrot. I didn't want her to vanish into the distance.

In 1913, a New Zealand engineer, William Calder, was appointed to do something about what had become the vanishing roads of Victoria. For two years, Calder and the other members of the new Country Roads Boards, McCormack and Fricke, travelled the length of every road in the state to see how bad they had become. Sometimes, the roads could only be negotiated by horse. Other times, their car, which they called Prudence, had to be coaxed through the mud. Some of Calder's adventures were scarcely less hair-raising than Hume's. The only difference was that Calder was supposed to be following roads that had already been made.

Calder thought that the main route between Sydney and Melbourne should be the road that runs through Gippsland, closer to the east coast, now called the Princes Highway. The Sydney Road was mainly for the benefit of local traffic. Even so, he was astonished by parts of it:

> Between Longwood and Wangaratta there are several fairly long sections which have originally been cleared and formed only, where the formation and in some cases the clearing is hardly discernible.

In the section further south, it was even worse. The road had deteriorated to such an extent that it no longer existed. Drivers had to find their way from tree to tree.

> Between Seymour and Longwood the old Sydney-road has practically been abandoned, and the traffic now follows a road parallel with the railway line. On this section, for considerable distances, the timber has not even been cleared, and the traffic has to wind its way in and out amongst the trees.

Calder ended up with the longest road in Victoria named after him, the one that links Melbourne, Bendigo and Mildura. He deserved it.

We got to Violet Town well ahead of our loose schedule, and went into the hotel to celebrate an easy day's work.

'What will you have?' I asked Jenny.

'The usual,' she said.

'That means metho and milk,' offered one of the drinkers.

Some of the patrons came across to congratulate me on my attractive companion. One man had seen her on the road and was going to pull over and offer her a ride.

'You mean a lift,' his mate corrected.

There was a wink in his tone which annoyed me.

'Yeah, a lift, that's what I mean.'

Then, the first man explained, he'd seen me huffing and puffing behind Jenny and realised I must have been her 'old man'. So he left us alone.

He asked me if I was one of the Kennedys.

'Do I look like JFK?' I asked.

'No, not him. He's dead.'

I had heard as much.

'No. Local mob. The Kennedys.'

I had to disappoint him.

'Don't be sorry, mate. It's not your fault.'

That night, we sat up to see the funeral of the Queen Mother. It was a funeral to die for.

Watching the solemn proceedings move at glacial speed and with glacial warmth, I felt sorry for the old Queen Mum. She was scarcely allowed to be human, even at her own funeral. At the end, a gentleman stood up and rattled off her many titles. He pronounced her 'most high, most mighty, most excellent'. Nobody acknowledged that she was none of those things now. The thing about pomp and circumstance, like everything else, is that you can't take them with you. Unlike other things, you can't leave them behind either. They just blow away like confetti.

For some reason, the Queen Mother's obsequies brought to mind a funeral I had conducted when I was a priest in an inner area of Melbourne. I was occasionally asked to say funerals for people who had died on the street or in dire circumstances, often on their own. Paupers' funerals take place every day of the year. Often I'd be the only person present other than the deceased and a bored undertaker who seldom did more than the bare minimum. I didn't blame them. It was a tedious day's work.

I always tried to do the full ritual and not to rush. It mattered in my mind that somebody should stop to observe the fact that one of our fellows had left our company. At least God knew this person, I always thought, even if nobody else did. And this funeral was no different, though it took place in 1997, on the day after that of the Princess of Wales.

The whole world had stopped for Diana, an outpouring of grief about which theses have been written. This was not going to be one of them.

Three of us stopped for Anton. First there was the undertaker. He brought in the coffin on a trolley and then retreated to the rear pew where he loosened his tie until he would be required again at the end of proceedings. I expected him to pull out the paper and start doing the crossword to fill in time. Second was me. The more casual the undertaker, the more solemn I became. On this occasion, I used all the incense, candles, holy water and prayers which I could lay my hands on. The undertaker looked at his watch several times during the service.

The third person present was Anton's next door neighbour. I asked him if he would like to say a few words, even if I would be the only person listening. He agreed. He stood up and addressed the coffin.

'Goodbye, Anton,' he said simply. 'I hope you are happy now. I hope you make some friends.'

Afterwards, the neighbour told me that this was the longest he had ever spoken to Anton. When he had first moved next door to Anton, he tried to develop a neighbourly relationship, but Anton showed no interest. He always waved over the fence but Anton never waved back. Every year, he put a Christmas card in Anton's letter box, but Anton never reciprocated. He had never once seen a visitor enter or leave Anton's house and had never heard a phone ring next door.

'He was a complete mystery. He was lucky he collapsed when he was doing his bit of shopping. They took him to hospital and he died there. He could have died at home and waited ages before anybody found his body. The odd thing was that he gave the hospital my name; he carried my phone number for emergencies. I got the shock of my life. It was like I was his next of kin. So maybe all those Christmas cards counted for something after all.'

We were moving along steadily at twenty kilometres an hour towards Seymour and proud of ourselves. We were enjoying the company of our own thoughts. I was ruminating about the Queen Mother's funeral.

'Have you ever thought of what you'd like at your own funeral?' I asked Jenny after a while.

She suggested that this wasn't something she needed to be planning with trucks speeding past the end of her elbow, dead animals on the shoulder of the road and memorials to accident victims coming upon us at regular intervals. A pig truck went past, smelling like death. We ploughed on.

In the early afternoon, we stopped at the roadhouse at Avenel where we stood in line behind half a dozen no doubt most excellent truck drivers. Nothing seemed to be happening. Wondering if there was a delay with service, I looked up ahead. A three-year-old boy was holding up the trucking industry of Australia as he made a painstaking choice between a green drink and a red one. His mother was frustrated but the truckies were patient.

'Go for the red,' said one.

'No mate, go for the lime,' said the bloke beside him.

This did not help to resolve the boy's indecision. Eventually he took the green one. The driver supporting green whistled his approval. The boy's mother turned red.

Back on the road, Jenny turned the morning question back on me. She asked me if I had ever thought what I would like to happen at my funeral.

'Don't you think that's jumping ahead a bit too far?'
'I guess so.'
'Don't you think we should be planning a wedding first?'
I looked over my shoulder. Jenny was smiling.
At that moment, three of the spokes in my back wheel decided they had had enough of carting *Anna Karenina* around. They all gave in at once.

SACRED COWS MAKE THE BEST HAMBURGERS
— Bumper sticker, Hume Highway

It was easy to decide what we wanted to do with the rest of our lives.

It was harder to decide where to spend the night.

First we had to get the buckle out of my rear wheel. The man in the bike shop in Seymour took a kindly interest. He looked at the bike Jenny was riding, which was the real McCoy, and then at the cheap one on which I was struggling to keep up.

'You two aren't together?' he asked.

We were.

'Oh, okay.'

He fixed the bike in the time it took to tell us a few useful facts. He told us the best saddles have a ridge down the middle.

'It stops the skin coming off anywhere. And I mean anywhere.'

He rode most days and averaged 38 kilometres per hour on the Hume. The other day, the wind had been good to him.

'You need to get some weight off that back wheel,' he said, poking me in the tummy with a bike pump.

He was right. I made a resolution on the spot. I dug *Anna*

Karenina out of the pannier once again and put her in a charity bin beside the train station opposite the bike shop. She was supposed to end up on the railway anyway, I thought.

We took a room at the Royal Hotel which offered what is euphemistically known as budget accommodation, meaning you had to negotiate a labyrinth of corridors and small staircases to find the bathroom. Once you got there, you didn't need thongs on your feet to stay above the water on the floor. You needed platform shoes. The bed felt like the front seat of an old Falcon. There was no TV but you could listen to the sound of mosquitoes all night. Hovell would have hated it.

The Royal Hotel, the oldest part of which was built in 1848, no doubt has a venerable place in the history both of Seymour and the road. But now it only brought to mind places we had visited friends who were down on their luck. Thinking of some of those friends made us feel sad. We wished we had stayed somewhere else. In the middle of the night, I got up to find the toilet. There was a man in a pair of shorts standing at the top of the stairs. He took a military pace towards the wall to let me past, stopping with his nose about an inch from the flaking plaster. When I came back, he was still there, staring intently at the wall. These days, many country hotels provide a place for people to live who would have trouble finding anywhere else, a lot of them struggling with mental illness. Give them credit for that. The pub also provides a bit of a community and some informal, if haphazard, support.

Once I was staying in an old pub in central west New South Wales as part of a retreat, a time of prayer and solitude. There was a large window from my room onto a wrought-iron balcony. I left the window open at night in an attempt to catch the breeze which, in the heat of summer, never seemed to come. Below me, the publican was abusing drunks, especially blacks, when they were slow to get moving at closing time. I dozed off for a while then, turning over in the middle of the night, saw a naked man standing over my bed. I was a little anxious about this. I didn't move. After a few minutes, the man scratched his balls and climbed back out through the window onto the balcony, farting as he left. The next morning, I told the publican what had happened.

'Old Zac,' he said. 'He won't harm you. Been here for years. Nowhere else to go.'

I noticed behind the bar, near the cigarettes, that the publican had a weekly pill dispenser, one of those ones with small windows for the medication you take at different times of the day. Zac's name was written clearly on it with a black marker. The publican was happy to let people drink their money and then abuse them for being drunk. But he also made sure that Zac got his medication. That's what these places are like.

The woman at the bar of Royal Hotel gave us a free beer because she wasn't happy with the way she had drawn our first ones. We sat with our drinks beside the pool table where a man with bare feet and torn shorts was playing a man in tidy overalls. The man in the shorts had a three-year-old son.

'I've come here to give the missus a break,' said the man, as he lined up his next shot.

At that moment, the little boy was frightened by a dog which had strayed in. The boy started crying and, as a result, his father missed his shot. He reacted angrily, telling the boy in black and white language that it would be his fault if he got bitten or eaten by the dog. Then it was his shot again.

The boy put the snooker triangle over his head and started toying with a broken chair, pretending that nothing had happened. He picked a cigarette butt out of an ashtray.

'He's already pretending to be brave,' said Jenny.

There was a laundromat a few doors from the pub. We returned to our suite and came back with the linen from our bed, having decided that it needed a wash as much as we did. There was a sign in the laundromat saying that due to health regulations, no horse blankets or animal rugs should be washed on the premises. We hoped we weren't breaking the rules.

Jenny talked about the great laundromats of London, many of which she had patronised during her sojourn on the Thames. Some were effectively social clubs. Others had clients who dressed up and did their hair and make-up before coming in. People studied in the laundromat, or wrote letters, or met friends, or sat in them to escape the cold. They were the chat-rooms of the pre-internet world. For the hour or so that it took to put your clothes through the machines, you could pretend to be whoever you wanted to be and others could do the same thing. Up to a point. Your laundry would eventually disclose your inmost secrets. It's hard to believe that a charming young man is completely unattached when he starts loading nappies into the tub.

We entertained each other with stories of the single life, which already seemed further behind us on the road than it really was.

Another customer arrived in the laundromat. She had a mountainous hairstyle and her washing accompanied her in a series of suitcases which were brought in from the car three at a time and then vigorously unpacked. I wasn't sure if she was going somewhere, returning from somewhere or if these were her regular laundry baskets. Before long, a man pulled up in another car out the front. His sunglasses sat high on his forehead. The minute he came out of the late afternoon glare into the gloom of the laundromat, he lowered them over his eyes.

'We have to talk, love,' he said to the woman. 'We have to talk now.'

'Not now, we don't,' she replied. 'Not here.'

'Why the hell not, love?'

'I don't believe in washing your dirty laundry in public.'

HEALTH IS MERELY THE SLOWEST POSSIBLE RATE AT WHICH ONE CAN DIE
— Bumper sticker, Hume Highway

Next day, Thursday, we went early to the supermarket to stock up on supplies for our last couple of days on the road. I inadvertently let the notebook in which I was keeping my record of the journey fall onto the conveyor belt along with the tinned tuna and cracker biscuits which had become our regular lunch. The supermarket must have had the same notebook in stock because it scanned without demur and I was outside again before I realised that I had been charged for my own diary. It cost me $1.50. I was peeved that my life was going so cheap.

A man approached us outside and asked how far we were going on the bikes. He longed to ride a bike along an old stock route that ran across the top of the Great Dividing Range from Cairns to Melbourne. Friends had done it. It had taken them three months and required them to pack a week's supplies at a time.

'A four-man tent weighs fuck all,' he assured us.

Without waiting for a reply, the man told us he was sick.

'I've got tumours like Christ.'

He mentioned the name of his disease but we had never heard of it.

'I'm not surprised. It affects one person in 200,000 and thirty women for every man. So I've had shit all luck.'

It's hard to know how to respond when a complete stranger comes up to you and, just because you are on a bike with loaded panniers, wants to tell you he is dying.

'I'll have a decent wake, that's one thing I know for sure.'

He said he could do without the pain.

'But it's not as bad as the pain when my woman went off with my mate. In the week I was diagnosed.'

The man wanted to accomplish something before his time was up.

'I want to build Australia's biggest toy.'

His dream was to create a huge model railway on a site he had selected on the Hume Highway, about ten kilometres north of Seymour. He hoped to see seven-year-olds come and play on the toy train with their grandparents.

'There'd be special accommodation for people to stay who didn't have anywhere else. They could work as volunteers in return for their keep. It might suit people out of work like your-selves.'

He gave us his card and said we could email him for free from the local library.

I couldn't remember the last time I had a hamburger for break-fast. Next to the Royal Hotel, separated by the width of a street, stood an old-fashioned burger joint which, it turned out, had been run for years by Stella Salakowski. The Caravan Cafe was an unembellished, squat brick building. Customers were sitting outside at weatherproof tables and chairs while the two women inside squeezed past each other. In the window we saw a number of newspaper clippings about the place.

According to these stories, having reached her late eighties, Stella Salakowski was now known far and wide as Mrs Sal, and was helped by her daughter, Barbara Zegir. But Mrs Sal had never aspired to make her mark as a small-order cook. She was born in New Jersey, then grew up in Poland as part of a Polish family. Barbara was born in Germany. The family arrived in Australia as refugees in 1950.

'We came with nothing. Not a thing,' they said when they saw us reading their story.

Once here, Stella had managed to find a good job in a guest house in Seymour and was doing well. Then, in 1956, her husband announced, to her surprise, that he had bought a food van. The owner, it seemed, had had chronic gambling problems.

Even today they thought this was a sad way to come into the business in which Mrs Sal had now been working for nearly fifty years. The caravan itself was gone and they'd been in the brick cafe for thirty-eight years.

Barbara told us she grew up in the place – she had been helping flip burgers since she was ten years old. In all that time, Mrs Sal had never changed the recipe for her burger patties. Nor had she divulged it to a living soul other than her daughter. They obviously relished this fact. Sometimes, the secret of success is simply having a secret.

Between burgers, Barbara said that the place has become a popular changeover point for families who've split up and now share responsibility for the care of children. When one parent is in Melbourne and another parent is in northern Victoria, it is not uncommon for them to meet at the Caravan Cafe on weekends or at the start and finish of school holidays, to talk and to transfer their children.

'I have watched a lot of those kids grow up,' said Barbara.

As customers came and went, we heard more of the story.

When Barbara's own two children went off to university, she

decided that she would do the same thing. She qualified in social-work and psychology – both useful around the Caravan Cafe. She said that she had saved marriages, sometimes by telling truck drivers that they were away too much and didn't do enough for their partners.

'I tell them they should take flowers home.'

Barbara told us she was the first woman elected to the Seymour Council, a position she held for four and a half years.

Both these women were widowed. Barbara's husband, an Albanian, had died of leukaemia nine years before. After his death, she said, she began to spend more time working with her mother. Mrs Sal's husband had died of cancer. The women were both young when their husbands died. Barbara was forty-six and Stella was fifty-two. They gave us the impression that work had been a balm, especially Stella. Barbara said that her mother had only closed the cafe one day since she took it over and that was to clean up after a flood. She had kept going during the flood itself, despite the fact that she was up to her knees in water. Later, when we asked if we could take a photo, we had to wait until Mrs Sal put on her apron. She wanted to be seen as a worker.

The photo was interrupted by the arrival of Wayne, a truck driver. Obviously a regular, he left his massive rig on the other side of the road and wandered across. Barbara brought his burger out to him and the pair talked knowledgeably about lawn bowls. Wayne then mentioned to Barbara that it had been his wife's anniversary the previous Sunday. Four years, he said, since she'd died, and left him with two young daughters; the younger of them was about to make her first Communion. They were missing their mum. So, we guessed, was he.

'It wasn't a steep learning curve when she died,' he said: 'it was like that.' He held his hand up, vertical.

'It was the same with me,' says Barbara. 'You just have to keep going.'

'You just have to keep going,' echoed Wayne.

Once the south road leaves Seymour, it heads south for the first time. It doesn't do so on any other part of its journey. It gets ready to make its second crossing of the Great Dividing Range; the first crossing takes place in the Southern Highlands of New South Wales.

As we rejoined the highway, Jenny started talking about the similarities between Mrs Sal and Mary Richardson, Henry Handel Richardson's mother. They were both, she said, women who came from other countries and found the going pretty tough once they got here. They knuckled down and survived. Not only that, they were determined to build something for their children.

We were discussing such things when Wayne slid past in his semi-trailer and gave us a friendly blast on his horn.

Then, leaving the freeway and following the old road, we reached Broadford, a place known for its paper mill, now closed. It had been a crucial industry to the town. The place was made from paper. The cafe where we had lunch still honoured the connection. The sandwiches tasted like cardboard.

Next we toiled uphill, past a monument to a pioneer apiarist, Frederick Beuhne, and into Kilmore. We were pretty chirpy and decided we were either getting fitter or that the mountains at this end of the journey weren't as steep as at the other. Both were true. In the time it had taken us to reach here from the north, erosion had taken another fraction of a millimetre off the range.

Do you want world domination with that?
— Bumper sticker, Hume Highway

Kilmore is almost within yelling distance of the outer suburbs of Melbourne which meant that Jenny and I could now stop yelling at each other. The closer we got to the city, the more reliable our mobile phones became and we found we could ring each other from bike to bike and save our voices. It was an enormous comfort to one's self-esteem to be taking calls once again, even if only from each other. My one call on the whole trip had come from a newspaper as we were watching the remains of the Queen Mother being most excellently removed from Westminster Abbey. The paper wanted me to write a piece on sex in the church. I replied that all the churches in Violet Town were closed at that hour so it would be difficult to do the research. There didn't seem to be much sex happening in the church I was watching on TV at the time either.

In the days before mobile phones, communication along the Hume was a challenge. The development of the overland mail service between Sydney and Melbourne had some of the elements of the mythical Pony Express. One of the forces behind that service was William Rutledge, the property speculator who gave Kilmore its name but never lived there. The former Hume Highway still intersects with Rutledge Street as it eases through the centre of Kilmore.

Rutledge was one of those Irish who become sentimental about places they don't have to live in, most of all Ireland. There were many towns called Kilmore in his native country, since the name means 'great church', and Rutledge's family home had been one of them. There is still plenty of evidence in this Kilmore of Irish culture, not least an annual Celtic Festival which was being advertised when we arrived.

Rutledge was born in 1806 and arrived in Sydney in 1829 where he prospered before hearing of further opportunities in Port Phillip. Having been the second person to bring stock overland from Sydney to the south, he then bought land in and around Melbourne and became one of the original members of the Melbourne Club. His land north of Melbourne was known as Rutledge's Special Survey, and is the current site of Kilmore. Rutledge had it in mind to encourage potato farming, a task he did more successfully in the Western Districts of Victoria near Port Fairy. He had realised that miners on the goldfields would need spuds and thus was among those who really did the gold rushes, the ones who woke up to the fact that there was more reliable money to be made out of supplying the wants of miners than there was out of mining. The story of Australia's transport magnates follows a similar pattern: there is as much to be made out of moving stuff as there is out of the stuff itself.

Rutledge diversified his interests and, at one time, had more coaches on the road in Victoria than the legendary Cobb and Co. He had extensive shipping interests. He was known as 'Terrible Billy' on account of his volatile temper and staccato language. He was in at the beginning of another great Australian tradition. In this country, nobody swears like a bullocky more than the bloke who owns the bullocks. If you want to hear real gutter language, the best place to look is the boardroom. It's the last vestige of egalitarianism.

Rutledge also thought money could be made in the communication industry.

The first mail between Sydney and Port Phillip ran in 1838 and was carried on horseback. One rider left Sydney heading south, another left Port Phillip heading north. They met at Howlong on the Murray, west of Albury, exchanged bags and returned to their departure point. It sounds easy. It wasn't. The northbound carrier then was John Conway Bourke and stories of how the mail got through lost nothing when he told them. One was of a horse being speared under him by an Aborigine. The horse struggled on until it expired in the waters of the Murray, leaving Bourke to bring the mail ashore as well as he could. He lost his clothes in the process, found shelter from marauding dogs in a tree where he was nearly shot by a settler – but the mail got through. It only cost ten pence then to send a letter overland between the two centres. You certainly got your money's worth. Bourke is one of those buried beside the road he shaped: his grave is in the Melbourne General Cemetery.

From 1839 to 1851, the postmen worked for William Rutledge. He replaced horses on the route with carts, an improvement which reduced the time a letter took to cover the distance from five weeks to three weeks. Rutledge once employed a mailman who managed to find his southbound counterpart without a problem. The pair celebrated the meeting by getting on the grog. Eventually, they went their respective ways. When they got home, they found they had returned with the same bags as they had taken with them: the mail from Melbourne ended up back in Melbourne.

Leaving Kilmore, with the scent of home in the air, we encountered one of the most cruel features on the Hume. The rise over the range is known as Pretty Sally, originally Pretty Sally's Hill.

In 1855, a visitor to Victoria, William Howitt, described his impression of this part of the road:

> *We were encountered by what is called the Big Hill or*
> *Pretty Sally's Hill, one of the most extraordinary hills for a*
> *road to pass over that can be conceived . . . drays with vast*
> *loads are toiling over this hill . . . The road at the last pinch*
> *went up an ascent which seemed very like the ascent of a*
> *pyramid . . .*

The real cruelty lies in the irony with which the feature was named. In the 1840s, one Sally Smith operated an illegal hotel at the foot of the hill. She made a living out of the fact that bullockies were unencumbered by drink-driving restrictions. Those about to tackle the hill welcomed a bit of dutch courage before the attempt; those heading in the other direction were glad of a place to celebrate, even one as rough as Sally Smith's premises were supposed to have been. Sally was, by all accounts, obese. She was regarded as ugly by many of her patrons. For obvious reasons she came to be known as Pretty Sally and the hill was linked to her.

In September 1847, Sally was alone in a spring cart on the road near Beveridge. The cart hit a log and flipped over. Sally was dead before help could arrive.

Sally Smith was among the first to die in a road accident on the highway.

Jenny and I stopped to take photos of ourselves on top of Pretty Sally, our last big hill, before heading down the other side. The steep decline was unnerving. Our brake pads were hot by the time we reached the foot of the hill. But we were on the homeward run now: signs of Melbourne's suburban sprawl were already in evidence and any minute now we expected to see the skyline in the distance.

There are many reminders along the road that Hume and Hovell or Hovell and Hume had passed this way before us. For the centenary of their expedition in 1924, there was a spate of unveilings. In a week-long festival between November 15 and 21, twenty-two monuments were officially sanctioned. On the whole, they are not very inspiring. In Euroa and Broadford we'd seen drinking fountains which no longer function. But a mile or two from Kilmore is a more impressive bluestone tower. This was the point at which Hume and Howell had first caught a glimpse of the sea, the moment at which they saw an end to travelling. They were ecstatic that, at last, they were going to make it. They were just as happy that they were soon to be relieved of each other's company. The bluestone tower is now in bushland. You can no longer see water from the top. You have to be satisfied with the view of the local graffiti.

At Beveridge on the outskirts of Melbourne, there is a park to celebrate the dysfunctional duo. It was not far from here that Claude Bossawa, a member of the troupe, suffered misfortune. Bossawa was not popular with the others. Reading between the lines, we'd decided that he was seen as 'slow-witted' and perhaps effeminate.

Bossawa is not mentioned by name in Hovell's journal. In his version of events published in 1853, Hume says that Claude supported Hovell in wanting to turn back when they were faced with difficulties.

> I also threatened to put Claude in the river if he did not cross it with me; at the same time seizing him by the throat, as if to make good my threat . . .

Later, Hume quoted a letter from a friend which described Bossawa as 'a chicken hearted fellow, in weight about nine stone four'. On the other hand, Hovell, in his reply, says that Bossawa was 'a practised and scientific bruiser' who would have killed

Hume except for the fact that Hovell, by virtue of his superior temperament, was able to keep them apart.

The names of Hume and Hovell's companions are commemorated in minor ways. Parts of the walking track which follows the original route are named after James Fitzpatrick and Harry Angel; both Fitzpatrick and Angel did well for themselves in later life and became landholders. William Bollard ran a hotel in Gundagai and later in Picton. Thomas Smith is thought to have become a police constable. Of the six, Thomas Boyd is best remembered on account of his appearance as an old man at the joining of the Sydney-to-Melbourne railway in 1883.

The names of all six were included in the memorial for the centenary of the expedition established at Lara, not far from Geelong, where they had mistakenly ended up. Hovell's navigational skills were less assured than his literary ones. They were supposed to be at Western Port.

Bossawa had to be carried the last part of the return journey to Gunning. He just made it home alive and then disappeared into obscurity. But he has one strange distinction. Bossawa pushed an odometer, also known as a perambulator, for almost the entire distance. It measured the miles, the yards, and sometimes the inches the men had dragged themselves. It was known disparagingly in the party as 'Claude's wheelbarrow'. Having served them stoutly, it gave up the ghost at Beveridge, on the outskirts of the modern city, where it fell apart. Hovell made a note of the occurrence: 'Perambulator hill, for here it was that it was broken to pieces.' Bossawa did not register on his scale of significance. But he had just driven the first wheeled vehicle between Sydney and Melbourne. He deserves a mention.

THE ONLY TIME THE WORLD BEATS A PATH TO YOUR DOOR IS WHEN YOU'RE IN THE BATHROOM

— Bumper sticker, Hume Highway

The road is made for cars and cars are made on this road. At Broadmeadows on the way into Melbourne you pass the headquarters of Ford Australia and the Ford Assembly Plant. It is a sizeable establishment. There are two carparks. One is full of uniform, shiny new cars, the other is full of a motley collection of vehicles in various states of repair and disrepair. One carpark is for the workers; the other is for their work.

Henry Ford created the modern world. He did not invent the car. Both Gottlieb Daimler and Karl Benz had produced cars in the mid-1880s. They were rivals then; their brand names, ironically, now belong to the same conglomerate. Ford did something more significant than invent the automobile. He invented the automobile consumer. The fact that he found a way in which cars could be mass-produced was certainly important. But with that he found a way in which human aspiration could be mass-produced to create the demand which he had set himself to supply. His assembly line did not just make cars. It supplied dreams.

Ford was born in 1863 and grew up on a farm in Dearborn,

Michigan. Dearborn is no longer rural; it is now part of Detroit, the city Ford defined. Ford was an industrialist yet he entertained an unreal reverence for nature. One of the most curious gatherings in America during World War I was comprised of Henry Ford, Thomas Edison and Harvey Firestone, the tyre magnate. The three industrialists went camping for a fortnight together every year. It was a major expedition. They found primal healing in the wild which gave them the energy they required to get back to their work of ripping into the environment and supplying machines for every need, real or imagined. Ford himself came to romanticise his rural upbringing. When he was rich, he had his childhood home rebuilt. He had the garden excavated to find shards of broken cups and plates his mother may have used, had them reproduced and put them on display.

You couldn't be Henry Ford and not be the subject of folklore. His mother died in childbirth when he was twelve. Soon afterwards, he noticed a self-propelled steam vehicle in the neighbourhood. He was instantly fascinated. It's hard not to conclude that he had found a substitute for the mother he'd lost and with whom he became obsessed.

Ford designed and built a number of cars before the famous Model T. His first, the gangly Quadricycle, appeared in 1896. But it was in 1908 that Ford fulfilled his vow to 'build a motor car for the great multitude'. Part of the car's purpose, ironically, was to enhance the buyer's appreciation of nature:

> . . . it will be so low in price that no man making a good salary
> will be unable to own one – and enjoy with his family the
> blessing of hours of pleasure in God's great open spaces.

The Model T was reliable, affordable, versatile and easy to drive. It was also impossible to lock your keys in. Within ten years, half the cars in the world were Model Ts. By the time production of them finally stopped in 1927, fifteen million vehicles had been sold. The

Model T had been customised to serve every conceivable purpose from taxi to hay cart, from ambulance to hearse. The car still has its devotees. In 2001, Model T drivers and owners gathered in Gunning for a rally. They came from far and wide; by the time they all assembled, 150 Model T Fords lined the showground oval. The owners said they never had trouble getting spare parts. It was easier to get them for a Model T than for many later model cars; they didn't even need to scrounge around for them second-hand. Such is the demand, that there are still places in the United States making parts for Model T Fords. It is possible to assemble an entire Model T from new parts. You can have a brand new antique if you want one.

The success of the Model T would not have been possible without the development of, first, the assembly line and, second, the moving assembly line. In the first instance a worker moved around and did the same job over and over; in the second instance the job came to the worker. This was more efficient and Ford was ruthless at that level. He specified the dimensions of the boxes in which parts he ordered were to be delivered to his factory because he wanted to use the wood in the crates to provide the flooring in his cars.

The Ford Company opened the Broadmeadows assembly plant on 27 January 1960. Until then, this was an area of market gardens. Now the government promised to extend a railway line to reach the new factory. Ford had come here because land was cheap and the new suburbs in the north of Melbourne offered a suitable workforce. Those suburbs had been created by 'new Australians'. They came to work on bicycles to make the cars they aspired to own. The plant came to have a significant impact on the economy, and it still does. It now employs about half the number of workers it did initially. But they make more cars. Call that progress.

The first cars assembled at Broadmeadows were Ford Zephyrs and Ford Anglias. But it wasn't long before Broadmeadows became the home of the Ford Falcon, one of the staples of Australian family life for forty years. Between 1960 and 2001, two and a half million of these vehicles rolled off the assembly line of Ford's plant at Broadmeadows.

Having spent the last fortnight dealing with the behaviour of cars when they grow up and leave home, it seemed only right to visit a maternity ward to see where they are born.

Adrian Ryan started work as a young man in the public relations department at the Broadmeadows plant in 1982. He'd grown up in northern Victoria. He remembers the Ford plant as one of the first signs of the approaching city when his family travelled the Hume to Melbourne. It was the point at which the kids started asking if they would soon see trams.

Not long after he started work, Ryan said, he noticed an old car lying in the wilderness at the back of the plant. It was quietly rusting in the long grass. Ryan made enquiries and found that this was the very first Falcon to have rolled off the line. By now it was over twenty years old and desperately unloved.

'Its tyres had gone and it was covered in birdshit,' says Ryan.

So Ryan had persuaded his employers to let him restore the car and display it at a motor show. After that, he began collecting bits and pieces of memorabilia.

In many ways, it was a counter-cultural thing to do. Henry Ford is renowned for having said 'history is more or less bunk'. That line is often taken out of context. It was uttered in the course of a trial during which Ford was accused of being an ignorant anarchist because he didn't know certain historical facts. He was arguing that history books were bunkum. But the line stuck. Ford spent years trying to salvage his reputation, so much so that he collected all sorts of historical artefacts to establish the kind of museum in which, as he thought, people could see and touch the past and not just learn about it through the prejudices of an author. It was a forerunner of the hands-on, interactive museum. Ford had a passionate interest in history, especially industrial history. His favourite historical subject was himself.

Nevertheless, Adrian Ryan pointed out that when any new model is produced a car company goes out of its way to destroy all the promotional material that pertained to the previous one. It doesn't want to confuse the public. A fortune is spent to create the impression of something new. All marketing, however repetitive, is targeted at the present.

'So much effort goes into preserving the future,' he said.

Ryan had gathered a lot of this discarded material and his accumulation is the basis of what is now the Ford Discovery Centre in Geelong.

'I simply asked people to send material my way before they chucked it out.'

The Ford Discovery Centre is elegant, the kind of place where the past looks brand new. Cars from different eras, some of them on loan to the centre, have been immaculately restored. TV monitors play Ford advertisements from bygone ages. Looking at generations of TV advertisements, it's obvious that the car industry has had little to do with helping people get around. It's main purpose has been to keep people interested in sex. Without the right car, none of us would ever have had a chance. Sex would have just rusted away.

Adrian Ryan works downstairs in a concrete bunker, out of sight of the public, surrounded by cyclone wire. His desk is an old door balanced on cartons of brochures. He is surrounded by bulging filing cabinets and overflowing boxes. It's hardly the showroom floor.

'You know,' Ryan said to us, 'Henry Ford got the concept for the moving assembly line from visiting an abattoir.'

Ford had seen carcasses swung around in a meatworks while

the butchers stood in one place to trim the meat as it came to them. His best idea was born in a slaughterhouse.

'Ford thought that instead of pulling something apart, the same idea could be used to put something together.'

The main building at Broadmeadows turned out to be almost as big as the town where I live. It covers 13.3 hectares – 34 acres. During a normal shift, 1,800 people work on one floor under the same roof. We joined a tour group, and found ourselves being taken around on a small train. We were given headphones so we could hear the commentary. The workers were also wearing ear protection. The place is noisy but the inhabitants work in a silent world.

Most of the people on our tour were new recruits to the company. We were all shown around by Geoff. He had started work at the Broadmeadows plant in 1962.

'It was the week the first Cortina came off the line.'

Geoff had retired twelve years before, but still helped with tours. We were not allowed into the paint shop because we'd all have had to change into lint-free clothing. Nor were we allowed to know what was under a huge tent outside: evidently a new model being kept under wraps.

The main building was a meal in itself. Geoff had every inch of the place measured and every screw counted. The conveyor belt was 11 kilometres long. There were 130 robots working on it. The robots were all arms, doubled-jointed and moving in measured spasms.

'The robots have been introduced gradually since 1982. All the people replaced by robots were given jobs elsewhere. The robots give us 100 per cent repeatability and they never get tired.'

Fifty or sixty trucks arrive every day with engines which are made at the Ford plant in Geelong. Other components are shipped in by suppliers, who must work under exacting pressure.

Deadlines are unbending, as the assembly plant only keeps half a day's stock of components on hand. This saves paying for storage space. New seats are delivered for installation every twenty minutes. If any part of the process takes more than a minute, that stage is duplicated to keep things moving. The result is anywhere between 400 and 500 new Falcons every day. It is only a percentage of the cars produced every day in Australia and a tiny fraction of the cars produced in the world.

Once our tour train stopped for a few minutes while Geoff checked on something. I watched one of the workers for a while. Every fifteen seconds, he turned around and pulled two cords through from the luggage compartment of an incomplete car into where the back seat would soon be fitted. Then, with the other hand, he pulled another cord in the opposite direction. He didn't need to look; he knew exactly where the cords would be. After he'd performed this operation, he turned on his heel through one hundred and eighty degrees to continue reading the newspaper that was open on a bench behind the assembly line. He read a few lines of a story and then, without looking at his watch, knew the precise second at which he needed to turn around to attend to the next car with the next three cords. He did this over and over. Just like in the movies. The first time he performed his manoeuvre it looked balletic. The tenth time it looked robotic. His expression never wavered, he never looked up and he never stopped reading.

I FISH AND I VOTE
I SHOOT AND I VOTE
I SHIT AND I VOTE
I PRAY AND I VOTE
— Bumper stickers, Hume Highway

I DON'T CARE AND I DON'T VOTE
— Bumper sticker, Hume Highway

There is plenty to look at as you inch your way into Melbourne. A major residential development at Craigieburn was promoting itself as 'the promised land'. They should have said 'the promised house'. The suburbaners who were creating it were rising to the most important challenge faced by contemporary builders: to put the largest possible house on the smallest possible land – a task which is accomplished by moving things indoors, such as pools, gardens and cars, which used to belong outdoors. Even then, there can be land left begging. So these bits are covered with lawn which arrives like carpet, wears like carpet and is occasionally vacuumed like carpet.

Any leftover interior space is filled with bathrooms. Most project homes have a bathroom for each bedroom and a spare one, just in case. All those bathrooms use a lot of water. The bathroom used to be a necessity tucked out of sight; it is now the major recreation precinct. People show them off. A real estate agent told me once that people don't buy houses, they buy kitchens and bathrooms. The house is just somewhere to keep them. The land is just somewhere to keep the house.

At the same time as people have become devoted to the improvement of their own private wetlands, public waterways have suffered neglect. Opposite the hoardings for the Craigieburn development was a sign advertising a new freeway soon be constructed in the area. It will replace the old Hume and, at the time we cycled past, was priced at $306 million. The new road is an inevitability. After all, Sydney has a freeway right into town. So Melbourne will want one as well. The cities are siblings. If one gets something, the other has to have it too.

There is no doubt that road access to Melbourne from the north has become a major problem. For Jenny and me, the most nerve-racking part of the whole journey was riding into town along the narrow highway. It was slow-moving, congested, polluted and unpredictable. We would have moved onto the footpath, which looked a lot safer, except for the fact that I wanted to say that I had ridden the whole length of the highway. I did not want to be disqualified on a technicality.

Something had to give. But a new freeway would not be without other costs, part of which involved the fate of Merri Creek, where we took our journey's last quiet moment.

Merri Creek is hardly one of the great waterways of the world. A trip along its entire length from Wallan to Dights Falls, where it meets the Yarra, might pale beside a journey up the Nile. But it's different when you see it through the eyes of Ann and Bruce McGregor. For twenty-five years or more they have been part of a group which has planted trees, organised clean-ups and lobbied councils and governments to stop Merri Creek vanishing. The results, we could see as we paused to breathe some real air, spoke for themselves. Merri Creek is not just a watercourse which could as well be replaced by a drain. It supports a unique natural environment. The best-known endangered species which calls Merri Creek home – the Growling Grass Frog. And there are plenty of other species too, both flora and fauna, which depend on it.

Ann and Bruce know Merri Creek like an old friend. One of its most interesting stretches, at Craigieburn East, is within sight of the current Hume Highway. Here, Ann and Bruce were able to point out rare native grasses, by name. They identified the voices of birds such as Reed Warblers, Moorhens and especially Kingfishers. They indicated gnarled river gums which have slowly carved themselves into elaborate natural sculptures over hundreds of years; a bluestone creek crossing which dates back to the century before last. Historian David Moloney has written about the site of a sheep station which was occupied by John Batman, the founder of Melbourne, in the very early years of the colony – that sheep station was surely close by. So archeological evidence of that settlement may well be waiting to be gathered.

Close to all this, there were stakes in the ground, marked with ribbons and colours, which indicated where the new F2 freeway into Melbourne will sweep all before it. They looked as innocent as stakes for grandma's tomato plants.

There were alternatives. In December 2001, Professor Bill Russell was among those who published a report on ways to improve access to Melbourne from the north. In late 2002, the Friends of Merri Creek took a case to the Federal Court to contest the freeway project. The group argued that the builders had not considered 'feasible and prudent' alternatives. Mr Justice Finkelstein handed down his decision in July 2003. The group described it as 'disappointing'.

'We didn't take an injunction,' said Max Sargent, the president of the group. 'We just didn't have the money to put up.'

It appears likely that, before long, both the Albury and

Craigieburn freeways will be open for trucks, cyclists and everything in between. Traffic will then be able to drive the entire length of the Hume and Hovell expedition, from Geelong to Sydney, without encountering a traffic light or stop sign.

PARKING IS SUCH SWEET SORROW
— Bumper sticker, Hume Highway

'If we ever cycle the road again,' I pointed out to Jenny, 'we won't have to stop.'

Jenny laughed. I knew we wouldn't be cycling this way again. Along the road, Jenny had once or twice expressed misgivings about throwing herself into something which was, after all, my silly idea. There were days when it was sheer hard work. If we had a fortnight to ride somewhere, there were far prettier and more soothing places we could have gone than the length of the country's busiest truck route. She wondered if her life would be swamped by my crazy ideas. She wanted to have a few of her own.

But along the way we had discovered a crazy idea which we both felt passionate about and could work on together. That was marriage. I guess it meant that if, in her old age, Jenny came up with the idea of travelling the road in a wheelchair, I'd have to come along too. There would be worse ways to be spending old age. I just hope they make panniers big enough for all the gear I'll need by then.

Hume and Hovell made it. There was nobody to welcome them at Corio Bay. It's possible that the escaped convict William Buckley, who was lurking around Point Lonsdale, not far from their journey's end, heard of their arrival on the bush telegraph. Buckley was a soldier who'd served against Napoleon but was sentenced in 1802 to fourteen years transportation for receiving a bolt of stolen cloth. He escaped from the fledgling settlement at Sorrento in 1803 and was presumed to have perished in the bush. But he enjoyed rude good health both on his own and in Aboriginal society until he introduced himself to John Batman, who was setting up the village of Melbourne, in 1835.

Buckley's story gives rise to the expression for an unlikely occurrence: 'Buckley's chance'. His survival was remarkable. No less remarkable was the apparent ease with which he rejoined white society once he discovered Batman. He went to Tasmania where he got a job as a storekeeper which, by any conventional psychological reckoning, he had Buckley's chance of settling into. But he held the same post for twelve years. He regained his ability to speak English and compiled various memoirs. In one set, he described himself during the years of his 'savage life' as 'a wild inhabitant of the wilderness, almost in reality'. Buckley had a rare gift. He could settle.

Hume was not so lucky. In 1867, over forty years after getting home, he was still trying to convince people that Buckley had come running after them, desperate to escape from paradise into the civilised desperation of his ill-humoured expedition. Buckley, according to Hume, was just a bit too late. They had already turned for home.

It was a pity. Buckley could have taken them back to his cave and taught them to sit still for a minute. 'How easy it is for the human being, as well as every other,' Buckley said to his ghost writer in 1852, 'to change his habits, taste, and I may add, feelings, when made the mere creature of circumstance.'

Jane Franklin, heading the other way, also made it. After six weeks on the roads of 1839, she was received 'cordially' by Governor Sir George Gipps and Lady Gipps. She found her accommodation satisfactory. Parties were organised to fete her. She took them as her due.

EVERYTHING IS POSSIBLE. THE IMPOSSIBLE JUST TAKES LONGER.
— Bumper sticker, Melbourne

We made it.

Some of our friends gathered in a hotel in Fitzroy to fete our modest achievement. We'd had the good sense to arrive about the time most people were finishing work on a Friday afternoon. We had the added sense to let everyone know that Jenny and I would be getting hitched in the spring. This meant that we didn't have to buy our own drinks.

Among our friends was Chris Nolan.

In 1996, aged twenty-eight, Chris was working as a lawyer in Hanoi. He had first gone to Vietnam on an Austrade fellowship and had made friends there. One night, he went out to dinner. The following day, his family received a call to say that Chris was in a coma in Hanoi hospital. He was not given much chance of survival. He had a suffered a multi-organ collapse and, because of a lack of oxygen during the extended period before he was found, he had sustained hypoxic brain injury. To this day, the cause of Chris's illness is unknown. Eventually he was airlifted to Singapore, then to intensive care at St Vincent's Hospital and then to an aged-care facility in North Fitzroy, near the pub where, now, we were already embellishing the story of our eleven days on the Hume.

What for many people would have been the end of the road has become the beginning of a new and difficult journey for Chris, his family and friends. For six months, Chris gave no evidence of being able to communicate with others. Neurologists suggested that he would remain a vegetable. Then one day, his cousin was talking in his room about a photo of an old truck from the family property at Meredith. Chris started laughing at the banter. He had emerged from his coma; sixty or seventy friends visited him over the next twenty-four hours.

Chris is unable to move. He can't see much and he can't speak. But he still laughs. He laughs when his mother, Mary, says that his friends don't want him to speak too soon because they have confided too many of their secrets to him. He also cries. He cried when one of his elderly room mates, Ben, died. Those close to him know how difficult he finds it when people treat him, in the language of people familiar with brain injury, as if he is 'not cognitive', as if he is not there. Chris uses a long blink for 'yes', although it often takes about fifteen seconds for him to respond. His negatives are harder to read. Little by little, some improvement in the movement of one hand gives hope that he might be able to use a switch to communicate. His progress has been slow but ground-breaking. One doctor commented that Chris made him wonder about other patients he had known whom he had dismissed as beyond rehabilitation.

Chris is an intimate part of the lives of people close to him. There are hundreds of young people living in nursing homes all over Australia, most of them survivors of road accidents. A teenager or twenty-something with an acquired brain injury resulting from a car accident tends not to attract the unalloyed sympathy that a young person suffering from cancer will attract. There are often unspoken questions about whether or not the victim was driving too fast, drinking too much or taking too little care. In other words, there can be an unstated element of blame. It is not as callous as thinking that they got what they deserved. Just a thought that the rest of us don't need the grace of God to avoid going there because the rest of us would be more careful.

The victims are parked in nursing homes, places which are seldom well suited to cope with the music young people like and the hours they keep. Like it or not, for most people nursing homes are close to the end of the line. Chris is nowhere near the end of the line.

Chris made his slow progress from the nursing home to the pub. It's a long trip for him.

'Chris, if you get a puncture,' says Eileen, the friend who lent Jenny her bike, 'I'm sure Michael can fix it for you.'

Chris blinks and smiles.

I look down at his wheels. They are just like ours, with spokes and rims and tyres. It just takes more to make his move. They make longer journeys than ours, but over shorter distances.

'How has Chris been today?' I asked Mary, his mother.

'He's been a bit restless.'

Six

The years ahead were never going to be easy for Cliff Young. He had spent sixty years learning how to live in his own company. Before long, however, Cliff married Mary Howell, thirty-five years younger than himself.

'If I had a feed for every kiss I'd had up until that stage of my life, I would have died of starvation.'

During their courtship, as they were out training, Cliff was stung by a bee on his penis. He was a modest gentleman who related proudly that he did not take advantage of Mary to relieve the situation. His mother was not happy about the match.

Westfield hosted a tacky re-run of the wedding and a reception in one of their shopping centres. A reporter who became a friend of Young's had the good grace, twenty years later, to say, 'We milked the Cliff phenomenon until a lovely tale about a simple bloke became silly and laughable . . . We were more childish than ever Cliff was.' The reporter was sorry that he had become involved in stunts such as booking the suite next to Cliff and Mary's to get a scoop of Cliff's views of marriage. Cliff himself maintained an innocence. He joked in his autobiography about the experience of losing his virginity at the age of sixty-two.

'It took a bit of time to get my act together. About two minutes, I reckon.'

Cliff wrote that he'd happily recommend sex to others in moderation. But he also laments that, as things developed, his marriage was to have a lot of problems.

'The cause of most of it was the darn phone.'

One day, Cliff was so sick of Mary talking on the phone that he told her she could pay the bill herself and he went home to his mother. He returned later in the day to try and bury the hatchet. Mary was still on the phone.

The couple separated in 1989 but 'remained friends'.

Young tried to repeat his success in the first ultra-marathon but was never able to do so. The following year, running the route in reverse from Melbourne to Sydney, he managed to complete the journey. But it cost him. He was now carrying the weight of celebrity as well. Crowds waited for hours in country towns as Cliff fell behind schedule. Local mayors asked to be woken at any hour of the night so they could welcome him. Kids rode their bikes alongside him. But Cliff just wanted to get it over with.

Only once more, in 1987, did Cliff finish the run along the Hume. That year it took him nine and a half days, almost twice as long as his original feat. But nothing to sneeze at. He was four years older by now. In November 1994, he was still able to run 150 kilometres in a day. In 1997, he set out to run around Australia. He covered 6,520 kilometres before giving it away. He was seventy-five. By then, Cliff was receding into the twilight of 'where are they now'. He retired to the Sunshine Coast in Queensland. The population had moved on. Eventually, Cliff suffered a stroke and was incapacitated. Over the same period, the Hume was body-building. It put on more and more muscle.

For the five days he ran the road in 1983, Cliff was the lightest traffic on it. He looked even more frail for the nine days he struggled in 1987. By then, he was almost a figure of derision. He was, many thought, a silly old man who didn't know when enough was enough and should have been content with his first victory. He was a mere insect compared to the trucks whose back-draught could lift him off his feet.

Cliff Young died in Queensland on Sunday night, 2 November 2003. He was a brief item on Monday morning's news which was mainly taken up with preparations for the Melbourne Cup to be run the following day. It is ironic that Australia's worst dressed athlete should have died at the start of Cup Week. He was eighty-one, had lived almost 30,000 days and was remembered for five of them.

But Cliff did something to the road. For a few days, when Cliff was running, the road took on a human character. It was both his companion and his adversary. He cast a spell over it. He was small enough to bring it to life.

BABY ON BOARD
— Bumper sticker, Hume Highway

The south road also heads north.

Mark Twain worked as a riverboat pilot on the Mississippi which meant becoming intimate with every nook and cranny of the river over 1,200 miles. It was highly skilled work, a job which both drew on and nurtured Twain's prodigious capacity for observation. In his time, a riverboat pilot earned as much as the Vice President of the United States. Pilots steered the economy of the union. Twain said that the river heading north was a different creature from the one heading south. The boats followed a different bank. The surface of the water told a different story:

> *The face of the water in time became a wonderful book, a book that was a dead language to the uneducated passenger, but which told its mind to me without reserve . . . it was not a book to be read once and thrown aside, for it had a new story to tell every day . . .*

The Hume Highway is not as subtle as Merri Creek, let alone the Mississippi. It was not carved by nature.

But the highway, like the river, is a different creature riding north than south. The hills catch different light, the sun is more likely to be behind you in the afternoon, parts of the north-bound road are not even visible from the southbound lanes. Heading north by car, I once noticed a roadside memorial to two priests who had died in a road accident on the Hume. I had known one of them slightly. The pair had been on their way to a meeting. Doubtless, their lives were full of meetings. The road does that. It turns banality into something else and doesn't give much notice. The memorial is not visible from the southbound carriageway.

A few months after we rode into Melbourne, Jenny and I were moving north. By that stage, we were married and I had got to the end of *Anna Karenina*. There is a character in it called Levin, another restless spirit. In the end, he decides that it is better to stay still and let the stars move in the heavens above him. It doesn't matter that the astronomers say that the stars are stationary and the earth is moving. You can be moving, but still at rest. Levin says that 'love saved him from despair'. Anna Karenina's tragedy is that she reaches her destination. She sets out for the railway to kill herself and she gets there. Levin doesn't get anywhere in particular. He surrenders to a sense of his smallness under the wide canopy of heaven.

The road begs the same question. On any given day, any traveller on it is only one among thousands. There isn't much point in that traveller thinking that the purpose of their journey, or the value of their cargo, or the importance of the people they are going to meet, really changes their significance. A car is just a tin can with wheels. Hurtling along at 110 kilometres per hour, it is a vulnerable place to be sitting. The experience of that fragility is significant for any individual, as is the humble realisation that they need never complete the journeys they set out upon. Not one roadside memorial on the Hume says where the people who died were going. They all mark the spot where they came to rest.

There are two common ways of musing about roads. The first is represented by the stage directions at the start of Beckett's *Waiting For Godot*.

A country road. A tree. Evening.

Vladimir and Estragon sit by the side of the road, exchanging small talk and banter, waiting for someone or something to turn up. They have no idea what it might be. They wait as passively as garbage bins. They are at the mercy of fate. The world, whatever that might mean, is indifferent to them.

A more common way of musing is represented by *The Wizard of Oz*. The yellow brick road will take you to the land of your dreams where you will find courage, brains and good heart. But in Frank Baum's fairytale, the Wizard of Oz points out to the Scarecrow that he does have brains. He just needs to use them, to wake up to the fact that 'you are learning something every day'. The Lion does have courage: 'true courage is in facing danger when you are afraid, and that kind of courage you have in plenty.' There was no need to go on a journey at all.

This way of thinking is widespread. Henry Ford didn't read much. But he did enjoy the essays of Ralph Waldo Emerson. Emerson believed that there was a universe within each individual and that the deity resided there. 'A man contains all that is needful to his government within himself,' said Emerson. He wrote an essay entitled 'The Over-Soul':

We know that all spiritual being is in man . . . there is no bar

> *or wall in the soul where man, the effect, ceases and God, the*
> *cause begins.*

Such words were music to Ford's ears. They told him he was God. *The Wizard of Oz* is sweeter music but it follows much the same melody.

Waiting for Godot represents a kind of fatalism in which people are powerless. They are roadside refuse. Godot never turns up. The *Wizard of Oz* represents a kind of individualism in which people are all-powerful. They can achieve anything and still be home in time for tea.

Neither of these ideas appeals to me.

I'll tell you what does.

The road can go in two directions at once. Maybe more. But the rest of us can only go in one. We are enriched by what we can't do and even more by what we choose not to do. The secret of being human is learning how to enjoy our limitations. Just about anyone can ride a bike from Sydney to Melbourne on their own. But it's impossible to squeeze the pimple in the middle of your back without help. If we could do everything, we wouldn't need other people and we wouldn't need a road. None of us is God. I just like to pretend sometimes that I am. Those have been the loneliest times.

Not long after I got to the end of *Anna Karenina*, Jenny was feeling unwell. We'd only been married for a few weeks. In spite of being a dumb male, I was learning to read the subtle body language of my intimate partner. By the time Jenny had been to the bathroom three times in one morning to throw up, I realised that she was not feeling her best. I was concerned that my presence in her life was having this effect already. She was no longer worshipping me. She was kneeling before the toilet.

We soon suspected that I was, indeed, partly to blame.

I was despatched to the supermarket to get a pregnancy test. I could have gone to the chemist near Jenny's flat, but the staff there were a bit too friendly. There are some things a couple prefers to keep between themselves and a disinterested checkout operator. I put the test at the bottom of a basket and covered it with a few groceries we didn't really need. I chose a checkout where the operator looked vacant. I assumed that everything from turps to toothpaste was just a barcode to her. I was wrong. She weighed the onions and carrots in a tired way. Then she saw the test kit. She stopped and smiled. It was like somebody had opened a window.

'It's not for me,' I explained.

She stopped smiling.

The test was positive. It's the only thing I have ever known to respond positively to being pissed on.

We made an appointment to see the doctor.

'Is this your first pregnancy?' she asked when we arrived.

It was.

'Do you want this pregnancy?'

I started crying. We both did. I'm not sure why. The doctor didn't press us for an answer. I guess some tears say yes and other tears say no and there's folk that know how to read them.

'I'm sorry,' I said, reaching for an excuse. 'I think I forgot to put money in the parking meter.'

Afterwards, we had a sandwich and talked about what we'd have for dinner that night and discussed a list of unimportant things.

'You know our lives are about to change,' said Jenny, cutting through a few layers of trivia.

More tears turned up. I'm sure they arrived from every-where all at the same time: anxiety and excitement, fear and faith, resistance and surrender, selfishness and love. It's not so easy to figure out some tears. They're on the doorstep and unloading their baggage before you can figure out what they've come for.

HEAVEN IS WHERE THE DONKEY FINALLY CATCHES THE CARROT
— Bumper sticker, Hume Highway

The trip north was more arduous than the one south. Some friends came round and helped us pack all of Jenny's belongings, including her car, into a crate. This was then loaded onto a truck bound for Gunning. The driver didn't do many long-distance deliveries. His girlfriend came along for the ride.

'What road do we take?'

'Just take the Hume.'

'That's the one that heads north, isn't it?'

'That's the one.'

We followed in my car. It was hot. The country along the road was deep in drought. We made regular stops. When we finally arrived, it was already dark. Our neighbours had been in to open the windows and air the house. A stranger had left a note under our door saying that one of our shrubs had blackspot and we should bathe it with the soapy water from our washing machine if we wanted to get rid of it.

'This is no place to hide, is it?' said Jenny.

The drought was cruel. The world looked like it was in pain.

The hills around town looked brittle; you could imagine they would snap under your foot. The country doesn't wear make-up. It speaks its truth baldly and doesn't lie. It was hurting.

But all over town, houses were being renovated. The value of property had escalated. One reason was the opening of the new freeway into Sydney. In one day, it had moved Gunning half an hour closer to the big smoke. Ten years before, the road had taken people away. Now it was bringing them back again. The road giveth and the road taketh away. People were finding the place. There was a new family in the old convent. The town was divided over a proposal to build an enormous roadhouse on the freeway.

'We're mortgage refugees,' a newcomer told me. 'It's cheaper here.'

'Ah, yes,' I said wisely, thinking back to the time just two years before when you could buy a house here for the cost of a car.

We called our little boy Benedict. St Benedict was a hermit who lived in the fifth century, at a time when the Roman Empire was collapsing. He lived in uncertain times. Everybody does. At the insistence of friends, Benedict emerged from his cave and agreed to lead a community of monks. He wrote a rule for them called, of course, *The Rule of St Benedict*. It is a humane and sensible approach to living.

Benedict thought that night-time was a natural time for prayer. The main reason for this, I think, was that he saw prayer as a form of listening. The first word in the Rule is 'Listen'. It begins by asking people to 'Listen with the ear of the heart'. Throughout the Rule the word 'listen' comes up again and again. It seems to be the only hard and fast instruction Benedict wanted to give. Perhaps that is why he said that spoken prayers should be brief. He didn't want people to be such chatterboxes that God couldn't get a word in edgeways:

We must know that God regards our purity of heart and tears of compunction, not our many words.

The one Psalm Benedict asked monks to say every single day was Psalm 94. It includes the words 'if today you hear God's voice, harden not your hearts'. For Benedict, the ear and the heart seemed to be joined together. We were learning that with our Benedict. Every time he laughed or cried or gurgled, it touched something in us.

St Benedict is often said to be the founder of Christian monasticism. I prefer to think of him as the man who called contemplative people in from the deserts and caves where they did a lot of weird stuff, much of it anti-social. One of them, St Simeon, lived on top of a pillar for thirty-six years. He stood all day, shouted sermons to people below and impressed them with his holiness by performing feats of extreme asceticism, such as hundreds of continuous genuflections. Simeon was typical of a movement. Benedict, on the other hand, had an even more radical idea; he challenged people to be home-makers. His rule is full of homely advice about how much to eat and drink, how much to sleep, how to look after the young, the old and the weak, how to forgive those you live with. He is well known for urging moderation in all things.

His rule suggests that people should be happy. In its time, this was uncommon sense. He hoped that his followers might grow in three areas in particular. He named them as humility, stability and hospitality. The last two come together. It's hard to make room for others unless you know where your own roots are; it's hard to answer the door if you don't belong inside. The most stable people are often the most hospitable.

Before our Benedict was born, one of our friends emailed us to say that the two things which every parent needs are a pair of ear plugs and a subscription to pay-TV. He said there was nothing decent on TV in the middle of the night (unless we liked the infomercials) and we would need something to occupy us when we were keeping vigil with our baby. Every parent knows that being up in the middle of the night is a bit of a drag. Holding a baby in the middle of the night, we were not always sure what to do or even whether we were going to cope. We dreamt of a wonderful future for Benedict but wondered how we would make it through the next day. All we could do was surrender.

But we also noticed how still the rest of the world is at that time. We noticed subtle sounds which, during the day, lie beyond consciousness. We counted the carriages on the interstate goods trains as they lumbered past; we noticed the small sounds of nature as it stirred from rest at some ungodly hour. More than anything, we listened to the road, a mile or more in the distance. The Hume Highway is alive at night. The trucks are hungry then. They pace up and down, covering their tracks over and over. On a clear winter's night, we could hear every noise they made. They moaned in the background, like the sea in rough weather. We listened to little Benedict close to us. We held him and wondered where his road would take him and where he would rest.

A NOTE ON SAUCES

The following sauces are available at Truckstop 31:

BBQ Sauce, Chilli Sauce Hot, Chilli Sauce Medium, Chilli Sauce Mild, Chilli Sauce Sweet, Chilli Sauce Sweet (with Ginger), Father's Favourite Sauce, Hickory Sauce, HP Sauce, Mint Sauce, Mustard Sauce, Oyster Sauce, Pepper Steak Sauce, Pick-Me-Up Sauce, Plum Sauce, Satay Sauce, Soy Sauce, Soy Sauce Low Salt, Spicy Red Sauce, Steak Sauce, Tabasco Sauce, Teriyaki Sauce, Thick Mint Sauce, Tomato Sauce, Worcestershire Sauce, Worcestershire Steak Sauce.

Apart from all those whose names are mentioned in the text, I owe an enormous debt of gratitude to many people. They are the real sauce. They include Bum Bag, Peter Bishop (and Varuna Writers House), Joe Bono, Ken Coggan, Barbara David, Lyn Dowling, John and Margaret Emery, Jenny Gleeson, Margaret Gleeson, Alan Gould, Sally Heath, Bill Jennings, Liz Kemp, Richard Leonard, Eileen McCormick, Shane Maloney, John Martis, Alex Mattea, Marcelle Mogg, David Moloney, Mel Morrow, Les Murray (especially for permission to quote from *The Burning Truck*),

Chris Nolan, Mary Nolan, Penny Russell, Alex Rutledge, Eddie Schubert (from VicRoads in Melbourne), Coralie Scott, Jack Waterford, Don Watson, Barry Whitney, Nona and Peter Willis, Mark Worsnop. Mike Coley and Simon Cook built a room for me to work in, without which this book would still be a pile of notes. Fran Bryson, my agent, Judith Lukin-Amundsen, my editor, and Nikki Christer, my publisher, Chris Mattey and Annie Coulthard all got out and pushed at different times.

For Sale

- One male bike. Low kilometres. Saddle may require attention.
- Well-thumbed copies of the following are also for sale by an indebted author. They will all fit comfortably into two panniers.

Peter Alexander, *Les Murray: A Life in Progress* (Oxford, 2000); W.K. Anderson, *Roads for the People: a History of Victoria's Roads* (VicRoads/Hyland House, 1994); Neil Baldwin, *Edison: Inventing the Century* (Hyperion, 1995); Judith Bassett, 'The Faithful Massacre at the Broken River, 1838' in *Journal of Australian Studies*, No. 24, May 1989; Phil Belbin and David Burke, *Changing Trains: a Century of Travel on the Sydney–Melbourne Railway* (Methuen, 1982); Geoffrey Blainey (ed.), *Henry Lawson* (Text, 2002); Les Carlyon, *Gallipoli* (Pan Macmillan, 2001); Axel Clark, *Henry Handel Richardson: Fiction in the Making* (Simon and Schuster, 1990); Manning Clark, *A History of Australia* (Melbourne University Press, various years); Manning Clark, *Henry Lawson: the Man and the Legend* (Sun Books, 1985); Frank Clune, *Journey to Canberra* (Angus & Robertson, 1960); David Day, *Chifley* (Harper-Collins, 2001); Michael Duffy, *Man of Honour: John Macarthur* (Macmillan, 2003); E.E. Dunlop, *The War Diaries of Weary Dunlop* (Penguin, 1990); Sue Ebury, *Weary – The life of Sir Edward Dunlop* (Penguin, 1994); Ralph Waldo Emerson, *Essays and Journals* (ed. Lewis Mumford) (Nelson Doubleday, 1968); Christopher Finch, *Highways to Heaven: the AUTO biography of America* (HarperCollins, 1992); Jeffrey Frost, *They Came like Waves: Long Distance Trucking in Australia*

(Kangaroo Press, 1997); Jean Field, *Grey Ribbon to the Border* (The Hawthorn Press, 1973); Tim Flannery (ed.), *The Explorers* (Text, 1998); Tim Flannery (ed.), *The Life and Adventures of William Buckley* (Text, 2002); Miles Franklin, *Old Blastus of Bandicoot* (Lothian, 1932); Miles Franklin, *My Brilliant Career* (Imprint Classic, 1990); Mary Gilmore, *Hound of the Road* (Angus & Robertson, 1922); John Hirst, *The Sentimental Nation: the Making of the Australian Commonwealth* (Oxford, 2000); Anne Holloway, *A Drive Around the Rutledge Survey* (Kilmore Historical Society, 1991); Stuart Hamilton Hume, *Beyond the Borders: an anecdotal history of the Hume and related pioneering families from 1790* (privately published, 1991); K.S. Inglis, *Sacred Places – War Memorials in the Australian Landscape* (Melbourne University Press, 2001); Ian Jones, *Ned Kelly: A Short Life* (Lothian, 1995); Robert Lacey, *Ford: the Men and the Machine* (Pan, 1986); Lao Tzu, *Tao Te Ching* (translated by D.C. Lau) (Penguin Classics, 1975); Henry Lawson *A Camp-fire Yarn; Complete Works 1885-1900* (ed. Leonard Cronin) (Lansdowne Press, 1984); Henry Lawson, *A Fantasy of Man: Complete Works 1901-1922* (ed. Leonard Cronin) (Lansdowne Press, 1984); Tempe Hornibrook Longmire, *A Glimpse of the history of Gunning* (privately published); H.G. Martindale and Niall Brennan, *New Crossing Place: the Story of Seymour and its Shire* (Shire of Seymour, 1982); Ross McMullin, *Pompey Elliott* (Scribe, 2002); Roger Milliss, *Waterloo Creek: the Australia Day massacre of 1838, George Gipps and the British conquest of New South Wales* (McPhee Gribble, 1992); Les A. Murray, *Selected Poems: The Vernacular Republic* (Angus & Robertson, 1976); Ann Moyal, *Platypus* (Allen & Unwin, 2001); Dr B.P. Parolin and Prof B.J. Garner, *Evaluation of the Economic Impacts of the Goulburn Bypass.* Report presented to Goulburn City Council, Goulburn Chamber of Commerce and Goulburn Business Enterprise Centre, June 1995; J.W. Payne, *Pretty Sally's Hill: a History of Wallan, Wandong and Bylands* (Lowden Publishing, 1981); Henry Handel Richardson, *Ultima Thule* (Penguin Books, 1971); W.H. Wilde, *Courage a Grace: a biography of Dame Mary Gilmore* (Melbourne University Press, 1988); A.B. 'Banjo' Paterson, *Singer of the Bush Complete Works 1885–1900* (ed. R. Campbell and P. Harvie) (Lansdowne Press, 1983); A.B. 'Banjo' Paterson, *Song of the Pen – Complete Works 1885–1900* (eds R. Campbell and P. Harvie) (Lansdowne Press, 1983); Annie Patterson, *Waterhole of Hope: a story of Sue Gordon Woods and St Joseph's House of Prayer* (Spectrum, 2001); Clive Probyn and Bruce Steele (eds), *Henry Handel Richardson: the letters. Vol. 3* (Miegunyah Press, 2000); Colin Roderick, *Henry Lawson: a life* (Angus & Robertson, 1991); Colin Roderick, *Banjo Paterson: Poet by Accident* (Allen & Unwin, 1993); Colin Roderick (ed.), *Rose Paterson's Illalong Letters 1873–p1888* (Kangaroo Press, 2000); Rachel Roxburgh, *Berrima Court House* (Berrima Court House trust); E.W. Russell, R. Bergmaier and D. Kilsby, *Melbourne's Northern Gateway: an Integrated Approach* (Melbourne Transport Forum, 2001); Clement Semmler, *The Banjo of the Bush: the life and times of A.B. Paterson* (Lansdowne Press, 1966); Peter C. Smith, *Tracking Down the Bushrangers* (Kangaroo Press, 1988); Leo Tolstoy, *Anna Karenina* (several copies available); Mark Twain, *Mark Twain in Australia and New Zealand* (Penguin Books, 1973); Liz Vincent, *Ghosts of Picton Past* (self published); Don Watson, *Brian Fitzpatrick: a Radical Life* (Hale and Iremonger, 1979); R.H. Webster, *Currency Lad: the story of Hamilton Hume and the explorers* (Ginninderra Press, 1999); Mark Whittaker and Les Kennedy, *Sins of the Brother: the definitive story of Ivan Milat and the backpacker murders* (Pan, 2001); G.A. Wilkes, *A Dictionary of Australian Colloquialisms* (University of Sydney Press, 1990); R.T. Wyatt, *The History of Goulburn, New South Wales* (Lansdowne Press, 1972)

Not for sale

A grateful author won't part with Alan Andrews' brilliant presentation of the journals and writings of Hume and Hovell: *Hume and Hovell, 1824* (Blubber Head Press, 1981). Nor does he want to lose Penny Russell's fine edition of the overland diary of Jane Franklin, which was compiled with help from earlier work by Roger Milliss: *This Errant Lady* (National Library of Australia, 2002). If I had my own copy of the *Australian Dictionary of Biography*, I'd hang on to that too.

Wanted to buy

Beresford Rea wrote a charming book called *Up and Down the Sydney Road: the Romance of the Hume Highway* (Georgian House, 1958).